CYRIL OF JERUSALEM

Cyril, Bishop of Jerusalem, preached his important and eloquent sermons at a time when the city was the focus of vital developments in the Church. A spectacular new liturgy was evolving in the basilica built by the Emperor Constantine; yet the city was also the centre of fierce struggles inside the Church, as the successors to Arius strove to impose their heterodox teachings, and neighbouring Caesarea fought to maintain its primacy.

This illuminating study begins with a comprehensive introduction to Cyril's life and works. It also considers the growing archaeological evidence for the Constantinian complex, centred on Calvary and Jesus' tomb, where Cyril preached. A full account of the rites he conducted there is given, along with an assessment of Cyril's thought in the context of fourth-century theological developments.

There follow up-to-date translations of a selection of Cyril's writings, mostly connected with the instruction of candidates for baptism, and focusing on the Creed and the liturgical rites. Also included are the text of a biblical sermon, and a fascinating letter written by Cyril to the Emperor Constantius. Accessible yet erudite, this volume will be a valuable resource for students and scholars of liturgy, theology and archaeology in the early Church.

Edward Yarnold, S.J. is a Research Lecturer at the University of Oxford. His numerous publications include *The Study of Liturgy* (co-editor, 1976 and 1992), *The Study of Spirituality* (co-editor, 1986) and *Truth and Authority* (with Henry Chadwick, 1977).

THE EARLY CHURCH FATHERS
Edited by Carol Harrison
University of Durham

The Greek and Latin Fathers of the church are central to the creation of Christian doctrine, yet often unapproachable because of the sheer volume of their writings and the relative paucity of accessible translations. This series makes available translations of key selected texts by the major Fathers to all students of the early church.

Already published:

MAXIMUS THE CONFESSOR
Andrew Louth

IRENAEUS OF LYONS
Robert M. Grant

AMBROSE
Boniface Ramsey, O.P.

ORIGEN
Joseph W. Trigg

GREGORY OF NYSSA
Anthony Meredith, S.J.

JOHN CHRYSOSTOM
Wendy Mayer and Pauline Allen

CYRIL OF ALEXANDRIA
Norman Russell

CYRIL OF JERUSALEM

Edward Yarnold, S.J.

London and New York

First published 2000
by Routledge
11 New Fetter Lane, London EC4P 4EE

Simultaneously published in the USA and Canada
by Routledge
29 West 35th Street, New York, NY 10001

Routledge is an imprint of the Taylor & Francis Group

Typeset in Garamond by
The Running Head Limited, Cambridge
Printed and bound in Great Britain by
TJ International Ltd, Padstow, Cornwall

British Library Cataloguing in Publication Data
A catalogue record of this book is available from the British Library

Library of Congress Cataloguing in Publication Data
Yarnold, Edward.
Cyril of Jerusalem / Edward Yarnold.
p. cm. – (The early church fathers)
Includes bibliographical references and index.
1. Theology–Early works to 1800. 2. Cyril, Saint, Bishop of Jerusalem, ca. 315–387.
I. Cyril, Saint, Bishop of Jerusalem, ca. 315–387. Selections. English.
II. Title. III. Series
BR65.C952 E5 2000
270.2′092—dc21 00-036638

ISBN 0–415–19903–4 (hbk)
ISBN 0–415–19904–2 (pbk)

CONTENTS

FIGURES

PREFACE

Having taught and written on Cyril of Jerusalem for more than thirty years, I was pleased to be given the opportunity of gathering together my thoughts on him when Dr Carol Harrison invited me to contribute a volume to the present series. I have several people to thank for helping me to bring this work to its conclusion: above all my *confrère* Robert Murray for reading the typescript and from his wide knowledge, especially of the Syriac fathers, making many valuable suggestions, some of which constraints of space unfortunately did not allow me to follow; Dr Alexis Doval, who in our many hours working together over his thesis confirmed my belief that the *Mystagogic Catecheses* are indeed attributable to Cyril; to colleagues at Campion Hall and Seton Hall where this work was written; and to John and Dawn Willson who provided hospitality and encouragement in the countryside of Provence while I was revising my translation.

I gratefully acknowledge permission to reproduce the two drawings from Dr John Wilkinson's *Egeria's Travels*, published by Aris & Philips, Warminster.

ABBREVIATIONS

ad Const.	*Letter to Constantius*
Adv. Haer.	*Adversus Haereses* (Against Heresies)
Bapt. Hom.	*Baptismal Homilies*
Cat.	*Catecheses*
CCSG	Corpus Christianorum Series Graeca
CCSL	Corpus Christianorum Series Latina
CH	A. Cameron and S.G. Hall, *Eusebius' Life of Constantine*, Oxford, Clarendon Press, 1999
Chron.	*Chronicon*
Com. Esa.	Commentary on Isaiah
Com. Matt.	Commentary on Matthew
CSEL	Corpus Scriptorum Ecclesiasticorum Latinorum
de ob. Theod.	*de obitu Theodosii* (On the Death of Theodosius)
de Syn.	*de Synodis*
Ep.	Epistle
ET	English Translation
FaCh	The Fathers of the Church, Washington DC, Catholic University of America Press, 1947–
GCS	Die griechischen christlichen Schriftsteller der ersten Jahrhunderte
GT	S. Gibson and J.E. Taylor, *Beneath the Church of the Holy Sepulchre Jerusalem*, London, Palestinian Exploration Fund, 1994
HE	*Historia Ecclesiastica* (History of the Church)
Hist. Rom.	*History of Rome*
JTS	*Journal of Theological Studies*
(de) Laud. Const.	*De Laudibus Constantini* (Praise of Constantine)
LCC	The Library of Christian Classics, London, SCM Press, 1953–
LXX	Septuagint

MC	*Mystagogic Catecheses*
OCA	Orientalia Christiana Analecta
OCP	*Orientalia Christiana Periodica*
Pereg.	*Peregrinatio Egeriae*
PG	J.-P. Migne, Patrologiae Cursus Completus, Series Graeca
PL	J.-P. Migne, Patrologiae Cursus Completus, Series Latina
PO	Patrologia Orientalis
Procat.	*Procatechesis*
RHE	*Revue d'histoire ecclésiastique*
RR	W.K. Reischl and J. Rupp (eds), *S. Patris Nostri Cyrilli Hierosolymorum Archiepiscopi Opera quae supersunt Omnia*, Munich, Libraria Lentneriana
SC	Sources chrétiennes, Paris, Éditions du Cerf
StPatr	*Studia Patristica*
VC	*Vigiliae Christianae*
Vit. Const.	*Vita Constantini* (Life of Constantine)

Introduction

1

CYRIL'S LIFE

We know virtually nothing about Cyril's early life. He was born shortly before that second spring in the history of the Church, when Constantine's vision of the Cross heralded his victory over his rival Maxentius in 312 and led him to embrace Christianity, granting the Church first a tolerated, and then an increasingly favoured position in the Roman Empire. Cyril would have been a schoolboy at the time of the Council of Nicaea in 325, and was ordained priest by Maximus who had become Bishop of Jerusalem shortly before the dedication of Constantine's great basilica there in 335.[1] Though W. Telfer suggested a Caesarean origin,[2] Cyril seems to have been a native of Jerusalem, for he was ordained to serve that church, and knew the appearance of the site before Constantine's basilica was built.

> For it was in a garden that he was crucified. For although it has been largely decorated with royal gifts, it was once a garden, and the signs and remains of it still survive. (*Cat.* 14.5)

> The phrase 'shelter of the rock' (Cant 2.14 (LXX)) refers to the shelter which at that time stood in front of the door to the Saviour's tomb, and had been hollowed from the very rock in the way that was customary here in front of tombs. It is no longer visible because some time ago the front chamber was chiselled away when the tomb was given the decoration it has today. For before the Emperor had set this magnificent structure over the tomb, there was a shelter in front of the rock. (*Cat.* 14.9)

Although the year in which Cyril became bishop cannot be established precisely, there are certain pointers to a date of about

350. His remark in the *Catecheses* that the Emperor Probus (276–282) reigned 'a full seventy years ago'[3] suggests that he had succeeded to the see of Jerusalem by the middle of the century; for although it was not unknown for a presbyter to deliver catechetical instructions (John Chrysostom's baptismal homilies at Antioch are an example) Cyril gives no hint that the 'bishop' in the *Catecheses* is any other than himself – in contrast to *Homily* 20, where the reference to 'our father's teaching' (*patrikēs didaskalias*) seems to imply that he had not yet become bishop. His accession was still recent when he wrote his Letter to Constantius in 351, which he calls his 'firstfruits', describing the apparition of a shining cross in the sky over Jerusalem (*ad Const.* 1).

Much uncertainty surrounds Cyril's succession to the see. According to one tradition two militantly Arian bishops of nearby cities, namely Acacius of Caesarea (the metropolitan see) and Patrophilus of Scythopolis, conspired to oust Maximus of Jerusalem because of his staunch defence of the orthodox faith, and appointed Cyril in his place (Socrates, *HE* 2.38; Sozomen, *HE* 2.20; 4.20). This version of the events evidently implies that Cyril himself had Arian sympathies, for, having succeeded in getting rid of Maximus, Acacius and Patrophilus would hardly have replaced him with one who was not kindly disposed to their own cause. St Jerome, who should have known what he was talking about as he was a resident in the Holy Land from the last months of Cyril's episcopate, gives a still more discreditable account of Cyril's succession, according to which Cyril, as an out and out Arian, was offered the see on Maximus' death on condition that he would repudiate his ordination at the hands of that bishop (Jerome, *Chron.*: PL 27.683). However, since Jerome's judgments of individuals were sometimes more emotional than judicious, he may have allowed his hostility to Cyril's successor John to colour his assessment of Cyril himself. Theodoret of Cyrrhus however gives a quite different account: he represents Cyril as 'an earnest champion of the apostolic decrees' of Nicaea, and says nothing about any Arian conspiracy to make him Maximus' successor (Theodoret, *HE* 2.22).

Nevertheless the circumstances of Cyril's succession cannot have been unquestionable. According to Theodoret the right-thinking Maximus had someone else in mind as his successor; one would not expect him to approve of a candidate who was acceptable to the Arian Acacius. Indeed, the bishops in their letter after the Council of Constantinople of 381 felt it necessary to vindicate both Cyril's orthodoxy and the validity of his consecration:

> Of the church at Jerusalem, mother of all the churches, we make known that the right reverend and most religious Cyril is bishop, who was some time ago correctly ordained by the bishops of the province, and has in several places fought a good fight against the Arians. (Theodoret, *HE* 5.9)

It would be no surprise or disgrace if Cyril had been a little slow to wake up to the dangerous implications of Arius' views. The Council of Nicaea was, after all, the first ecumenical council, and the Church at large did not at once recognize the decisive authority of its novel definition that the Son was 'of the same substance (*homoousios*)' as the Father. Even such a defender of orthodoxy as Hilary of Poitiers claimed to have had no knowledge of Nicaea or the *homoousion* until the eve of his exile in 357 (Hilary, *de Syn.* 91); while St Athanasius himself, for all the persecution he endured at the hands of the Arians, was slow to take the term *homoousios* into his own writings. Eusebius, Acacius' predecessor at Caesarea, seems to have regarded the Arianizing Council of Jerusalem, which reinstated Arius in 335, as at least equal in authority to the Council of Nicaea, which had condemned him (and arraigned Eusebius himself) ten years earlier. We shall have more to say about Cyril's orthodoxy below in section 5.

However much Cyril owed his appointment to sympathy with Acacius' Arian convictions, his relationship with his metropolitan soon changed, as he entered into a dispute with Acacius 'concerning his [Acacius'] rights as a metropolitan, which he claimed on the ground of his bishopric being an apostolic see' (Sozomen, *HE* 4.25). The seventh canon of Nicaea had done little to clarify the issue when it decreed that, in view of ancient custom, the bishop of Aelia (Jerusalem) should have 'the succession of honour', while at the same time the metropolis was to retain its proper rank.[4] This dispute influenced the protagonists' attitude to the religious significance of the places chosen by providence as the theatre on which the drama of salvation-history was enacted: whereas Cyril sought to exploit the significance of Jerusalem as the Holy City, Acacius' predecessor Eusebius had focused more widely on the Holy Land, which included Caesarea as well as Jerusalem.[5] Cyril's letter to Constantius on the appearance of the Cross in the sky over Jerusalem should perhaps be read against this background as an opportunistic attempt to enlist the Emperor's support on the side of the Holy City.

According to Sozomen the scope of this dispute widened, so that the two bishops exchanged accusations of heresy, with Cyril charging

Acacius of Arianism, and being charged in return of holding that the Son is 'of like substance with the Father'. We shall see in the fifth section of this Introduction that even in the *Catecheses*, which should be dated no later than the early 350s, Cyril already saw the need to refute some of the key Arian theses, though he never included Arius or his followers in lists of heretics. Acacius strengthened his case against Cyril with allegations that he had restored communion to several deposed bishops and illegally sold church property to raise funds during a famine (Sozomen, *HE* 4.25); and when for two years Cyril persisted in his refusal to appear before his metropolitan, Acacius deposed him in 357. Thereupon Cyril appealed to the secular authorities, a step which the historian Socrates regarded as unusual, though Touttée shows that such an appeal was not unparalleled.[6] He spent this first exile at Tarsus, but he was allowed to make his appeal at the Council of Seleucia (359), where according to Sozomen he joined the moderate anti-Arian party of Basil of Ancyra and Eustathius of Sebaste, who, while avoiding the Nicene *homoousios*, preferred to say that the Son was 'of similar substance (*homoiousios*)' with the Father – the very view which, as we have seen, Acacius had detected in Cyril.[7] The Council deposed Acacius, allowing Cyril to return to his see, only to become an exile again the following year once Acacius had persuaded Constantius, an Arian sympathizer, that Cyril had sold to a dancer a vestment presented by the Emperor's father Constantine to Bishop Macarius, so that it became a stage prop.[8] However, when Constantius died in November 361, Julian the Apostate, becoming sole emperor, showed his superiority to the Christians he despised by recalling all the bishops who had been banished in the previous reign.[9] The place of Cyril's second exile is not known, though when he was again restored, his journey home took him through Antioch, where he rescued a young Christian who had been imprisoned and tortured by his pagan father, and smuggled him back to Jerusalem in his carriage.[10] The imperial clemency did not however deter him from resisting Julian's attempts to restore the Jewish Temple in Jerusalem; he received providential assistance from a storm which damaged the rising building, and was regarded as a portent (Socrates, *HE* 3.20).

On the death of Acacius of Caesarea (c. 365), Cyril carried the war into the rival camp and sent two candidates for the vacant see, the successful one being his own brother Gelasius. However, the success of this attempt to reverse the domination of Caesarea over Jerusalem was short-lived, for Gelasius was soon deposed and replaced by the Arian Euzoius.[11] Worse was to follow. In 367 Valens, another Arian sympathizer, succeeded as Emperor of the Eastern provinces and reactivated the sentences of banishment imposed by Constantius. Thus Cyril went into exile for the third time. However, when Valens' reign ended in 378, his successor Gratian soon recalled the exiled bishops.

At the end of this third exile – he had been in banishment for some fifteen out of the preceding twenty-two years – Cyril returned to find the church in Jerusalem rent by schism. Gregory of Nyssa, who visited the city in 379, described the religious strife and moral decay which he found there, apparently shortly before Cyril's arrival.[12]

> There is no form of immorality that they do not venture to commit – to say nothing of prostitution, adultery, theft, idolatry, poisoning, envious disputes, murder . . . nowhere is murder taken so lightly as it is in those parts . . . I had promised to confer with the heads of the holy churches in Jerusalem, because their affairs were in confusion and a negotiator was needed.

The *Mystagogic Catecheses*, which Cyril delivered in his last years in Jerusalem, give no hint of this stormy background.

At the Council of Constantinople in 381 Cyril emerged as one of the leaders of the homoousians; though Sozomen and Socrates, in keeping with their unfavourable accounts of Cyril's original succession to the see of Jerusalem, maintained that he first needed to renounce his earlier 'Macedonian' position.[13] The charge is plausible, in so far as Cyril, like Macedonius, preferred to speak of the Son as 'like' the Father rather than as 'consubstantial' with him; there is no parallel in Cyril's works to Macedonius' denial of the divinity of the Holy Spirit.[14] Nevertheless the bishops who met in the same city in the following year included in their synodical letter an expression of confidence that Cyril had been 'canonically ordained [or appointed] by the bishops of the province', and praised 'the good fight he had fought in several places against Arianism' (Theodoret, *HE* 5.9); but, as has been suggested above, the fact that such a declaration was necessary implies that some doubt had been expressed. The year of Cyril's death was traditionally given as 386, but P. Nautin has shown that the text of Jerome, *De Viris Illustribus* 112, on which the date was based, suggests rather a date of 387.[15]

2

JERUSALEM[1]

Jesus was crucified outside the walls, but close enough to the city to provide a public spectacle. All four evangelists name the site the 'Place of a Skull', and all save Luke give its Aramaic name 'Golgotha'. Although the name is sometimes explained in reference to the shape of the hill on which Jesus died, none of the gospels refers to a hill. A later tradition links the name with Adam's skull, which was said to be buried there; in one version of the legend, Christ's blood trickled down to the skull and so redeemed Adam and the whole race.[2] Gibson and Taylor argue that, since the present rock of Calvary is 'too narrow to permit three crosses, and is too steep to allow easy access', Jerome was probably right to explain the name as a common term for a place of execution.[3] The two authors accordingly conclude that Golgotha was the name of the place where Jesus was crucified (all four gospels speak of the 'place (*topos*) of a Skull'); the mound of rock was a prominent feature of the area, but not the very spot of the crucifixion.

John speaks of the sites of Calvary and the Tomb as a 'garden'; Cyril himself confirms this tradition.[4] There are however signs that the Tomb was set within a quarry. Not only does Cyril add the word 'quarried (*lelatomēmenon*)' to Luke's reference to a 'tomb carved from the rock' (*en mnēmati laxeutōi*),[5] but archaeological investigations of what has long been identified as the site of the crucifixion and the burial suggest that, within an extensive quarry covering an area of 200m by 150m, a band of inferior rock was left unquarried, and used partly as a place of execution, partly as a place of burial, and partly as a cultivated garden. Although in Jesus' time it lay outside the city walls, when the walls were redrawn in the middle of the first century AD, it now lay inside them. Gibson and Taylor speak of 'numerous other examples of Early Roman tombs near Jerusalem which were similarly cut into the scarps of abandoned or partly disused stone quarries' (GT 61). The so-called Tombs of Zachariah (second century BC) and Absalom (first century AD), which are still plainly visible from the city walls, are Jewish examples of elaborate tombs carved out of the living rock. Commenting on the prophetic text 'in the shelter of the rock' (Cant 2.14 (LXX)), Cyril explains that the text:

> refers to the shelter which at that time stood in front of the door to the Saviour's tomb, and had been hollowed from the very rock in the way that was customary here in front of tombs. It is no longer visible because the front chamber was then cut away to give the tomb the decoration it has today. (*Cat.* 14.9)

When the Roman Emperor Titus crushed the Jewish revolt in AD 70, he destroyed the city of Jerusalem. The gospels record Jesus' prophecy that 'not a stone will be left upon a stone' (Mt 24.2), but the words are not literally true, for at least some of Herod the Great's gigantic masonry was left in place, and can still be seen at the Western Wall of the Temple and elsewhere. In Cyril's day even more of the Temple walls were still standing, so that he believed that the prophecy was still awaiting its fulfilment before the coming of the Antichrist:

> The Antichrist will come when in the Jewish Temple a stone does not remain on a stone, as the Saviour proclaimed. For when their age leads all the stones to collapse or they are knocked down with a view to rebuilding or for some other reasons – I am not referring to the stones of the outer perimeter, but those of the Temple inside, where the cherubim stood – then he is to come amid all his lying signs and portents. (*Cat.* 15.15)

In 130–132 Hadrian refounded Jerusalem as a pagan Roman city, thus provoking the second Jewish revolt led by Bar Kochba in 135. Hadrian gave the new foundation the name Aelia Capitolina: 'Aelia' after the Emperor's second name, and 'Capitolina' in honour of the three Roman 'capitoline' gods Jupiter, Juno and Minerva. There is no certainty about the location of the customary temple honouring these three gods: Gibson and Taylor place it to the north of the Temple Mount, on the site of the fort of the Antonia; they cite the evidence of the third-century historian Cassius Dio and a statement by Jerome that an 'idol of Jupiter' stood on the Mount.[6] On the Mount itself two statues of emperors seem to have been set, that of Hadrian being on the very site of the Holy of Holies.[7] For the forum of the new city a site next to the quarry was chosen; the quarry itself was filled in and paved over. It seems to have been used as a sacred precinct for Venus, with a temple for that goddess at its northern end. Eusebius, recalling what he had seen with his own eyes, relates that over the cave which had served as the Lord's tomb:

> above the ground they constructed what could be described with terrible truth as a tomb for souls, building a gloomy alcove for dead idols in honour of the licentious demon Aphrodite [Venus], and then pouring cursed libations there over impious and profane altars. (*Vit. Const.* 3.26)[8]

Gibson and Taylor conclude there was 'a temple precinct made up of several shrines containing idols pertaining to the multifaceted cult of Venus'.[9] This goddess in fact seems to have been much more prominent in the devotion of the pagan city than the Capitoline trinity after which it was named.

Though the level of the pavement was raised, completely covering the Tomb, it appears that the tip of the rock of Calvary remained visible, and was crowned with a statue of Venus, for Eusebius, in an early work written before Constantine's building began, reports that Golgotha is 'pointed out in Aelia to the north of Mount Sion', while Jerome later states that 'on the rock of the cross a statue of Venus made of marble was venerated by the pagans'.[10] Coins show a statue of the goddess standing on what Gibson and Taylor believe to be a 'rocky outcrop'.[11] The visible rock would help to pinpoint Christian traditions concerning the site.

The main credit for rescuing the holy places from these profanations belongs to Constantine, but his mother Helen took a part in the process. Eusebius describes how this intrepid old lady, when in her seventies or even her eighties, travelled to Palestine,

> an old woman with the vigour of youth and outstanding good sense, to visit the Holy Land and to inspect the nations, cities and peoples with the wise benevolence which befitted an empress. When she had offered the worship which was due to the Saviour's footprints, in accordance with the prophetic text: 'Let us worship at the place where his feet stood' (Ps 131 (132).7), she immediately bequeathed

> to posterity the fruit of her personal devotion. (Eusebius, *Vit. Const.* 3.42)

Eusebius attributes to her the foundation of the churches at the site of the Nativity at Bethlehem, and on the Mount of Olives at the site of the ascension and of the cave where 'the Saviour of the universe' was truly said 'to initiate his votaries into the secret mysteries' (*Vit. Const.* 3.43); her son supported her in these enterprises. However, the construction of the third set of buildings, those at the Holy Sepulchre, Eusebius attributes to Constantine alone (*Vit. Const.* 3.25–40). Ambrose, however, and after him Socrates and Sozomen, give Helen a share of the credit, as did the pilgrim Egeria, who attributed the decoration of the buildings to Constantine 'under the supervision of his mother'.[12] However, the fact that Cyril in the middle of the century, while speaking of the cross in two different works, makes no mention of Helen must cast some doubt on her involvement.[13] As Eusebius narrates the events, the Emperor,

> being assuredly inspired by the Holy Spirit, did not allow the place we have spoken of to remain hidden by all sorts of polluted material, as the enemy plotted, and to be left forgotten and unknown; he would not yield to the ill-will of those who were responsible for this action. Calling upon God to work with him, he ordered the place to be cleared, for he believed that through his own efforts the ground which the enemy had defiled should be foremost in enjoying the fruits of the good God's magnificence. (*Vit. Const.* 3.26)

The site of Calvary was marked by the statue of Venus set on the top of the rock; in the two centuries since the building of Aelia, the site of the Tomb seems to have been forgotten.[14] Consequently Constantine's original plan seems to have been simply to remove the pagan pollution from Calvary, knocking down the buildings, destroying the idols, and removing the rubble. But, not content with this,

> the Emperor, under divine inspiration, ordered his workmen to excavate to a great depth the very soil which formed the foundations, and to remove it with all the rubble to some place a great distance away, because it had been contaminated by the bloodshed of demonic worship. (Eusebius, *Vit. Const.* 3.27)

What followed next seems to have been unforeseen. When all the material had been removed and the original level reached,

> Then, beyond all hope, the sacred and all-holy memorial of the Saviour's resurrection came to light, and the cave which is the holy of holies began to reveal the image of the Saviour's return to life. (*Vit. Const.* 3.28)

The main church which Constantine subsequently built on the site became known by this name 'Memorial' (Martyrium).

This account by Eusebius of these events is remarkable for his systematic refusal to speak of Golgotha or the wood of the cross. He says nothing of the rock of Calvary so dishonoured by the statue of Venus which crowned it, or of its uncovering, or of its subsequent decoration and integration into the general scheme of the buildings. He describes the site as 'the most blessed spot of the Saviour's resurrection in Jerusalem', 'that divine memorial of immortality' (*Vit. Const.* 3.25, 26). Constantine's building is 'a house of prayer, worthy of God, around (*amphi*) the cave of salvation' (*Vit. Const.* 3.29). Cyril, by contrast, repeatedly refers to the events connected with Calvary and takes every opportunity of drawing his listeners' attention to the rock.

Constantine reacted with such speed, says Eusebius, that it was as if he had planned to build a church there all along. He instructed the governors of the Eastern provinces to erect a sumptuous building there at his own expense. He also sent instructions to the Bishop of Jerusalem, Macarius, in a letter which Eusebius quotes at length. It begins as follows:

> Nicetas [Victor] Constantine the Great, Augustus, to Macarius. So great is our Saviour's grace that it seems impossible to find words to do justice to the present marvel. For it truly surpasses all wonder how the token of that most holy Passion lay hidden for so many years buried under the earth, until through the destruction of our common enemy it was destined to shine once more on his liberated servants. For if everyone throughout the world with a reputation for wisdom came together with the purpose of making a pronouncement that was worthy of the event, they would not be able to match the smallest part of the truth. For the nature of this wonder transcends every nature capable of human reasoning as much as heavenly things are by nature

> more powerful than earthly. Accordingly this has always been my one and only aim: that, just as the true faith is revealing itself every day in new wonders, so all our souls, with all virtue and harmonious eagerness, should become more earnestly devoted to the holy law. So I think it is clear to everyone, and I want you especially to be convinced of this, that there is no other cause that is dearer to me than to erect beautiful buildings to grace that holy place which, by God's command, I have freed from the weight of the foul idol which had been set on top of it – that place which from the beginning was made holy by God's judgment, and was revealed as holier still since he brought to light the proof of the Saviour's Passion. (*Vit. Const.* 3.30)

It is notable that in this letter Constantine, like Cyril but in contrast with Eusebius, places the emphasis on the crucifixion. He makes no explicit mention of the cave-tomb or the resurrection; he describes the object which was so unexpectedly unearthed as 'the token (*gnōrisma*) of that most holy Passion', and 'the proof (*pistin*) of the Saviour's Passion'.

What was this unexpected find of the token of the Passion? The words can hardly refer to Calvary itself, as the summit of the rock had remained visible for the last two centuries since the foundation of Hadrian's city, and no new marvel could have been revealed when its full height was laid bare. Constantine's words are not well chosen if they are intended to apply to the Tomb, for it is hard to see how a rock cave in a disused quarry could count as proof of the Passion. Eusebius himself hints at the solution to the puzzle in the speech *de Laudibus Constantini* which he delivered in 336 in honour of the thirtieth anniversary of the Emperor's accession, and which is likely to be a more reliable reflection of Constantine's intentions than the *Life*, which was published after the Emperor's death. This is the earlier and briefer account of the events:

> With regard to the province of Palestine, in the middle of the Jewish royal city, at the very Martyrium of the Saviour, he endowed a huge house of prayer and a holy temple in honour of the saving sign with rich ornament and all kinds of decoration; and the memorial of everlasting memory and the trophy of the great Saviour's victory over death he honoured with embellishments which are too great to be described.

Eusebius then proceeds to speak of the Emperor's munificent treatment of the 'three mystic caves', namely of the Nativity, of the Ascension,

> and in the one that lay between them, proclaiming the saving victory that followed his whole struggle. The Emperor adorned all these caves, proclaiming the saving sign to all mankind. (*Laud. Const.* 9: PG 20.1369–72)

It is most natural to understand the 'saving sign' in these quotations as a reference to the cross,[15] while the 'memorial' is the tomb. Accordingly the 'token' and the 'proof' of the Passion which the letter speaks of will likewise be the cross. Eusebius himself, despite his reticence in the *Life*, in his address in praise of Constantine refers to the cross with which the Emperor confronted his opponents as 'the saving and life-giving sign'; it is 'a wonder to speak of, wonderful indeed to conceive' (*Laud. Const.* 9, 10 (PG 20.1364, 1372)). Cyril's allusions to the wood of the cross in the *Letter to Constantius* and the *Catecheses* show that devotion to the holy wood was well established by the middle of the century; the Letter states explicitly that the discovery was made during Constantine's reign.[16] The feast of the finding of the cross was a major celebration in Jerusalem by the last years of Cyril's episcopate, being celebrated on the same day as the dedication of the basilica, and, like Easter and the Epiphany, honoured with an octave (Egeria, *Pereg.* 48–9).

We have other evidence of Constantine's devotion to the sign of the cross which had led him to victory over Maxentius. Eusebius tells us he used to carry a 'tabernacle of the cross' with him on his campaigns, and set up a jewelled golden cross in a prominent position in his palace in Constantinople (*Vit. Const.* 2.12; 3.49). One long chapter of Eusebius' *de Laudibus Constantini* refers repeatedly to the honours the Emperor paid to 'the saving and life-giving sign', 'the sign that brings victory', 'the great trophy' (*de Laud. Const.* 9 (PG 20.1364–9)). He had such a devotion to Christ's nails that he incorporated one into his helmet and another into his horse's bit.[17] It is the feast of the Passion, rather than the resurrection, which Constantine says in his *Speech to the Assembly of the Saints* is 'brighter than the light of the sun, and brings restoration of decayed bodies'. In the course of the same speech he quotes a Sibylline acrostic verse in Greek, the initials of which give the words: 'Jesus Christ, Son of God, Saviour, Cross'.[18]

Perhaps the finding of the cross took place in this way: Constantine's original plan, as described in his letter to Macarius, had been to honour the site of Calvary, which was marked by the statue of Venus, by freeing it 'from the weight of the foul idol which had been set on top of it'; this plan was then extended to the clearing away of the foundations and laying bare the bedrock. The work of excavation unexpectedly revealed the cross, which the Emperor then decided to honour by building the basilica of the Martyrium. Later in the process the cave-tomb was discovered and identified, and incorporated into the design, as we shall see.

The earliest description of the buildings is that written in 333–334 by an anonymous pilgrim from Bordeaux, who gives a characteristically jejune account of them when their construction was nearing completion:

> but on the left is the hillock (*monticulus*) of Golgotha, where the Lord was crucified. About a stone's throw from there is the crypt where his body was placed and rose again on the third day. In the same place a basilica (or royal building [*dominicum*]) has recently been built by order of the Emperor Constantine. It is of wonderful beauty, and has a cistern beside it, from which water is drawn, and a bath beside it, where the infants are washed.[19]

The Pilgrim's impression is thus of the mound of Calvary and the cave-tomb, both presumably set in the open, with the basilica next to them, with a separate baptistery.

The Martyrium was consecrated in 335. The occasion was a double triumph for Eusebius over his orthodox Jerusalem rivals; for not only did he apparently assume the leading role, making 'elaborate speeches (*poikilais . . . dialexesi*)', but the occasion was taken to readmit Arius and his followers to communion at Constantine's request.[20] Eusebius' detailed but puzzling description of the now completed buildings in his *Life* of Constantine can be set between that year and 339, the year of his own death. A tentative plan is sketched out in Figure 1.

Eusebius' description fills in the details that are missing from the Pilgrim's laconic account, though, as we have seen, he omits all reference to Calvary, and emphasizes the importance of the Sepulchre.

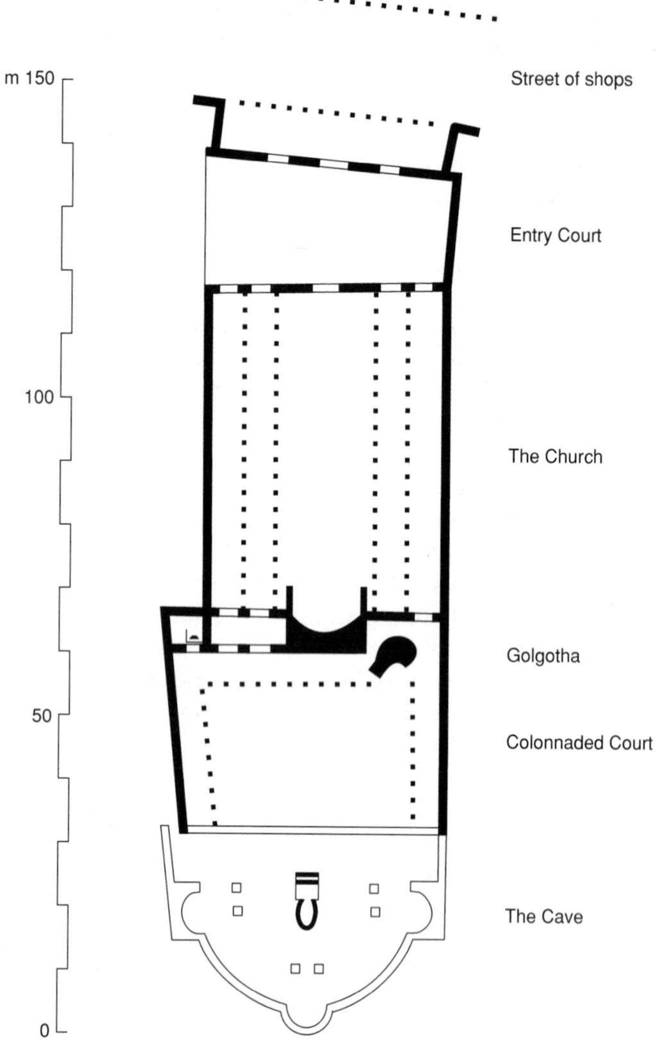

Figure 1 The Church of the Martyrium as described by Eusebius (see Introduction, sect. 2, p. 15). The top of the plan is to the east; the apse and sanctuary are at the west end. Eusebius fails to mention the jewelled cross and other decoration with which Constantine adorned Golgotha. The plan does not show the Church of the Anastasis (resurrection) which was built later round the Tomb, which on the plan is called the Cave; nor does it show the baptistery, which was probably built to the south of the Colonnaded Court. Redrawn after Figure 6 in John Wilkinson's *Egeria's Travels* (Aris & Philips, 3rd edn 1999).

> So first of all, as the head of the whole complex, he adorned the holy cave, that divine memorial at which the radiant angel announced publicly the rebirth revealed through the Saviour. So the Emperor in his generosity began by decorating it, as the head of the whole, with choice pillars and abundant ornamentation, embellishing it with every kind of splendour. (*Vit. Const.* 3.33–4)

Ample archaeological evidence indicates a chamber with a pointed roof fronted by a railed balcony, from which, according to Egeria's description, the bishop addressed the neophytes.[21] It was set in a 'vast space in the open air', which was paved and surrounded with a portico on three sides (*Vit. Const.* 3.35). On the fourth side, opposite the cave, lay the basilica.

> It was an extraordinary work, raised to an immense height, with its length and breadth extended to the full. The inner walls of the building were covered with sheets of polychrome marble; the outer face of the walls gleamed with polished stone fitted together at the joints, and made a wonderfully beautiful sight in no way inferior to the appearance of marble. Overhead on the roof, lead formed a protective covering for the outer structure, as an effective protection against the winter rains; the inner surface of the ceilings was fitted with carved panels, which were fitted together and covered all over with shining gold, so that like a great sea they extended over the whole basilica, and made the whole temple seem to shine with glittering lights. (*Vit. Const.* 3.36)

Two lines of pillars ran along each side of the church, and to the east three gates opened on to a colonnaded courtyard; its outer gates, 'exquisitely decorated', gave on to the forum, and 'afforded passers by an astonishing glimpse of what was to be seen within' (*Vit. Const.* 3.39).

> At the opposite end from the doors, as the head of the whole building, a dome extended over the top of the basilica. It was encircled by twelve columns: the same number as the Saviour's apostles. The tops of the columns were adorned with huge silver bowls, a beautiful offering which the Emperor had made personally to his God. (*Vit. Const.* 3.38)

Reconstructions which depict this dome as if it were the customary curving roof of an apse are misleading. Eusebius' word for dome is *hemisphairon*, a hemisphere; the curved ceiling of an apse would be only a quarter-sphere. Moreover, if my translation is correct, the dome 'extended over the top of the basilica' (*ep' akrou tou basileiou ektetamenon*), which is not an accurate description of the curved roof of an apse. Telfer's suggestion that the dome is a *baldachin* built over the altar and rising *up to* the roof is less faithful to the Greek, which suggests a dome *over* the highest part of the building.[22] Gibson and Taylor, following H.A. Drake, suggest that the purpose of the dome was 'to enshrine the place, somewhere beneath the apse or altar, where the wood of the cross was discovered';[23] this might be the explanation of the strange alignment of the buildings. If all this is correct, the dome which is a prominent feature in two early representations of the buildings, namely the apsidal mosaic of S. Pudenziana at Rome (c. 400) and the Madaba Map (sixth century; see cover photo) would be this crowning dome which dominated the Martyrium.

Although the Bordeaux Pilgrim and Eusebius both make it clear that the Tomb stood in the open air, by the time of Egeria's visit in the 380s it had been contained within a separate building known as the resurrection (*Anastasis*). Gibson and Taylor point out that the traditional view that this new chapel was a rotunda crowned with a dome has no evidence to support it; these features cannot be attested until the reconstruction by Monomachus in the eleventh century.

> The archaeological evidence suggests that it was a semi-circular building. Since, according to our analysis of the Madaba mosaic, it is not shown there, it is likely that the Anastasis was not especially high or imposing . . . The roof may have been fairly flat, like that of both the Arian and Orthodox baptistries in Ravenna.[24]

However, though Gibson and Taylor may be right about the roof, they cite no conclusive evidence for the semi-circular shape, which would apparently leave too little space for large congregations to meet in front of the Tomb, as the liturgy required. It seems to me more likely that the Anastasis was a circular, low-roofed structure (see Figure 2). As it would be surprising if the Madaba Map did omit so important a building, one wonders whether it might be represented out of position to the right of the dome, as there was no space to fit it in the correct position on the mosaic?

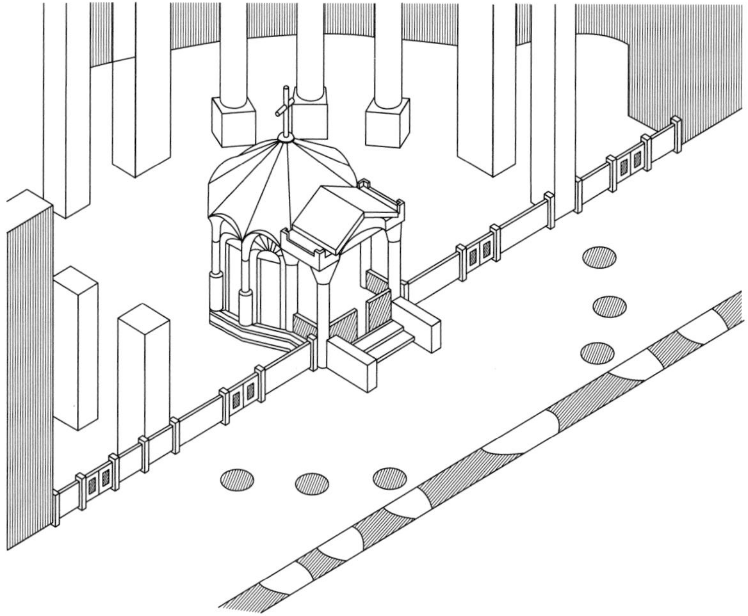

Figure 2 A reconstruction of the Anastasis, the church built round the Tomb. The outer and inner chambers of the Tomb, and the railings described by Egeria (p. 17) are shown. Redrawn after Figure 11 in John Wilkinson's *Egeria's Travels* (Aris & Philips, 3rd edn 1999).

How then are the two mosaic representations to be interpreted?[25] The domed building to the left of the S. Pudenziana mosaic has been identified as (a) the hypothetical Rotunda added over the Tomb (L.H. Vincent); (b) the circular Church of the Ascension on the Mount of Olives, known as the Imbomon (W. Pullan); (c) the apse of the Martyrium (K.J. Conant); (d) a complete dome over the sanctuary of the Martyrium let into the roof of the church (Gibson and Taylor). Pullan ingeniously suggests that the outer viewpoint of the Rotunda does not feature in the Pudenziana mosaic because it depicts schematically its curved *interior*, with the risen Christ on his throne replacing the Tomb; this would however presuppose a high degree of artistic sophistication in a Roman congregation if they were to understand the mosaic in this way. The apparently octagonal building to the right of the mosaic Pullan and some others take to be the octagonal shrine at the west end of the Church of the Nativity at Bethlehem. However, the Bethlehem shrine was attached to the main basilica, whereas the building in the mosaic is free-standing. Could it possibly be the Tomb or a domeless Anastasis? Evidently the last word on the subject has not yet been said.

As we have seen, Eusebius makes no mention of Golgotha or the finding of the Cross. Walker suggests various reasons for this silence: as a scientific historian Eusebius was not convinced that what was found was the real Cross; he was reluctant to do anything which might enhance the influence of Jerusalem over against Caesarea.[26] Perhaps a more significant explanation can be found in Eusebius' theology, which emphasizes the resurrection rather than the crucifixion: for him the site is 'the place of the saving resurrection', 'that wonderful memorial of immortality' (*Vit. Const.* 3.25, 26). In fact, he tells us that Constantine's plan was to construct a new Jerusalem confronting (*antiprosōpos*) and opposite (*antikrus*) the old one, with the Tomb as the Holy of Holies.[27] J. Wilkinson suggests that this was the controlling idea in the construction of the buildings, though subsequent generations lost sight of it.[28]

Cyril's Letter to Constantius indicates that the discovery of the Cross seems to have occurred some time during the clearing of the site and the construction of the Martyrium.

> In the time of your blessed father Constantine of happy memory, the saving wood of the cross was found in Jerusalem when God's grace rewarded the piety of his noble search with the discovery of the hidden holy places. (*ad Const.* 3)

As we have seen, Constantine's intention to honour the 'saving sign' confirms the view that the cross was found at this time. The tradition that it was Helen who made the discovery does not appear until the works of Ambrose at the end of the fourth century;[29] later still legends were recounted about the ingenious methods which she used to make the identification.[30] (Excavations indicate that the present subterranean chapels of St Helen and the Finding of the Cross were not part of Constantine's design, but were simply a natural hollow which the builders filled with rubble (cf. GT 76).) But how *was* the Cross identified? Ambrose speaks about the honour which Constantine paid to Christ's nails.[31] Was it the discovery of wood and nails together which made Constantine so sure that what was found was indeed the 'token' of the Passion?

For a description of the way Constantine's builders decorated the rock of Calvary we have to look beyond Eusebius. The rock was situated at the south-eastern corner of the open space between the

Martyrium and the Tomb. The builders left enough of the original rock visible for Cyril to be able to speak of:

> Golgotha here, the pre-eminent, which is still visible today and still shows how the rocks were split because of Christ that day. (*Cat.* 13.39)

By Egeria's time (37.1) this rock was crowned by a cross, which is presumably to be identified with the jewelled cross of the Pudenziana mosaic; she describes how the bishop's throne could be set up there, which is perhaps what the mosaic depicts, with Christ taking the place of the bishop. The whole area was given the name of 'Before the Cross'. Egeria also refers to an area 'behind the cross'; scholars debate whether this name refers to the whole Martyrium or a special small chapel.[32]

3

WORKS

Apart from some fragments and some evidently spurious writings,[1] there are only four works which are widely agreed to be authentic works of Cyril:

(a) *The Sermon on the Paralytic*, a meditative homily which Cyril preached during the liturgy, apparently while still a presbyter; for the words to 'our father's teaching', if the reading is genuine, seem to refer to Cyril's bishop.[2] The sermon contains allegorical exegesis of a type which Cyril generally avoids in his later works. We shall return to Cyril's treatment of Scripture in section 5.

(b) *The Letter to Constantius*, which Cyril wrote to the Emperor in 351 (or possibly 350) shortly after his accession to the see of Jerusalem (his 'firstfruits', nn. 1, 7), on the occasion of the miraculous appearance of a luminous cross in the sky over Jerusalem during the Easter season on 7 May (n. 4). Cyril, surely remembering (though without mentioning) the vision of the Cross which heralded the victory of the Emperor's father Constantine over Maxentius in 312, represented the apparition as an assurance of divine support in Constantius' war against the usurper Magnentius. The apparition is attested by the historians Philostorgius and Sozomen, as well as an anonymous Arian mid-fourth-century source.[3]

The Letter is written in the most contrived court rhetoric, in marked contrast to the plainer style of Cyril's other writings.

(c) The baptismal instructions, namely the *Procatechesis* delivered to the candidates who at the beginning of Lent had just given in their names for baptism, and eighteen *Catecheses* providing these same candidates with the doctrinal instruction they needed before baptism. They can be dated to about 350, either just before or just after Cyril became bishop.

There is some evidence that the text of the *Catecheses* which has come down to us does not contain the original version of the work, but has incorporated later liturgical changes, which in at least one instance have been set inconsistently alongside the original version. At the end of the last *Catechesis* the reader is first given the impression that a final explanation of the rites will be offered shortly before they are celebrated:

> But when the holy day of Easter comes, the day when your charity will be enlightened in Christ through the 'washing of rebirth', you will receive, God willing, the further teaching you will need: concerning the devotion and order with which the called should enter; the purpose of each of the holy mysteries of baptism; the devotion and order with which you should proceed from baptism to God's holy altar, where you will enjoy the spiritual, heavenly mysteries. In this way your soul will be enlightened in advance through instruction on every point, and you will learn how sublime the graces are which you will receive from God. (*Cat.* 18.32)

Yet in the next section we are told that these instructions will be given in the week after the sacraments are received:

> After the holy and saving day of Easter, starting on Monday every day of the following week, after the assembly you will enter the holy place of the resurrection, where, God willing, you will hear further catechetical instructions. (*Cat.* 18.33)

There follows a list of subjects, much of which parallels the list in the preceding section.

(d) The five post-baptismal *Mystagogic Catecheses*, containing Cyril's main explanation of the rites of initiation, of which baptism, anointing with chrism and first communion form the chief parts. These are not part of the same collection as the Lenten baptismal instructions; some MSS, including Syriac and Armenian translations, contain the *Catecheses* without the *Mystagogics*; others contain both but show by the titles that they are regarded as separate works.[4] (Some MSS also omit the *Procatechesis*.) The tenth-century Monacensis 394 regarded the *Catecheses* as a complete text, as the following note between the *Catecheses* and the *Mystagogics* shows (though the later Marcianus gr. II.35 and Ottobonianus 220, which reproduce part of the note, transfer it to the end of the second work):

> Many other catecheses were delivered each year, both before baptism and after the neophytes had been baptized. But these were the only ones which certain devout people took down in writing while they were being delivered in the year 352[5] of the Incarnation of our Lord and Saviour Jesus Christ. You will find explained in them point by point (*ek merous*) according to the Scriptures all the essential dogmas of the faith which people need to know, arguments against the Greeks and the circumcised and the heresies, and every kind of Christian moral teaching, by the grace of God.

Moreover, since in most of the MSS the title introducing each of the *Catecheses* states that the instruction was 'improvised' (*schediastheisa*), but the same is not said of the *Procatechesis* or the *Mystagogics*, this change of style in the titles suggests that we are dealing with what were considered two or even three distinct works, since it does not seem likely that it was only the *Catecheses* which were improvised.

By contrast with the *Procatechesis* and the *Catecheses*, the authenticity of which has never been disputed, the attribution of the *Mystagogics* to Cyril has from time to time been called in question, first during the post-Reformation controversies by Protestant writers who were embarrassed by their strong sacramental teaching.[6] Doubts were revived by T. Schermann in 1911, and more recently by W.J. Swaans, who gives a history of the debate, W. Telfer, E. Bihain, G. Kretschmar, A. Renoux, A.A. Stephenson and J. Wilkinson. Several of these authors attribute the *Mystagogic Catecheses* to John of Jerusalem, who occupied the see from Cyril's death until 417, though it is sometimes conceded that John may have done little more than to adapt the mystagogic instructions to which Cyril refers in *Cat.* 18.33. Stephenson however not only hints that the author may have been neither Cyril nor John, but even suggests that the place may not have been Jerusalem; but in this regard his is a lone voice.[7] The main arguments which have been raised against Cyril as the author of the *Mystagogic Catecheses* are these:

(1) While the ancient MSS attribute the *Catecheses* to Cyril, none attributes the *Mystagogics* to him alone (though, of course, when they are attached to the *Catecheses*, as they sometimes are, no such separate attribution would be necessary). Some give no author's name at all; of the Greek MSS, the earliest (Monacensis 394) attributes the *Mystagogics* to John; another of almost equal antiquity

(Ottobiensis 86) originally bore only John's name, with Cyril's added by another hand. Several later MSS attribute the *Mystagogics* to both bishops, but are probably copying Ottobiensis 86. An early Arabic translation in the tenth-century Sinaiticus 22 also carries the name of John alone.[8] Whereas several fifth-century writers, such as Rufinus and Theodoret, quote the *Catecheses*, one has to wait until the second half of the sixth century before finding in Eustratius a quotation from the *Mystagogics* ascribing them to Cyril.[9] By contrast, no ancient MS ascribes the *Mystagogics* to Cyril alone.

(2) Certain liturgical features of the *Mystagogics* seem out of place as early as about 350, when the pre-baptismal instructions were written; these include:

- the inclusion of the Lord's Prayer in the Eucharist;[10]
- the language of awe applied to the Eucharist (*MC* 5.4, 9);
- the explanation of the Eucharist in terms of a change in the elements from bread and wine to Christ's body and blood through an epiclesis of the Holy Spirit;
- the association of the Holy Spirit with the anointing with chrism;
- prayer for the 'Emperors'.[11]

(3) There seem to be various discrepancies between the pre- and post-baptismal instructions. Most notable are the differences in the ways the two sets of addresses explain the gift of the Holy Spirit: in the *Catecheses*[12] it seems to be conferred by a laying-on of hands imparting a 'seal' at the moment of baptism, and is linked with Pentecost; in the *Mystagogics* the Spirit is imparted by a post-baptismal chrismation with little reference to a seal, and reflecting not Pentecost but Jesus' baptism.[13] There are differences in style between the pre- and post-baptismal works: Stephenson finds the style of the Mystagogics 'jejune' and 'poverty-stricken', in contrast with the 'notable mastery of language, a quite rich vocabulary and some imagination' shown by the author of the *Catecheses*.[14] While the *Catecheses* contain many verbal echoes of the *Procatechesis*, such echoes are much harder to find in the *Mystagogics*.

(4) The programme set out in *Cat.* 18.33 for the forthcoming post-baptismal instructions does not exactly correspond to the contents of the *Mystagogics*.

However, many of these objections brought against Cyril as the author of the *Mystagogics* disappear if they were not delivered in the same year as the pre-baptismal instructions, but some thirty years later towards the end of Cyril's episcopate. The liturgical features which seem out of place in the middle of the fourth century are much easier to accept in the 380s, while the dramatic events of those decades may account for a development in Cyril's theology. The most thorough case for the attribution to Cyril has been made by Alexis Doval.[15]

The MS attributions are not decisive against Cyril. More than three centuries before any extant MS of the *Catecheses*, we have seen Eustratius quoting a passage from the *Mystagogics* and attributing it to Cyril; seven MSS of an Armenian florilegium quote the same passage together with the Cyrilline attribution.[16] Moreover the fact that the *Catecheses* seem to have been better known in antiquity than the *Mystagogics* may be due to the different circumstances in which the two sets of sermons were written down. The note at the end of the last *Catechesis* in the Monacensis 394 codex, quoted above, indicates that the *Catecheses* were taken down by a shorthand-writer as they were delivered; if the *Mystagogics* on the other hand were notes made by the preacher himself, they would probably not bear his name, which would have to be supplied by the copyist perhaps centuries later.

The differences in the style of the two sets of addresses can be explained by similar factors. The title of each of the *Catecheses* shows that they were 'improvised', which means that the preacher spoke without a prepared text, and that his words were taken down in delivery by the shorthand-writer. The *Mystagogics*, on the other hand, are not described in their titles as improvised, and indeed their evident 'jejune' character suggests that what we have is a summary of the preacher's words. Often points are touched upon, but not developed. A clear example of this is the telegraphic summary of trinitarian doctrine in connection with the descent of the Holy Spirit on Jesus in the Jordan, 'like resting upon like'.[17] It is consequently a surprise when we read the pilgrim Egeria's description of the rapturous reception which the *Mystagogics* inspired in their hearers.[18] Nevertheless there are points in the text of the *Mystagogics* where a point is elaborated on paper with emotive rhetoric, as in the preacher's exclamation of wonder at the grace of baptism:

> What a strange and wonderful thing! . . . What unmeasured love this showed for mankind! Christ received the nails in his pure hands and experienced pain, and grants me salvation through sharing his experience without the pain and the toil.[19]

The attribution to John now appears implausible. He was celebrated as a follower of Origen, who was attacked by St Jerome precisely for his acceptance of Origen's teachings.[20] However, the attempt to prove any but the most tenuous Origenistic features in the *Mystagogics* has proved unsuccessful. Even A.A. Stephenson, who is convinced that Cyril was not the author of the *Mystagogics*, admits that:

> The case for John's authorship is less strong than the case against Cyril's. For John seems to have been a cultured Origenist of some renown, and the *Mystagogiae* do not seem to be very markedly Origenist.[21]

There is extant an Armenian version of a sermon attributed to John which shows little affinity in style or thought to the *Mystagogics*;[22] moreover, the statement in *MC* 3.1 that the Son and the Spirit were 'like' seems to contradict one of Origen's tenets.[23]

There are in fact notable correspondences between the pre-baptismal addresses and the *Mystagogics*.

(a) There are common features of *style*. Favourite words and metaphors (e.g. those drawn from perfume)[24] occur in both sets of writings. In both *Catecheses* and *Mystagogics* the vivid metaphor of falling over a precipice is used to express danger.[25] Both sets of sermons exhibit a delight in poetic justice, as can be seen by comparing what the *Catecheses* have to say about the fate of Nebuchadnezzar:

> He had nails like a lion, for he had stolen the holy things; he had a lion's mane, for he had been a rapacious, roaring lion; he ate grass like an ox, for he was like cattle, not knowing who had given him his kingdom; his body was bathed in dew, because he had seen dew extinguish fire but had not believed (*Cat.* 2.18)

with the *Mystagogics*' account of the plight of Lot's wife, who 'was turned into a pillar of salt, pilloried for all eternity' (*MC* 1.8), and of hunters,

> who expose themselves to wild beasts in order to indulge their wretched stomachs; to pamper their bellies with food they become themselves food for the stomachs of wild beasts . . . Avoid the races, a mad spectacle which unseats the soul. (*MC* 1.6)

Both sets of writings display a taste for word-play. This taste is evident in the last two quotations from the *Mystagogics:* being made a pillar of salt (*stēlē . . . halos*), Lot's wife was 'pilloried' (*estēliteumenē*) as a reminder of the bitter (literally 'salty', *halmuran*) concerns of life. The spectacle at the races is 'unseating' (*ektrachēlizon*) for the soul as well as the body. The same addiction to word-play can be observed in the pre-baptismal addresses. The *Procatechesis* contains this pun on the word 'catechumen' (*katēchoumenos*), which is derived from the Greek *ēchē* (sound or echo):

> Even now let your ears seem to ring (*katēcheisthai*) with that glorious sound (*ēchēn*) which the angels will raise when you gain salvation. (*Procat.* 15)

Similarly in the *Catecheses* Cyril finds an apt explanation for Manes' name in the Persian word for 'dispute' and the Greek word for 'madness' (*mania*) (*Cat.* 6.24).

(b) There are also significant common *theological* features.

(i) Both sets of sermons speak of Old Testament figures as *types* of Christ.[26] In the *Catecheses* Joshua is said to have 'prefigured' Jesus (*tupon epheren*) (*Cat.* 10.11); in the *Mystagogics* Moses, in leading the Israelites to freedom through the water of the Red Sea, is the type (*tupos*) of Christ who saves his people through the water of baptism, while the blood of the paschal lamb which wards off the destroying angel is the type of Christ's blood which drives away demons (*MC* 1.3). The same terms occur in both groups to express the contrast between the type and the reality: both speak of the reality as *noētos*, *pneumatikos*, *mustikos*, as opposed to what is *sōma/sōmatikos* or *phainomenos*.[27]

(ii) Both sets of sermons express a theory of the double effect which sacraments produce, namely on the body and the soul. In the *Catecheses* Cyril applies this analysis to the waters of baptism:

> For since a human being is twofold, being a composite of soul and body, the purification also is twofold: incorporeal for the incorporeal, and bodily for the body. And the water purifies the body, and the Spirit seals the soul. (*Cat.* 3.4)

In the *Mystagogics* Cyril applies the same analysis to the Eucharist:

> In the New Testament there is the bread of heaven and the cup of salvation, which sanctify both body and soul. Just as

> the bread is suitable for the body, so the Word is adapted to the soul. (*MC* 4.5)

(iii) The very epiclesis theology which has been used as an argument against Cyril as the author of the *Mystagogics* is in fact already to be found in a less developed form in the *Catecheses*. The most developed trinitarian form of epiclesis is to be found in *MC* 5.7, in which God (the Father) is asked to send down the Holy Spirit upon the eucharistic bread and wine, so as to bring about Christ's presence:

> when we have sanctified ourselves through these holy hymns, we call upon the God who loves mankind to send down the Holy Spirit on the offerings so as to make the bread Christ's body and the wine Christ's blood, for whatever the Holy Spirit touches is made holy and transformed.

Similar less developed epicleses are to be found in other passages in the *Mystagogics*: in *MC* 1.7, where as a result of the invocation of the Trinity the bread and wine become Christ's body and blood; in *MC* 2.3, where the 'invocation of God' gives exorcised olive-oil power to purify and drive out the powers of the Evil One; and in *MC* 3.3, where the invocation of the Holy Spirit changes ordinary bread into Christ's body and the *muron* into Christ's grace:

> Beware of imagining that this is ordinary ointment. For just as after the invocation of the Holy Spirit the bread of the Eucharist is no longer ordinary bread but the body of Christ, so too this holy *muron* is no longer ordinary or, so to say, common ointment, but Christ's grace which imparts to us his own divinity through the presence of the Holy Spirit.

Already in *Cat.* 3.3 the names of the three Persons are similarly connected with an epiclesis, in this case over the baptismal water, though as in *MC* 1.7 and 2.3 the roles of the Persons are not clearly distinguished.

> Do not regard the font as ordinary water (*mē hōs hudati litōi prosechе tōi loutrōi*), but regard the spiritual grace which is given with the water. For just as the offerings on [pagan] altars are ordinary (*lita*) by nature, but become contaminated by the invocation of idols, so by contrast after the

> ordinary (*liton*) water has received the invocation of the Holy Spirit and Christ and the Father, it acquires the power of holiness.

Some of these epicletic passages from both groups of addresses contrast the 'ordinary' material of everyday life with the material transformed for sacramental use. In the *Catecheses* the water of the font is not to be conceived as 'ordinary' (*litōi*) water; one should fix one's mind on 'the grace given with the water' (*Cat.* 3.3). In the *Mystagogics* the eucharistic bread and wine after the epiclesis are no longer 'ordinary' (*litos*) or 'mere' (*psilois*) bread and wine, and the *muron* is no longer *psilon* and *koinon* but Christ's grace.[28] An elliptical construction occuring in *Cat.* 3.3 quoted above, namely the use of the verb *prosechein* ('direct'), with the noun *noun* ('mind') omitted, is to be found also in the *Mystagogics*:

> So do not regard them as ordinary bread and wine (*mē proseche oun hōs psilois tōi artōi kai tōi oinōi*). (*MC* 4.6)

(iv) Both the *Procatechesis* and the *Mystagogics* compare the rite of insufflation in exorcism with the kindling of a flame:

> As goldsmiths achieve their effect by directing their breath into the fire through narrow pipes and blowing on the gold hidden in the retort and stimulating the flame underneath, so too the exorcists inspire fear through the Holy Spirit and, so to speak, enkindle the soul inside the retort of the body. Our enemy the devil departs. (*Procat.* 9)

> For just as the breathing of the saints and the invocation of God burns like the fiercest flame and chases away the demons, so too the invocation of God together with prayer gives this exorcised oil such power that it can burn away the traces of sin and even chase away the hidden powers of the evil one. (*MC* 2.3)

Both groups explain the efficacy of baptism by Christ's contact with the water of the Jordan. In the *Procatechesis* the water is 'Christ-bearing'; in the *Catecheses* 'Jesus sanctified baptism by being baptized himself', and crushed the serpent's head in the Jordan; in the *Mystagogics* he 'imparted contact with his divinity to the waters' of the Jordan.[29]

(c) There are notable points of resemblance in spirituality expressed by the pre- and post-baptismal works.

(i) A tender sympathy with the suffering Christ is evident in both sets.

> All the same, people can never weary of hearing about the Master's crown, especially at this holy place of Golgotha. For while others can only hear, we see and touch. So let no one grow weary; take up your arms against your enemies for the sake of the cross. Set up your faith in the cross as a standard against its opponents. When you are about to discuss Christ's cross with unbelievers, first let them see you make the sign of Christ's cross with your hand, and their objections will be silenced. Do not be ashamed to acknowledge the cross, for angels glory in it, saying: 'We know whom you are seeking, Jesus the Crucified' (Mt 28.5). Can't you say, angel: 'I know whom you are seeking: my Master.' 'But', he replies confidently, 'it is the Crucified whom I know.' For the cross is a crown, not a disgrace . . . You can see the place of Golgotha? You express your assent with shouts of praise; see that you never deny it in a time of persecution. Do not rejoice in the cross only in times of peace; preserve the same faith even in times of persecution. Don't be Jesus' friend in times of peace, and his enemy in times of war. (*Cat.* 13.22–3)

> What a strange and wonderful thing! We did not literally die, we were not literally buried, we did not literally rise again after being crucified. We experienced these things only in symbols and representations; but salvation we experienced literally. Christ was really crucified and really buried and literally rose again, and all of this he did for our sake so that we might gain salvation literally. What unmeasured love this showed for mankind! Christ received the nails in his pure hands and experienced pain, and grants me salvation through sharing his experience without the pain and the toil. (*MC* 2.5)

(ii) Both sets of sermons encourage a reaction of awe. The *Procatechesis* explains how the exorcists 'inspire fear' (*phobon*: *Procat.* 9); the *Catecheses* speak of the 'truly great fear' (*phobos . . . alēthōs megas*: *Cat.* 16.1) which is spoken of in the gospels. This emphasis on awe is more developed in the *Mystagogics*. Both the renunciation of the devil and the Eucharist are described as a 'most awesome moment' (*tēn phrikōdestatēn hōran: MC* 1.5; 5.4); the Eucharist itself is 'the holy and most awesome sacrifice' (*tēs hagias kai phrikōdestatēs . . . thusias*: *MC* 5.9). We shall return to the subject of awe in the section on Cyril's liturgy.

Other arguments have been put forward in favour of dating the *Mystagogics* to the last few years of Cyril's life.

(i) C. Beukers has argued that the prayer 'for kings, for our armies and allies' (*MC* 5.8) suggests a time when Cyril was in Jerusalem during a reign of two emperors, which would suggest either 364–367 or after 378; in addition the reference to 'allies' points to a period after 382, when the Visigoths became allies of the Roman Empire.[30] (However it is possible that the mention of prayers for kings is derived from 1 Tim 2.2, and so has no reference to any contemporary political situation.)

(ii) It has been argued that, since St Ambrose's *de Sacramentis*, which was composed about four years after Cyril's death, seems to have been influenced by the *Mystagogic Catecheses*, there would be insufficient time to account for this influence if the *Mystagogics* were the work of Cyril's successor.[31]

In view of the consistencies of style, theology and spirituality which we have indicated, the most plausible hypothesis seems to be that the *Mystagogics* are indeed the notes of instructions Cyril gave towards the end of his episcopate. Differences would then be due to the evolution of a mind over some forty years, and to the different circumstances in which the sermons were produced. The MS attributions are not decisive; however, if the *Mystagogics* were found in Jerusalem only after Cyril's death, the attribution to his successor John is not surprising.

4

LITURGY

Cyril's long episcopate was a period of perhaps unique liturgical creativity, due to historical circumstances as well as his own inventiveness. He must have been born within a few years of the Church's emergence from the shadows of persecution; as a boy he shared in the excitement of the discovery of Christ's cross and his tomb, and he was ordained priest in Constantine's great basilica a very few years after its dedication in 335. By the end of his episcopate in 387 a colourful and moving liturgy had developed in Jerusalem; and, although we have no way of discovering precisely how much of the credit for it belongs to him, his sermons show that he knew how to exploit to the full the liturgical possibilities of the most sacred site in Christendom.[1]

Cyril's own addresses are not the only evidence we possess concerning his practice and understanding of the liturgy. There is also an eye-witness account of the Jerusalem liturgy written by the pilgrim who is now generally known by the name of Egeria. Her work shows that she was a member of a religious community from Spain or the south of Gaul who wrote for her sisters an account of her three-year tour of the biblical lands. As the one, incomplete MS in which the work has come down to us does not tell us the author's name, for its opening pages are missing, the name 'Egeria' was given her as the result of informed guess-work. The first editors at the end of the nineteenth century gave her the name 'Silvia', the sister of Rufinus of Aquitaine, whom Palladius speaks of as a pilgrim;[2] another conjecture was 'Galla Placidia', but this failed to gain general acceptance. In 1903 M. Férotin, observing the close correspondence between her itinerary and that of the woman pilgrim who was the subject of a letter written by the Spanish monk Valerius in the seventh century, argued that the women in the two writings were identical.[3] However, although most scholars have accepted Férotin's suggestion, there remains uncertainty concerning the pilgrim's name, for the MSS of Valerius' letter give her name in several forms. For a while advocates were found for the forms 'Aetheria', 'Etheria' or 'Eucheria', but scholarly opinion now favours the form 'Egeria'; and so we shall call her. The period of her pilgrimage has been fixed precisely as 381–384 by P. Devos,[4] and thus falls within the last few years of Cyril's long episcopate. In her breathless and ungrammatical Latin she provides invaluable information about the liturgical setting of Cyril's sermons.[5]

INITIATION

Since Cyril's addresses never speak of the baptism of babies, it seems likely that the normal practice was to defer the baptism of the children of Christian parents until they were old enough to choose to be baptized. Whether or not J. Jeremias was right to argue that infant baptism was regularly practised in the first two centuries – K. Aland wrote a detailed refutation of the theory – from early in the third century there is evidence for the practice in many parts of the Church.[6] In the middle of the fourth century, however, it seems as if the baptism of babies was generally abandoned for several decades; between 329 and 354 there are many examples of saints who had one or both parents Christians, but were nevertheless not baptized until they were grown up, such as Gregory of Nazianzus (a bishop's son!), Basil the Great, Ambrose and Augustine. It is possible that there is a connection between what Jeremias calls this 'crisis' and the new freedom from the threat of persecution which Christians were enjoying.

The information Cyril gives us about the celebration of initiation in Jerusalem throughout his episcopate does not tell us how candidates were treated before they gave in their names for baptism at the beginning of Lent. From the third century we have references from different parts of the Church to a three-year catechumenate in Rome (Hippolytus), and in Egypt and Palestine (Clement and Origen);[7] on the other hand, Augustine, who was born in North Africa about this time, was received into the catechumenate as a child, but not baptized till many years later. It is impossible to say, however, if either of these arrangements was in force in Jerusalem. L. Dujarier believes that the purposeful programme of instruction which extended over the three years in the early Church was crammed by Cyril into the few weeks of Lent, and necessarily was lacking in depth.[8] W. Harmless however shows that Dujarier overlooked the effect of the prolonged period as catechumens; for even if there were no longer the organized catechetical classes which are evident in the *Apostolic Tradition*, the catechumens attended the Sunday liturgy and heard the readings and the homily before they had to leave the assembly.[9] Cyril asks the candidates for baptism to look back to this period in their lives:

> Up till now you have been called a Catechumen,[10] one who hears from the outside. You heard hope, but you didn't see it. You heard mysteries, but you didn't understand them. You heard the Scriptures, but you didn't understand their depth. But now you are hearing a sound not from outside but from within, for now the Spirit lives in you and makes your mind God's home. (*Procat.* 6)

Augustine later described a rite of admission into the catechumenate which consisted of the tracing of the sign of the cross on the candidate's forehead, a laying-on of hands, the administration of salt on the tongue, and exorcism.[11] Cyril gives us no indication however whether these rites were performed in his church.

Cyril's instructions commence at the beginning of Lent with the enrolment of the catechumens who wish to be baptized at Easter. He gives the impression that the rite had by the middle of the century become something of a formality, so that little rigour was exercised in selecting the candidates for baptism:

> We are the servants of Christ. We welcomed you. We had the responsibility of doorkeepers, but we left the door open. Perhaps you came in with your soul spattered with the mud of your sins and with stained intentions. You came in; you were passed; your name was recorded. (*Procat.* 4)

Egeria however describes a more formal investigation:

> For those who give in their names give them in before the first day of Lent, and a presbyter records everyone's name, that is, before the eight weeks during which, as I have said, Lent is observed.[12] When the presbyter has recorded everyone's name, shortly afterwards on another day of Lent, that is, on the day on which the eight weeks begin, the bishop's

> chair is set in the middle of the Greater Church, that is the Martyrium; the presbyters sit on seats on either side of him, and all the clergy stand. Then the candidates[13] are brought in one by one, the men with their godfathers and the women with their godmothers.[14] Then as they come in one by one, the bishop questions their neighbours in these words: 'Is he good-living? Does he respect his parents? Does he avoid drunkenness and vanity?' And he asks at least about each of the vices which are more serious in a person. If the bishop establishes that the person is above reproach in each point of his inquiry before the witnesses, he writes down the person's name with his own hand. But if a charge is brought against anyone, the bishop orders them to depart, saying: 'Let him amend his life, and when he has done so, then let him come to the font.' In these words he inquires about both men and women. (*Pereg.* 45)

Perhaps therefore over the years between the *Procatechesis* and the *Mystagogics* Cyril perceived the need to be more rigorous in the selection of candidates.

Once the applicants' names have been accepted for baptism they are no longer known as catechumens but 'candidates for enlightenment'.[15] Nevertheless they still have to attend regular catechetical instructions, which have a double purpose: On the one hand they provide a systematic instruction in doctrine:

> Imagine catechesis is a building. If we don't make the house secure by strengthening the building with clamps in the proper order to prevent gaps appearing or the structure becoming unsound, even our earlier efforts will be wasted. Stone must follow stone and corner fit corner in the right order. We must smooth away irregularities if the building is to rise. In the same way we bring you, so to speak, stones of knowledge. You must learn about the living God; you must learn about judgment; you must learn about Christ; you must learn about the resurrection. I shall have many things to say in order: first I must explain them piecemeal, only later in their mutual connections. If you don't join them together into a single whole, remembering what comes first and what second, I will have performed my task of building, but the structure you have will be unsound. (*Procat.* 11)

On the other hand they will receive ammunition to use against opponents:

> You are being given weapons to use against the power ranged against you, weapons against heresies, against Jews and Samaritans and pagans. (*Procat.* 10)

During this period before baptism the candidates also had to attend regular exorcisms, in the course of which they were breathed upon in order to inspire sacred awe and to drive away the devil; during this rite the candidate's face was veiled.[16]

Egeria describes this Lenten process:

> For it is the custom here that during these forty days of fast those who are seeking baptism are first exorcised early in the morning by the clergy as soon as the morning dismissal from the Anastasis has taken place. The bishop's seat is at once placed at the Martyrium in the Greater Church, and all the people to be baptized, both men and women, sit in a circle near the bishop, and their godfathers and mothers stand in their place; and if any of the people want to listen, they all come in and sit down – but only the Faithful.[17] But the catechumens are not present while the bishop teaches the law, which he does in this way: for these forty days beginning with Genesis he goes through all the Scriptures, first expounding them literally, and then explaining the same spiritually. Similarly with regard to the resurrection and faith, everything is similarly explained during these days. This is called catechesis . . . The result is that in these places all the Faithful follow the Scriptures when they are read in church, because they are all taught for these forty days, i.e. from the first to the third hour, since the catechesis lasts three hours . . . When the dismissal has taken place after the catechesis about the third hour, the bishop is at once escorted with hymns to the Anastasis, and the dismissal takes place about the third hour; thus they are taught for three hours a day for seven weeks. (*Pereg.* 46)

Since the extant *Catecheses* would not take anything like three hours to deliver, the time was presumably taken up with repeating the talks in Syriac, in explanations and discussions in small groups, and in exorcisms and prayers.[18] After the five weeks, Egeria states, the candidates 'receive the Creed'; as it has been kept secret from them up to this point, they are now taught it by heart, but are not allowed to write it down. Cyril gave directions for this 'handing over of the Creed', which took place at the end of his fifth *Catechesis*:

> I want you to memorize it word for word, and to recite it very carefully among yourselves. Do not write it down on paper, but inscribe it in your memories and in your hearts. (*Cat.* 5.12)

From this point, Egeria tells us, the bishop begins to explain the Creed to them, as he had the Scriptures, 'first literally and then spiritually' (*Pereg.* 46.3).

Egeria's account of the contents of the catechesis raises problems. (a) There is nothing in Cyril's *Catecheses* corresponding to this systematic exposition of the whole Bible; perhaps this is because the instruction was so informal that a text was not preserved. (b) It is difficult to reconcile the time-table Egeria gives for the instructions on the Scriptures and the Creed with the text of Cyril's *Catecheses*. If, as she says, no instructions were given in the eighth week (*Pereg.* 46.4), and the instructions on the Creed did not begin until the end of the fifth week, it is hard to see how the thirteen which exist could have been fitted in, especially as they do not seem to have been given every day.[19] (c) We shall discuss in section 5 below Cyril's treatment of the literal and spiritual senses of Scripture; but what does Egeria mean when she speaks of the literal and spiritual senses of the Creed? What Cyril does do is to explain how the truths about Christ are foreshadowed in the Old Testament; perhaps this is her understanding of the spiritual sense of the Creed.

Although Cyril does not tell us this, we know from Egeria that towards the end of Lent the candidates had to appear before the bishop in the Martyrium and show him that they had learnt the Creed by heart:

> The bishop's seat is placed at the back of the apse behind the altar, and there they come one by one, the men with their godfathers and the women with their godmothers, and recite the Creed to the bishop. When the recitation of the Creed to the bishop is completed, the bishop addresses them all in these words: 'During these seven weeks of Lent you have learnt the whole law of the Scriptures and also

> heard about faith; you have heard also about the resurrection of the flesh and a full explanation of the Creed, at least as far as was permitted to you as catechumens. But matters of deeper mystery, that is, concerning baptism itself, you are not allowed to hear, since you are still catechumens. And lest you should think that anything is done without good reason, when you have been baptized in the name of God, you will receive instruction in the Anastasis throughout Easter week after the dismissal from the church.[20]

The final sentence is confirmed by Cyril's remarks towards the end of the last *Catechesis*:

> After the holy and saving day of Easter, starting on Monday every day of the following week, after the assembly you will enter the holy place of the resurrection, where, God willing, you will hear further catechetical instructions. You will receive further teaching about the reasons for everything that is done, and you will receive proofs from the Old and New Testaments.[21]

Cyril's *Mystagogics* contain ample information about the rites of initiation celebrated at the Easter Vigil. To appreciate the impact of the rites, we should remember that the candidate will have received no precise information about what to expect. Cyril's account begins with the candidates' entry into the outer hall of the baptistery, which was probably to the south of the Holy Sepulchre. There they each hear a voice coming out of the darkness – Cyril repeatedly emphasizes the voice of the instructor – telling them to stretch out their hand and renounce Satan, presumably repeating the formula phrase by phrase, 'as though he stood there before you' in the west, the home of darkness (*MC* 1.2). Next they are turned to face the east from which the Easter sun is shortly to rise and bidden to make a brief profession of faith, which takes the place of the traditional act of loyalty to Christ. They thus announce to the devil that they are transferring their loyalty from him to Christ – an act which, in an age when the devil was taken seriously, must have required a degree of courage.

The candidates then enter the baptistery itself, where they strip. Although Cyril attributes their freedom from embarrassment to their recovery of the innocence of Paradise, one must remember too that it was dark and the sexes were probably segregated. Their whole bodies are then anointed with exorcised olive-oil; Cyril sees this rite not only as a protection against devils (this was the customary explanation) but also as a symbol of a 'share in the richness of Christ' (*MC* 2.2–3). Baptism follows in the usual form: the candidate is immersed three times after professing faith in God the Father, Son and Holy Spirit. The baptized re-enact the Lord's three days in the tomb, and themselves die and are reborn (*MC* 2.4). Coming up from the font, the neophytes are clothed in a white baptismal robe (*MC* 4.8), and anointed with perfumed oil called *muron* or chrism; in this way they share Christ's Messianic anointing, and, like Christ after his own baptism, receive the Holy Spirit (*MC* 3.1). Finally they attend the whole of the Eucharist for the first time, for catechumens and candidates for baptism had to leave the church after the liturgy of the word. In the course of this Eucharist they hear for the first time the Lord's Prayer; later in St Augustine's Hippo the Prayer was taught before baptism in a rite which paralleled the handing over of the Creed.[22]

We have seen how at the end of Lent Cyril promised that he would explain the rites of initiation in the week after Easter. Egeria also speaks of daily instructions 'throughout those eight days, i.e. from Easter to the octave' (*Pereg.* 47.1). In fact, however, there are only five *Mystagogics*; which suggests that here and perhaps elsewhere Egeria's account may not be completely accurate.[23] She gives her sisters a charming description of Cyril as he delivered these last instructions:

> When the Easter season arrives, throughout those eight days, i.e. from Easter to the octave, after the customary dismissal from the church and procession with hymns to the Anastasis, a prayer is said immediately, the people are blessed, and the bishop stands leaning on the inner rail in the cave of the Anastasis, and explains everything which took place at baptism. At that time no catechumen is present; the only ones to enter the Anastasis are the neophytes and the Faithful who wish to hear of the mysteries. The doors are shut, to prevent any catechumen from getting in. As the bishop explains and recalls each point, the shouts of applause are so loud that they can be heard even outside the church. For truly he unfolds the mysteries in such a way that no one who hears them explained in his way can be left unmoved. (*Pereg.* 47.1–2)

EUCHARIST

Since catechumens regularly attended the first part of the Eucharist, departing after the readings, homily and intercessions, Cyril's description begins at the point which was unfamiliar to them, namely the celebrant's washing of his hands, apparently to the accompaniment of Psalm 25 (26) ('I shall wash my hands among the innocent') and the kiss of peace. Cyril's reference to the command to be reconciled before making an offering suggests that the Offertory followed.[24] Next came the Preface with the customary introductory dialogue, concluding with the Sanctus (*MC* 5.4–6).

The rest of the Eucharistic Prayer presents an important problem. Its structure seems to be:

- epiclesis, or invocation of the Holy Spirit to change the bread and wine into Christ's body and blood (n. 7);
- intercessions for the living (n. 8);
- commemoration of the dead and intercessions for them (nn. 9–10).

However, can there really have been no Institution Narrative and no prayer of Anamnesis (commemoration) and Offering, both of which are indispensable features of later Eucharistic Prayers? It is true that, since Cyril gives us only a paraphrase and not the complete text, it is possible that the 'missing' sections did form part of his Prayer, but for some reason were omitted from his summary. However, this seems less likely, as the phrases 'then' and 'after this' which introduce each of the three sections set out above seem to indicate that the list is meant to be exhaustive. Thus after giving a paraphrase of the Sanctus, Cyril continues:

> Then, when we have sanctified ourselves through these holy hymns, we call upon the God who loves mankind to send down the Holy Spirit on the offerings so as to make the bread Christ's body and the wine Christ's blood, for whatever the Holy Spirit touches is made holy and transformed. (n. 7)

With apparently no space left for the Narrative and Anamnesis the text continues:

> Then, after the completion of the spiritual sacrifice, the worship without blood, we call upon God over this sacrifice of propitiation for the peace of all the churches . . . (n. 8)

A number of commentators have therefore taken Cyril's Eucharistic Prayer to be but one of several without Institution Narratives, such as the *Didache* and the Liturgy of SS. Addai and Mari,[25] so that the later Jerusalem liturgy of St James would be a composite of Cyril's prayer with the 'missing' sections added later from other sources. Nevertheless, whatever be the case with primitive liturgies, comparison with other examples from Cyril's period makes it unlikely that a liturgy as late as the 380s would be without Institution Narrative or Anamnesis-Oblation.

For this and other reasons it seems more plausible to suggest that Cyril's 'completion of the spiritual sacrifice' included some form of Institution Narrative and Anamnesis-Oblation. There is no evidence that at this date the Eucharistic Prayer was thought to be composed of epiclesis, Narrative and Anamnesis *as distinct modules*. Cyril probably takes it to be composed of two sections: the first, sacrificial section being followed by the intercessions 'over' the sacrifice. In this way the structure of Cyril's Prayer would resemble that of the Egyptian Liturgy of St Mark, in which, after the conclusion of the Sanctus, 'heaven and earth are full of your glory', God is asked to 'fill' the sacrifice through the descent of the Holy Spirit (epiclesis), because of Christ's words and deeds at the Last Supper (Narrative), in consequence of which the sacrifice is offered in proclamation (Anamnesis) of Jesus' death and resurrection.[26]

After the Eucharistic Prayer there follow:

- the Lord's Prayer (nn. 11–18)
- holy communion (nn. 19–22).
- a prayer of thanksgiving (n. 22).

DAILY OFFICE

Although Cyril's own writings give no account of the celebration of the Office in Jerusalem, Egeria describes it in detail. The first liturgical hour is that of the Vigil celebrated before cockcrow by the monks and virgins in the Anastasis, in the presence of laypeople, perhaps pilgrims like herself; it consists of psalms said responsorially, antiphons and prayers. At daybreak the bishop arrives with the clergy, enters the cave of the resurrection, and pronounces prayers and blessings; he then comes out from the cave, and stands within the railing to bless and dismiss the people individually. The same pattern is followed at noon and the ninth hour (3 p.m.). At the tenth hour in the presence of the bishop the Lucernarium is celebrated, at which the candles are lit from the flame which burned perpetually inside the cave; then a deacon reads a list of people who are to be prayed for, and to each name a large choir of children replies '*Kyrie Eleison*'. The bishop blesses the catechumens and the Faithful separately, then goes in procession to the jewelled cross that stood on the rock of Calvary, and again blesses the catechumens and the Faithful. Finally the procession moves 'behind the cross' to the Martyrium, where the blessings are repeated.[27]

On Sundays the worship is much more elaborate, and participation in it calls for considerable stamina. The people assemble in the Martyrium before cockcrow so as not to be late, and sing psalms (*ymni*) while they wait for the doors of the Anastasis to be opened.

> But as soon as the first cock crows, the bishop comes down and enters the cave in the Anastasis; all the doors are opened and the whole crowd comes into the Anastasis, where countless lights are already shining. When the people have come in, one of the priests recites a psalm and everyone responds, and then a prayer is said. Again one of the deacons recites a psalm and a prayer is said in the same way; then a third psalm is recited by one of the clergy, a prayer is said for the third time, and [the needs of] all are called to mind. So when these three psalms have been recited and the three prayers have been said, at once thuribles are carried into the cave of the Anastasis, and the whole basilica of the Anastasis is filled with their fragrance. Then the bishop stands there inside the railings, takes the gospel, goes to the door[28] and personally reads the account of the Lord's resurrection. As soon as the reading begins, the cries and the groans of all the people are so loud, and there is so much weeping that even the most hardened person could be moved to tears because the Lord suffered so much for us. So after reading the Gospel, the bishop goes out and is escorted with psalms to the Cross, and all the people go with him. There once more a psalm is recited and a prayer said; again he blesses the Faithful, and the dismissal takes place. As the bishop leaves, everyone approaches his hand.[29] Thereupon the bishop retires to his house, and from that time all the monks return to the Anastasis, and psalms and antiphons are recited until it is daylight; with each psalm or antiphon a prayer is said. For every day the priests and the deacons take turns in watching at the Anastasis with the people.

> Any laymen or laywomen who wish remain there until it is daylight; those who prefer not to, return home and take some more sleep.
>
> When it is daylight, because it is Sunday, there is a procession to the Greater Church which Constantine built, the church at Golgotha behind the cross, and everything is done as is customary everywhere on Sunday. All the same, because it is the custom here for any of the priests who are in their seats to preach if they wish, and after them the bishop preaches – these homilies are given every Sunday in order to train the people continually in the Scriptures and the love of God – while these homilies are being delivered there is a long wait before the dismissal from the church is given, and so it does not take place before the fourth or even the fifth hour.

The bishop then leads the Faithful, but not the catechumens, back into the Anastasis, where 'thanks are given to God' – which may be a reference to the Eucharist. It is getting on for noon before the service is over (*Pereg.* 24.8–25.1).

FEASTS

Egeria shows how much use Cyril made of the sacred sites connected with each feast, though the incomplete state of the MS leaves gaps in our knowledge. Pentecost Sunday was celebrated at Sion (the Upper Room) rather than the Martyrium (*Pereg.* 25.6). Christ's birth was celebrated at the Epiphany:

> It would be impossible to describe the decoration that day of the churches of the Anastasis, the cross or in Bethlehem. You can see nothing there but gold and jewels and silk. The hangings you see are of gold-embroidered silk; the curtains you see too are of gold-embroidered silk. The sacred vessels of every kind brought out that day are gold and jewelled. And how could one calculate or describe the number or weight of the candles, the candelabra, the lamps and the various sacred vessels? (*Pereg.* 25.8)

The feast was celebrated for eight days. On the fourth day the celebrations were held in the Eleona instead of the Martyrium, on the fifth at the Lazarium, dedicated to Lazarus at Bethany, on the sixth at Sion, on the seventh in the Anastasis, and on the eighth at the Martyrium again. Throughout the week the church at Bethlehem was decorated in the same way, and joyful celebrations were held there.[30] Forty days after the Epiphany the Presentation was commemorated, with the appropriate readings from St Luke (*Pereg.* 26).

Egeria describes the observance of Lent and Holy Week in great detail. What is now called Palm Sunday was celebrated at the various sacred sites: at the Lazarium, where the gospel passage recounting Mary's anointing of Jesus' feet (Jn 12) was read, and the Mount of Olives, first at the Eleona (at the cave where Jesus taught) and then at the Imbomon, the place of the Ascension. At the eleventh hour, after the reading of the Palm Sunday gospel, the bishop and the people went in procession down from the Mount and through the city to the Anastasis.

> For all the people go in front of him with psalms and antiphons, repeating the response: 'Blessed is he who comes in the name of the Lord.' And all the children in the region, including those who are too young to walk, and their parents hold them at their necks – all holding branches, some of palm-trees, others of olive-trees. And in this way the bishop is escorted in the same way that the Lord was escorted then . . . and in this way, slowly, slowly, so as not to tire the people, it is already evening by the time they reach the Anastasis. (*Pereg.* 31.2–3)

On the Monday, Tuesday and Wednesday there were long services of psalms, readings and prayers, lasting from 3 to 7 p.m. On the Tuesday there was a night visit to the Eleona, where the bishop read from St Matthew the discourse Jesus gave on the Mount of Olives after his entry into Jerusalem: 'See that no one leads you astray' (Mt 24.4). On the Wednesday night in the Anastasis a priest read from outside the rails of the tomb the gospel account of Judas' bargain to betray Jesus.

> And when this passage is read the cries and the groans of the whole congregation are so loud that no one can fail to be moved to tears at this time. (*Pereg.* 34)

On the Thursday afternoon, the Eucharist was celebrated twice, first in the Martyrium, then in the open courtyard 'before the cross'

– the only occasion in the year, Egeria tells us, when the Eucharist was celebrated there.[31] The people, having been warned to assemble at the Eleona in the first hour of the night, 'for a very tiring experience faces us tonight', 'all hurry to return home to eat', before climbing the Mount of Olives. They remain there till midnight, engaged in psalms, prayers and readings of the gospel passages in which 'the Lord spoke to the disciples on this day, seated in the very cave which is in this church'; they then move on to the Imbomon, to the place of the Ascension, for more hymns, readings and prayers. At cockcrow the procession moves on to 'the place where the Lord prayed', where there is an 'elegant church', where the gospel account of the Agony in the Garden is read; then all, 'up to the smallest infant', descend with the bishop to Gethsemani,

> where, because of the size of the crowd, and wearied by the watching and worn out by the daily fasting, because they have to descend so high a mountain, slowly, slowly, they come with hymns to Gethsemani. More than two hundred church candles have been prepared to provide light for all the people.

There the account of Jesus' arrest is read, once more amid cries and groans and tears, which can almost be heard in the city. The procession reaches the city gates at first light, where:

> everyone without exception is waiting there, older and younger, rich and poor. On that day above all no one leaves from the vigil to the morning.

From there they move to the cross, which they reach by daybreak, where the account of the trials of Jesus is read. The bishop then addresses some words of encouragement to the people:

> Go to your own homes now, each one of you, and rest for a little while, and be ready here about the second hour of the day; and from then until the sixth hour you can see the holy wood of the cross, and believe that it will be profitable to each one of us for our salvation. (*Pereg.* 36)

First, however, the devout go to Sion to the column where Jesus was scourged. The veneration of the wood of the cross takes place 'behind the cross', where the oblation has been celebrated the day before.[32]

> The bishop sits on his seat with a table covered with a cloth in front of him; the deacons stand round the table. A box of silver and gold is brought, containing the holy wood of the cross. It is opened and brought forward, and the wood of the cross and the title are placed on the table.

The bishop presses on the ends of the holy wood, while the people file up and bow to kiss it. Deacons stand around to guard the relic, because a pilgrim was said to have bitten out a piece of it.

> So in this way all the people file by one by one, bending and touching the cross and the title first with their forehead and then with their eyes, and so they kiss the cross and pass on, but no one stretches out a hand to touch it.

Here follows the veneration of Solomon's ring and the horn which held the oil with which the kings were anointed (*Pereg.* 37.1–3).

At midday, wet or fine, they reconvene before the cross in a 'very big and quite beautiful courtyard', where the bishop's chair is set, for a three-hour service of psalms and readings of all the passages in the Gospels, Epistles and Acts which deal with the Passion, as well as the Old Testament prophecies.

> In this way during those three hours all the people are taught that nothing took place which was not foretold, and that nothing was foretold which was not fully fulfilled . . . At each of the readings and prayers the emotion and the groaning of all the people is so great that it is a wonder; for there is no one, old or young, who does not lament for those three hours that day to an extent that cannot be imagined at the thought of what the Lord suffered for us.

The service concludes with John's account of the Lord giving up his spirit. Another service in the Martyrium follows. Although everyone is tired,

> the people who wish – or rather can – do keep vigil there [in the Martyrium] until morning, but the clergy do keep vigil there, at least the stronger or younger among them. (*Pereg.* 37.4–9)

A large number of people kept vigil for part of the time.

On the Saturday the usual offices are performed at the third, sixth and ninth hours. The vigil itself Egeria does not describe, as it was celebrated in the same way in her own home, noting only that the newly baptized in their white robes go with the bishop from the baptistery to the Anastasis, before joining the congregation in the Martyrium. After the Easter Vigil the people revisit the Anastasis, where the Easter Gospel is read again. On the afternoon of Easter Sunday there is a procession to Sion, where John's account of Jesus' appearance to the Apostles in the Upper Room is read (*Pereg.* 38–9).

During Easter Week the churches are decorated as for the Epiphany. Every day the bishop, the clergy, the religious (*aputactitae*), the neophytes and any others who wish climb the Mount of Olives and visit the Eleona and the Imbomon, returning to the Anastasis for the Lucernarium. On Low Sunday all the people take part, after which they proceed to Sion for the reading of the Gospel about the appearance to Thomas and the other Apostles. For the seven weeks after Easter there is no fasting.

Pentecost Sunday is a a very strenuous day for the people.[33] After the usual Sunday Eucharist in the Martyrium, the whole congregation 'without exception' (*usque ad unum*: *Pereg.* 43.2) proceeds with psalms to Sion, so as to arrive at precisely the third hour. Then the account in Acts of the descent of the Holy Spirit at that hour is read, after which the Eucharist is celebrated. After a short rest, the people all climb up to the Imbomon, 'so that not a single Christian remains in the city'. There the Scripture passages about the Ascension are read. From there the procession goes to the Eleona, then down the hill to the Martyrium, which is not reached until the second hour of the night, for the procession moves 'slowly, slowly . . . in case their feet get tired' (*Pereg.* 43.7). By the light of two hundred candles they enter the Martyrium through the great doors which face the forum. From there they go to the Anastasis and the cross, and finally to Sion, where there are more readings, psalms and prayers.

> Thus very tiring efforts are borne on this day, since vigil was kept at first cockcrow at the Anastasis, and from that point there has been no respite throughout the day; and all the ceremonies are prolonged to such an extent that it is midnight by the time everyone returns home after the dismissal takes place on Sion. (*Pereg.* 43.9)

Another octave was celebrated, Egeria tells us, for the annual celebration of the Dedication of both the Martyrium and the Anastasis

(*Pereg.* 48–9). However, Egeria may be mistaken here, since the Anastasis was not built by Constantine, but later during the episcopate of Cyril. The date was between 12 and 15 September, and coincided with the celebration of the Finding of the Cross. It also coincided with that of the dedication of the Roman temple of Jupiter Capitolinus, who had been one of the patrons of the pagan city of Aelia Capitolina; this fact supports the theory that Constantine intended his buildings at Jerusalem to match and outshine the pagan rites. The name 'Encaenia' (Dedication) is derived from the Septuagint text of 2 Chron 7.9, which recounts Solomon's dedication of the Temple.[34] People came from as far afield as Egypt and Mesopotamia for the celebration; 'more than forty or fifty bishops' took part. The churches were decorated as sumptuously as at Easter and the Epiphany. Processions went on different days to the Eleona and other sites as during the other octaves.

LECTIONARY

At the head of each of Cyril's baptismal addresses except the *Procatechesis* the MSS note the Scripture reading, to which the preacher sometimes subsequently refers. Cyril's lectionary corresponds almost exactly with the readings prescribed in the Old Armenian Lectionary for the use of the Armenian community in Jerusalem. This document has survived in three recensions, the earliest MS, which is in Yerevan, the Armenian capital, dating from the beginning of the fifth century, only about twenty years after Cyril's death; the other two MSS, from Paris and Jerusalem respectively, date, according to A. Renoux, between 417 and 439.[35]

The Armenian Lectionary does more than just set out the passages read at the various services; it also confirms many of the details Egeria gives concerning the particular church in which each service is held. In addition it provides us with information about the observance of saints' days in Jerusalem, which perhaps Egeria reported in a section of her *Peregrinatio* which has not survived.

MYSTERIES[36]

Historians have given the name *disciplina arcani* (the discipline of secrecy) to the practice of keeping the central rites and formulas hidden from those who were not members of the Church. This sense of reserve is already apparent in the Gospels: 'Do not give what is holy to the dogs, or throw your pearls before swine' (Mt 7.6). In the fourth century however this plea for reverence developed into a widespread and systematic command not to reveal the Christian mysteries to pagans or even catechumens. Thus the unbaptized had to leave the congregation before the eucharistic section of the liturgy; hence the distinction between the Mass of the catechumens and the Mass of the Faithful. Apart from the baptismal and eucharistic rites, the secrecy extended to the Creed, which in Jerusalem was not taught until a few days before baptism, and the Lord's Prayer, which was kept secret until the Easter Eucharist.[37] Especial care was taken not to commit the secrets to writing. Before teaching the Creed to the baptismal candidates, Cyril warned them not to write it down (*Cat.* 5.12); later Pope Innocent I instructed another bishop that the Kiss of Peace should be given 'after everything which I am not entitled to make public' (*Ad Decentium*, 1.4: PL 20.553). Accordingly in Jerusalem the candidates went through the rites of initiation without any preliminary explanation; it was not until the week after Easter that Cyril taught the newly baptized the meaning of these rites in the *Mystagogic Catecheses*. Egeria describes the enthusiasm with which these instructions were received:

> the bishop stands, leaning on the inner railing in the cave of the Anastasis, and explains everything which is done at baptism . . . And as the bishop explains and recalls each point, the shouts of applause are so loud that they can be heard even outside the church. For truly he unfolds all the mysteries in such a way that no one who hears them explained in this way can be left unmoved. (*Pereg.* 47.1–2)

Cyril gives reasons for this practice. It is better pedagogically to witness the rites before learning their meaning: 'I saw clearly that seeing is much more convincing than hearing.' Only now are they 'able to understand the more divine mysteries' (*MC* 1.1). Although St Ambrose followed the same practice in Milan, in other places the practice was different; St John Chrysostom, for example, instructed the candidates in advance, 'so that you may go from here with knowledge and a more assured faith' (*Bapt. Hom.* (Stavronikita) 2.12).

Closely associated with the *disciplina arcani* was the use of the liturgy to inspire awe. Thus Cyril describes both the renunciation of the devil and the Eucharistic Prayer as an 'awe-inspiring moment'; the consecrated bread and wine are the 'awe-inspiring sacrifice' (*MC* 1.5; 5.4; 5.9); as early as the *Procatechesis* he relates how the exorcists 'inspire fear' (*Procat.* 9). In practice Cyril seems deliberately to have performed the rites in such a way as to foster this experience of awe, as his explanation of the Renunciation shows:

> Nonetheless you hear a voice telling you to stretch out your hand and say to him as if he were there before you: 'I renounce you, Satan.' I want to tell you why you stand facing west, for you need to know. The west is the quarter from which darkness appears, and Satan is himself darkness and exerts his power in the dark. (*MC* 1.4)

This defiance cast in Satan's face in the darkness of the baptistery must have been a particularly spine-chilling experience. In fact all the initiation-rites must have had a cumulative effect of this kind. Even before giving in their names for baptism, the candidates had heard mysterious hints of great secrets and privileges that lay before them. In the *Procatechesis* and the first *Catechesis* Cyril summarizes these enticements:

> The baptism which lies before you is a great matter. For prisoners it means ransom; for sins forgiveness; the death of sin; new birth for the soul; a shining garment; a holy, indelible seal; a chariot to heaven; the food of paradise; the grant of royalty; the grace of adoption. (*Procat.* 16)

> Acquire the pledge of the Holy Spirit through faith, so that you may be received into the everlasting tabernacles. Approach the mystic seal, so as to be recognizable to your Master. Be numbered among Christ's holy and spiritual flock, to be set apart on his right hand and to inherit the life which has been prepared for you. (*Cat.* 1.2)

The same concern for the emotive power of the liturgy can be seen in Cyril's exploitation of its celebration at the very places where each saving incident took place. In addition to the Martyrium, the Anastasis and the rock of Calvary, there were services at Sion, the Lazarium, the Eleona, the Imbomon, the place of the Agony, and that of the Arrest; there were also visits to Bethlehem:

> people can never weary of hearing about the Master's crown, especially at this holy place of Golgotha. For while others can only hear, we see and touch. (*Cat.* 13.22)

Egeria's repeated descriptions of the cries and the groans which the people were moved to utter during the Easter services is testimony to the emotive power of the celebrations.

Long before Cyril's time this exploitation of religious awe had been a feature of the Greek and Roman mystery-religions. The very word 'awe-inspiring' (*phrikōdēs*), which literally means 'causing a shiver' or 'making the hair stand on end', had formed part of the vocabulary of the pagan mysteries; in these initiation was performed through secret rites in which the candidates took part in the re-enactment of episodes in the life of a god or goddess, generally involving death and resurrection. One of these rites to which the word 'awe-inspiring' was applied was the celebration of the mysteries of the corn-goddess Demeter or Ceres.[38] These mysteries commemorated Demeter's loss of her daughter Persephone (Proserpine), who had been carried off by Dis (Pluto), the god of the underworld. While the goddess was mourning her loss, she refused to allow the wheat to grow; but eventually Persephone was reunited with her mother for eight months in every year, which symbolized the period of growth. Every year in commemoration of Demeter's loss and recovery of her daughter, at the time of the autumn sowing the Athenians performed ceremonies at Eleusis, which included rites of initiation. Although little is known about the details of these secret rites, it seems that the candidate was required to re-enact Demeter's search for Persephone, fasting, sitting with veiled face on a fleece-covered stool beneath a winnowing-fan, and given a spiced or drugged drink called *kykeon*. Much play was made of the alternation of light and darkness:

> Proserpine is sought in the night by the light of torches. Once she is found the whole rite ends amid rejoicing and the waving of torches.[39]

A climax of the ceremony seems to have been the contemplation and handling of a sacred object, perhaps a golden ear of wheat. Thus Clement of Alexandria records the following profession of faith made by the initiates:

> I fasted; I drank the *kykeon*; I took out of a box, handled and put away in a basket; I took out of the basket and put into the box.[40]

Although the original purpose of the Eleusinian rites was to obtain from the gods the seasonal rebirth of the crops, their aim was eventually extended to include a blessed afterlife. In the words of Aristides, whom we have quoted above:

> The effect of the festival is not only immediate pleasure or release from past misfortunes; with regard to death they have fairer hopes that they will enjoy a happier existence and not lie in the darkness and mud that are in store for the uninitiated. (*Eleusinios* 259)

The great Roman orator Cicero, who was himself initiated into the Eleusinian mysteries, pays this tribute to their power:

> Your Athens was the source of many great and wonderful benefits to the human race; but I think that none is greater than those mysteries which refined our uncouth rustic lives and made us humane and gentle. (*de Legibus* 2.26)

The mysteries owed their effectiveness to the emotive power of the rites. According to a catch-phrase that was attributed to Aristotle, 'those undergoing initiation are not expected to gain knowledge (*mathein*) but an experience (*pathein*) and a disposition'.[41]

Christian initiation, as practised by Cyril at Jerusalem, bore striking resemblances to these pagan rites.

- The *disciplina arcani*, which, as we have seen, existed already in embryonic form in New Testament times, seems to have been extended and systematized;
- Cyril's eventual practice of conferring the rites of initiation without previous explanation, on the grounds that 'seeing is much more convincing than hearing', recalls Aristotle's principle that the initiates are influenced by 'experience' rather than 'learning'. The very terms 'mystagogic' and 'mystagogy' are borrowed from the pagan mysteries (*MC* 1.1; 2.1).
- Cyril seems to have striven to create a dramatic effect on the candidates like that of the pagan mysteries. As we have seen, he used the same terms to express religious awe as they did, and he practised the same techniques. There have been preliminary mysterious hints, the effects of protracted fasts and sleeplessness, daily moral exhortations and exorcisms, constant prompting by the godparents, all of which have conspired to raise the candidates to a pitch of expectation. Finally at the Easter Vigil after prolonged prayers, they are led into a corner, where a voice

comes out of the darkness commanding them one by one to turn on the devil, point at him, and reject him to his face, then to turn to Christ and swear allegiance to him; they remain only half comprehending as they find themselves stripped, anointed from head to toe, pushed three times under the water; then, after fragrant oil has been poured on their heads, they are dressed in white and led to the tomb of the risen Lord, then into the Martyrium, the church which is the witness to the Passion, where they are greeted with joy and for the first time take part in the secret rites of the Mass, and receive for the first time the bread and wine over which have been said the Lord's words: 'This is my body . . . my blood' – and all without any explanation.

- Just as the Eleusinian initiate re-enacted the experiences of Demeter as she searched for her daughter, so Cyril makes much of the fact that baptism involves a sharing in Christ's Passion. While linking his ideas with Romans 6.3–4, he gives the text a peculiar twist by dwelling on the sharing in Christ's sufferings, and not just his death. In stripping for baptism the candidates imitate Christ in his nakedness on the cross (*MC* 2.2). The short walk from the outer room of the baptistery to the font recalls Jesus' passage from Calvary to the tomb (*MC* 2.4). The triple immersion recalls his three days in the tomb:

> we were not literally buried, we did not literally rise again after being crucified. We experienced these things only in symbols and representations; but salvation we experienced literally . . . What unmeasured love this showed for mankind! Christ received the nails in his pure hands and experienced pain, and grants me salvation through sharing his experience without the pain and the toil. (*MC* 2.5)

This accumulation of points of resemblance between Cyril's baptismal practice and the pagan initiation rites confirms Hugo Rahner's belief that there was here and elsewhere a conscious attempt to assimilate into Christian practice some of the liturgical techniques of the mystery-religions.[42]

If any one person is to be singled out as the original thinker behind this scheme, the most likely candidate is Constantine.[43] Before his conversion the Emperor had been a devotee of the one god symbolized by the Unconquered Sun,[44] and had been initiated into various mysteries. He now transferred his allegiance to Christ and adopted the cross as the emblem of Christ's victory and his own.[45] Accordingly he determined to transfer Rome from the protection of the pagan gods to that of Christ, and eventually founded a new, Christian Rome at Byzantium. Throughout the empire Christian mysteries were to replace the old pagan ones. Jerusalem, the place where the Christian hero-god had died and risen, and where one could revere the sacred objects connected with his sufferings, above all the cross, Golgotha and the tomb, was the perfect place for the foundation of a Christian mystery-shrine, which superseded the pagan ones and provided the ideal location for the celebration of the Christian rites of initiation.[46] To Jerusalem were added Bethlehem and the Mount of Olives. As Eusebius explains it, Constantine's master-plan was this:

> Choosing in this region three places which were honoured by three mystical caves, he set about adorning them with opulent buildings.[47]

Constantine had already erected many churches before work began on the Palestinian buildings, beginning with the Lateran basilica in Rome in 313. In the mid-320s, however, he began a new style of church, such as the basilicas of St Peter and St Paul in Rome, incorporating a martyr's tomb or a sacred place. A. Grabar suggested that this new style was derived from pagan cult-centres for the worship of heroes, in which the tomb of the hero was sometimes contained in a crypt within a round or polygonal structure, and set beneath an altar or shrine.[48] The three churches in the Holy Land conformed to this new type. The buildings at Bethlehem and the Eleona incorporated respectively the caves of the Nativity and the teaching of the mysteries; in Jerusalem the Martyrium was built over the spot where the cross was found, and the tomb set apart in a cave-like structure outside.

Since the Martyrium had been dedicated for some fourteen years by the time Cyril became bishop, he cannot take all the credit for the devising of the imaginative liturgy which was celebrated there. However, he seems to have exploited and developed what he inherited; and to Constantine's buildings in the Holy Places he added the churches at Sion, the Anastasis and the Imbomon. Pilgrims like Egeria spread his influence throughout the Christian world.

5

CYRIL'S USE OF SCRIPTURE, AND HIS THEOLOGY

Since Jerusalem was a point of contact between Greek- and Syriac-speaking Christians, it is no surprise that Cyril's theology shows numerous points of affinity with both Antiochene and Syriac writings. Thus his Christology is in some respects in the tradition of Antioch, while his use of typology and imagery has many parallels in Syriac literature.[1]

THE USE OF SCRIPTURE

Cyril subscribed to a form of *scriptura sola* doctrine, stating categorically that every doctrinal statement must be based on the Scriptures: 'let us not presume to speak of what is not in Scripture' (*Cat.* 16.24).

> For where the divine and holy mysteries of the Creed are concerned, one must not teach casually without reference to the sacred Scriptures, or be led astray by persuasive and elaborate arguments. Do not simply take my word when I tell you these things, unless you are given proof for my teaching from holy Scripture. (*Cat.* 4.17)

The Creed summarizes the Scriptures which contain the whole of doctrine (*Cat.* 5.12).

Cyril's method of interpreting Scripture had more in common with Antioch than with Alexandria. The Alexandrian Fathers, following Philo, Clement and Origen, influenced no doubt by the methods which the literary critics of their city employed to expound the Homeric poems, were quick to seek a philosophical or spiritual message beyond the literal interpretation of a passage, and in doing so were prone to attach a deep, allegorical significance to each detail of a narrative. Thus for Origen the 'two measures' which the pots at Cana contained refers to the two senses of God's word, 'the soul meaning and the spiritual meaning'.[2] The Antiochenes, on the other hand, while suspicious of the arbitrary nature of allegory, were not opposed to every kind of 'spiritual' interpretation, provided that the historical narrative was respected.[3] Thus John Chrysostom appealed not only to verbal prophecy but also to 'prophecy expressed in terms of things'.[4]

It is this Antiochene method which Cyril adopts and develops. In the *Catecheses* he repeatedly regards events in the Old Testament as prophecies of the circumstances of Jesus' Passion and resurrection, providing 'testimonies (*marturias*) concerning the cross', and 'proofs (*apodeixeis*) concerning the resurrection' (*Cat.* 14.2). His aim is not 'to perform an allegorical (*theōrētikēn*) exposition of the Scriptures, but to deepen our faith in things we already believe' (*Cat.* 13.9). For example, the Old Testament provides the key to understanding the details of the resurrection (*Cat.* 14.5):

> Do you want an indication of the place? It says again in the Song of Songs: 'I went down to the nut-garden' (Cant 6.10 (11)). For it was in a garden that he was crucified. For although it has been largely decorated with royal gifts, it was once a garden, and the signs and remains of it are still present. 'A garden enclosed . . . a spring sealed' by the Jews who said: 'We have remembered that that deceiver said while he was still alive: "after three days I shall rise." So give orders for the tomb to be made safe.' And later: 'They went and made the tomb safe with the guard, sealing the stone' (Mt 27.63–4, 66). There is a saying which applies to them neatly: 'You will judge them to your rest' (Job 7.18 (LXX)). What is the sealed spring? What is the meaning of the 'spring of the well of living water' (Cant 4.15 (adjusted))? It is the Saviour himself, about whom Scripture says: 'With you is the spring of life' (Ps 35 (36).9).

Underlying this exegetical method is a theory of salvation-history resting on two presuppositions. The first is that God's saving action is a continuous whole, so that what he has accomplished in the Old Testament gains its true significance as a preparation for his work in the New. A hermeneutic of this sort was already familiar to St Paul, according to whom the misfortunes which befell the Israelites in the desert were types or symbols (*tupoi*) of our situation:

'these things befell them symbolically (*tupikōs*) but were written as a warning for us' (1 Cor 10.6, 10). Adam was 'a symbol (*tupos*) of the one to come' (Rom 5.14). So too in 1 Peter the salvation which comes to us through baptism is symbolized by (*antitupon*) the safety which the ark provided for Noah and his family amid the water of the Flood (1 Pet 3.21).

The second presupposition of this method is that the symbol provided by the Old Testament event is less 'real' or 'true' than its application in the life of the Church. To transfer one's gaze from the crossing of the Red Sea to baptism is to pass from symbol (*tupos*) to reality (*MC* 1.3). Our baptism is an 'image' (*eikōn*) and 'imitation' (*mimēsis*) of what happened 'really' (*ontōs*, *alethōs*), of Christ's Passion and resurrection (*MC* 2.5). Solomon was anointed as a prefiguration (*tupikos*) of the anointing which Christians receive in reality (*alethōs*).

Cyril does not develop this typological interpretation of Old Testament events and persons until the *Mystagogics*, where he uses it in various ways and extends it beyond the Old Testament to other areas:

- The Old Testament type (e.g. the blood of the lamb at the Exodus) points to an event in Christ's life (the shedding of Christ's blood) (*MC* 1.3).
- The Old Testament type (e.g. the Red Sea; the anointing of Aaron and Solomon) points to an event in the sacramental life of the Church (baptism, post-baptismal anointing) (*MC* 1.3; 3.6).
- The sacramental event (e.g. baptism, anointing) is an imitation or image of or participation in an event in the life of Christ (the Passion, anointing with spiritual – *noētōi* – oil) (*MC* 2.5–6; 3.2).
- The sacramental event (e.g. receiving bread and wine, washing hands) is a sign or symbol (*tupos*, *sumbolon*) of an effect in the order of grace (sharing Christ's body and blood and becoming of one body and blood with him, purification from sin) (Mt 4.3; 5.2; 5.20).

THEOLOGY

Space is not available here for a complete summary of Cyril's teaching; nor is one necessary, as he provides his own in the fourth *Catechesis*. We shall be content with selecting four major themes: theological language, the Trinity, Christology and sacramental theology.

Theological language

The inadequacy of human language to describe God is a recurrent theme in Cyril's writings. He develops his idea most fully in the opening paragraphs of *Cat.* 6. 'For in what concerns God the height of knowledge is to confess one's ignorance' (*Cat.* 6.2). There is much in creation we cannot explain; how can we presume to give an account of the Creator? Cyril gives more than one reason why God is hidden from us: we often find it impossible to express analytically in words complicated facts which we recognize by insight; God's 'substance' (*hupostasis*) or 'nature' (*phusis*) is hidden from us, even though we know enough from his works for our needs (*Cat.* 6.5; 9.2). Thus in his analysis of the statement that the Father 'begot' the Son, Cyril warns the listener against an anthropomorphic understanding of the word and against curious speculation (*polupragmonein*):

> So will you speculate about matters which even the Holy Spirit has not written of in the Scriptures? If you are ignorant of what is written there, will you speculate about what is not written? (*Cat.* 11.12; cf. 11.8–13)

The purpose of theology is 'to glorify the Lord, not to explain him' (*Cat.* 6.5).

Trinity

The pastoral and liturgical orientation of Cyril's theology helps to explain why he never became deeply engaged in theological controversy over the Trinity. In the *Catecheses* he expresses regret at the schisms which were dividing the Church, but shows little interest in the doctrinal issues involved. Thus, speaking on the signs of the Second Coming, he advises the candidates not to bother with the theological issues which lead to schisms:

> If you hear that bishops are proceeding against bishops, and clerics against clerics, and congregations against congregations, even to the point of bloodshed, do not be disturbed. It was foretold in Scripture. So pay no attention to what people are *doing*; attend to what is *written* in Scripture. (*Cat.* 15.7)

The early Arians could regard him as a man who posed no threat; his clashes with Acacius were perhaps concerned more with ecclesiastical politics than with dogma. He never includes Arius or his followers in lists of heretics. Although Rufinus thought it characteristic of Cyril's episcopate that he 'varied sometimes in faith, more often in communion',[5] J. Lebon seems to be right when he suggests that this judgment is only half true: though Cyril's 'communion' varied, in so far as he changed his allegiance from the Arian to the anti-Arian party, his faith remained unchanged.[6]

Nevertheless there are points at which, even as early as the *Catecheses*, Cyril's intention seems to be to refute an Arian tenet. He rejects the Arian watchword: 'There was once when the Son was not.'[7] According to St Athanasius, the Arians had argued from Phil 2.9 ('therefore God has highly exalted him . . .') that Christ became God and Son as a 'reward of virtue', through advancement (*prokopē*) and improvement in humility (*c. Arianos* 1.37, 40); Cyril by contrast, apparently anticipating Athanasius by several years, states that Jesus 'did not gain the rank of Lord by advancement (*prokopē*) but possesses it by nature' (*Cat.* 10.6).

It seems unlikely that Cyril was ever expressly opposed to the *homoousion*, as A. Harnack and A. Stephenson suggest.[8] It is, however, true that the word occurs only once in his works, namely in the formal conclusion to the Letter to Constantius (8), where he refers to 'the holy and consubstantial Trinity'. This passage is surprising for several reasons. First, one would not expect to find Cyril speaking in these terms to the Arian sympathizer Constantius, especially as he seems concerned to win the Emperor's favour. Moreover, whereas the Nicene Creed speaks of the Son as consubstantial with the Father, this passage describes the whole Trinity as consubstantial, a use of the term which was not officially adopted until the Council of Constantinople (381).[9] Even in the late *Mystagogic Catecheses* Cyril speaks of the Spirit as 'like (*homoiou*)' the Son, rather than 'consubstantial' with him (*MC* 3.1). Presumably it is reasons such as these which led Stephenson to conclude that the term 'consubstantial' in the Letter to Constantius is 'certainly an interpolation'.[10]

Still, granted that it was not to be expected that Cyril would describe the Spirit as 'consubstantial' as early as the *Catecheses* or the Letter to Constantius, it is clear that he already believed in the Spirit's full divinity: 'the Only-begotten Son shares in his Father's divinity together with the Holy Spirit' (*Cat.* 6.6). However, he explicitly renounced any attempt to express this truth in scientifically exact terms:

> There is one God the Father, one Lord, his Only-begotten Son, and one Holy Spirit, the Paraclete. This is all we need

> to know, without inquiring curiously about nature or hypostasis. For if it had been in Scripture, we would have spoken of it; let us not presume to speak of what is not in Scripture. (*Cat.* 16.24)

However, Cyril has many ways of formulating his understanding of the Trinity without recourse to the controversial *homoousios*. The language of the Gospels and the Creed ('I believe in one God, the Father . . .') encourages him to apply the name of God pre-eminently to the Father: 'One should not think of God without thinking of him as Father' (*Cat.* 6.1). Like Justin and the other Logos-theologians, Cyril explores the process of speech as an analogy for the begetting of the Father's Son or Word (*Cat.* 11.10).

Cyril has various ways of expressing the Son's equality with the Father. 'For the Son is in everything like (*homoios*) the Father' (*Cat.* 11.18; cf. 4.7). The Son is eternally begotten: he has an *archē* in the the sense of an origin, but not a beginning in time (*Cat.* 11.20). His glory and his worship are identical with the Father's; their wills are inseparable.[11] Jesus' words: 'I and the Father are one' (Jn 10.30) mean that they are one in the dignity of their Godhead, in their reign, in unity of wills and operations; the Father creates through the Son (*Cat.* 11.16).

Thus Cyril envisages the Son as in a sense subordinate to the Father, though equal to him. The Father is the principle or beginning (*archē*) of the Son (*Cat.* 11.30). The Son 'honours' the Father, and obeys him.[12] It is by the Father's decree that he rules over the world he has created (*Cat.* 10.5).

Christology

Cyril kept apart from speculative controversy about the nature of Jesus Christ, just as he did about the Trinity. Nevertheless his treatment of the Saviour in his addresses implies a firm Christology, for he wanted to show his hearers how to assess various heresies, and to make them see the significance of what had taken place 'here in Jerusalem'. Thus we find him affirming against the Docetists the reality of Jesus' earthly existence:

> The humanity he assumed was not an appearance only or an illusion, but true. He did not pass through the Virgin as if through a pipe, but truly took flesh from her and was truly

> nourished by her milk . . . For if the Incarnation was an illusion, so too was our salvation. (*Cat.* 4.9)

There is no hint of the hesitations which even orthodox theologians sometimes showed about asserting that Jesus experienced real suffering:

> You must believe too that this Only-begotten Son of God came down from heaven to earth because of our sins, assumed a humanity subject to the same feelings as ours, and was born of the holy Virgin and the Holy Spirit. (*Cat.* 4.9)

> Christ was really crucified and really buried and literally rose again, and all of this he did for our sake so that we might gain salvation literally. What unmeasured love this showed for mankind! Christ received the nails in his pure hands and experienced pain, and grants me salvation through sharing his experience without the pain and the toil. (*MC* 2.5)

In his comments on the Creed he is equally explicit about the distinction between Christ's humanity and divinity, and about the unity between them. Cyril does not draw the conclusion that every event in Jesus' life had both a divine and a human dimension, but like Tertullian he attributes some of Jesus' experiences to the divinity and others to the humanity:

> Christ was twofold: man in appearance, and God, but not in appearance. As man he ate truly as we do, for he had the same fleshly feelings as ourselves; but it was as God that he fed the five thousand from five loaves. As man he truly died; but it was as God that he raised the four days dead body to life. As man he truly slept on the boat; but it was as God that he walked on the waters.[13]

SACRAMENTAL THEOLOGY

In addition to what has been said above concerning Cyril's celebration of the liturgy and his use of typology, two more points need to be made. The first concerns the importance he attached to the epiclesis (the invocation of the Holy Spirit). In the most fully worked out formulation of this, the celebrant calls upon the Father to send down the Holy Spirit, so as to make Christ present or active in a sacrament. This trinitarian form is evident in Cyril's account of the epiclesis at the Eucharist:

> we call upon the God who loves mankind to send down the Holy Spirit on the offerings so as to make the bread Christ's body and the wine Christ's blood, for whatever the Holy Spirit touches is made holy and transformed. (*MC* 5.7)

The same process is at work with the water of the baptismal font:

> after the ordinary water has received the invocation of the Holy Spirit and Christ and the Father, it acquires the power of holiness (*Cat.* 3.3)

and the *muron*:

> just as after the invocation of the Holy Spirit the bread of the Eucharist is no longer ordinary bread but the body of Christ, so too this holy *muron* is no longer ordinary or, so to say, common ointment, but Christ's grace which imparts to us his own divinity through the presence of the Holy Spirit. (*MC* 3.3)[14]

The second point concerns Cyril's explanation of Christ's eucharistic presence in realistic, almost materialistic terms. The bread and wine are 'transformed' by the Holy Spirit; if one loses a particle of the Eucharistic bread, 'it is as if it were part of your own body that is being lost' (*MC* 5.7; 5.21). When we receive holy communion, 'we become Christ-bearers, as his body and blood are spread around our limbs' (*MC* 4.3). The sacrament benefits the body and the soul in different ways:

> In the New Testament there is the bread of heaven and the cup of salvation, which sanctify both body and soul. Just as the bread is suitable for the body, so the Word is adapted to the soul. (*MC* 4.5)

In receiving the sacrament the communicants apply the bread and wine to their senses:

> Before you receive, carefully bless your eyes with the touch of the holy body . . . While your lips are still moist, touch them with your hands and bless your eyes, your forehead and your other senses. (*MC* 5.21–2)

Christ is present as a 'sacrifice of propitiation', because of which the intercessions included in the Eucharistic Prayer have a special efficacy,

> for we believe that great benefit will result for the souls for whom prayer is offered when the holy and most awe-inspiring sacrifice lies on the altar. (*MC* 5.8–9)

Translations

TEXTS

Although Cyril's writings are not extensive, there has not been space in this volume for a complete text of his works. I have chosen to include the whole of the *Letter to Constantius*, the *Homily on the Paralytic*, the *Procatechesis* and the *Mystagogic Catecheses*. From his only other, and longest, surviving work, the Lenten *Catecheses*, I have chosen the central instructions on Christ's incarnation, passion and resurrection, adding sections from the third instruction on baptism, the whole of the fourth, which is a summary of Christian faith, sections from the fifth, which precedes the formal delivery of the Creed to the candidates, and from the sixth on the One God, together with Cyril's final remarks before the people proceed to baptism. I have based these translations on the following texts:

Homily on the Paralytic, Procatechesis, and Catecheses: S. Patris Nostri Cyrilli Hierosolymorum Archiepiscopi Opera quae supersunt Omnia, ed. W.K. Reischl and J. Rupp, Munich, 1848–60.

Letter to Constantius: 'L'Épître de Cyrille de Jérusalem à Constance sur la vision de la Croix (BHG^3 413)', ed. E. Bihain, *Byzantion* 43 (1973), pp. 264–96.

Mystagogic Catecheses, ed. A. Piédagnel, SC 126 *bis*, Paris, 1988.

I have noted the few occasions when I have not followed the readings contained in these editions.

I have made my own translation of the Scriptures. For the Old Testament Cyril naturally uses the Septuagint (LXX). I have indicated the passages in which the LXX reading differs significantly from that of the Hebrew, which is the basis of most English translations. Although Cyril is often inexact in his quotations, I have not indicated this unless the variation is significant.

LETTER TO CONSTANTIUS[1]

This letter can be dated to 351, and is the 'first offering' of Cyril's episcopate. Several motives may have prompted him to write this letter. He may have felt the need to assert his loyalty to Constantius early in his episcopate, as the Emperor suspected Athanasius of supporting the other side.[2] *Secondly, Cyril may have anticipated a potential clash with the Emperor over the Arian party, which Constantius supported, and sought to win his favour in this way. Thirdly, the vision gave him an opportunity of enhancing the position of Jerusalem over against Caesarea (see Introduction, sect. 1).*

Letter of Cyril, Bishop of Jerusalem, to the Emperor Constantius on the sign which appeared in the sky.

Cyril, Bishop of Jerusalem, to the most pious Constantius Augustus, most favoured by God. Greetings in the Lord.

1 This, the first offering of a letter which I have sent from Jerusalem to your Majesty, favoured by God, is as honourable for you to receive as it is for me to send. It will not bear a message of flattery but a report of the heavenly vision God has sent us; it will not be skilfully composed of persuasive rhetorical phrases but in the words of the holy gospels it will testify to the facts as they occurred.

2 It often happens that others at their own expense send golden crowns adorned with gleaming gems to crown your honoured head. But we shall not offer you an earthly crown, for earthly gifts come to an earthly end. Our purpose is to bring with all speed to your Piety's attention the display of divine energy that took place in the sky over Jerusalem during your reign so favoured by God.[3] I do not presume to imagine that I am leading you from ignorance to divine knowledge: your piety already equips you to instruct others. My hope is rather that you may be confirmed in the knowledge which you already possess, and that, when you learn how God has honoured the imperial destiny which you have inherited from your

ancestors with a richer, heavenly crown, you may now more than ever give fitting thanks to God the universal King, and face your enemies with greater heart when you understand how the miracle which has occurred in your time gives concrete proof that your reign is the object of God's love.

3 In the time of your blessed father Constantine of happy memory and most favoured by God, the saving wood of the Cross was found in Jerusalem when God's grace rewarded the piety of his noble search with the discovery of the hidden holy places.[4] But you, most pious Lord Emperor, have surpassed your father's piety with an even greater reverence for the divine, and in your time miracles have now appeared no longer from the ground but in the heavens: the trophy of the victory which our Lord and Saviour Jesus Christ, the Only-begotten Son of God, won over death – I refer to the blessed Cross – has been seen flashing like lightning over Jerusalem.[5]

4 In these holy days of the Easter season, on 7 May at about the third hour, a huge cross made of light appeared in the sky above holy Golgotha extending as far as the holy Mount of Olives. It was not revealed to one or two people alone, but it appeared unmistakably to everyone in the city. It was not as if one might conclude that one had suffered a momentary optical illusion; it was visible to the human eye above the earth for several hours. The flashes it emitted outshone the rays of the sun, which would have outshone and obscured it themselves if it had not presented the watchers with a more powerful illumination than the sun. It prompted the whole populace at once to run together into the holy church, overcome both with fear and joy at the divine vision. Young and old, men and women of every age, even young girls confined to their rooms at home, natives and foreigners, Christians and pagans visiting from abroad, all together as if with a single voice raised a hymn of praise to God's Only-begotten Son the wonder-worker. They had the evidence of their own senses that the holy faith of Christians is not based on the persuasive arguments of philosophy but on the revelation of the Spirit and power (cf. 1 Cor 2.4); it is not proclaimed by mere human beings but testified from heaven by God himself.

5 Accordingly we citizens of Jerusalem, who saw this extraordinary wonder with our own eyes, have paid due worship and thanksgiving to God the universal King and to God's Only-begotten Son and shall continue to do so, and we have prayed at length in the holy places for your blessed reign and shall likewise continue to do so. However, since it was our duty not to consign these heavenly revelations to silence, I have made haste to communicate the good

news to your godly Piety by means of this letter, so that to the excellent foundation of the faith that is already yours you may add the knowledge which comes from the recent divine manifestations. Thus may you conceive a firmer hope in our Lord Jesus Christ, and, as one who has God himself for an ally, with your wonted boldness and courage and with all eagerness may you bear the trophy of the Cross, the boast of boasts, carrying forward the sign shown to us in the skies, of which heaven has made an even greater boast by displaying its form to human beings.[6]

6 In accordance, Emperor most favoured by God, with the testimony of the prophets and the words of Christ contained in the holy Gospels, this miracle has been accomplished now and will be accomplished again more fully. For in St Matthew's Gospel the Saviour granted his blessed apostles knowledge of future events and through them foretold to their successors in the clearest of statements: 'And then the sign of the Son of Man will appear in the sky' (Mt 24.30). When you take up the divine book of the Gospel, as is your custom, you will find recorded there the prophetic testimonies to this event. I urge you, my Lord, above all people, to devote more frequent study to these words, because of what follows in this passage. For our Saviour's predictions demand our most reverent attention if we are not to suffer harm from the power which opposes us.

7 These words of mine, Emperor most favoured by God, are the first offering which I send you; they are my first address from Jerusalem to you, our most noble and pious fellow-worshipper of Christ, the Only-begotten Son of our God and Saviour, of Christ who accomplished the salvation of the world in Jerusalem according to the sacred Scriptures, who in this place trod death underfoot and wiped away the sins of mankind with his own precious blood, who bestowed life, immortality and spiritual grace from heaven on all who believe in him. Guarded by his power and grace, distinguished by greater and more glorious achievements of piety, rejoicing in the royal issue of noble sons,[7] may you receive protection from God himself, the universal King, the source of all goodness, through a succession of many peaceful years, so that together with all your family you may remain the glory of Christians and of the whole world.

8 May the God of all things keep you in good health for us and endow you with every virtue. May you continue to show your customary benevolence towards the holy churches and the Roman Empire. Augustus and Emperor most favoured by God, may you and all your family rejoice in still greater rewards for your piety through a succession of many years of peace.[8]

HOMILY ON THE PARALYTIC BY THE POOL

1 Wherever Jesus appears, there also is salvation. If he sees a tax-collector seated at the counter, he makes him an apostle and an evangelist; if he is buried among the dead, he raises them; he gives sight to the blind and hearing to the deaf. When he walks around the pools, it is not to inspect the buildings but to heal the sick.

2 In Jerusalem there used to be a sheep-pool with five porticos, four surrounding the pool, the fifth in the middle, where there lay a great crowd of the sick. There was much unbelief among the Jews. The Physician and Nurse of souls and bodies granted healing in due order, tending first the man who had long been sick so that he might experience the speediest release from his sufferings; he had been lying there not for a day or two, or even a month or a year, but for thirty-eight years. Having become well known to the onlookers in the course of his lengthy illness, he was able to display the power of the healer, for everyone knew him because of the length of time he had been paralysed. Though the Supreme Physician was revealing his power, he was despised by those who took it in bad part.

3 As he walked round the pool, he saw. He didn't learn by asking questions: his divine power supplied what was lacking. He saw, without asking, how long the man had been lying there; his eyes taught him what he already knew before he saw it. For if with regard to what was in the heart he had no need for anyone to ask him about man (for he knew for himself what was in man (cf. Jn 2.25; 16.30)), all the more was this true with regard to diseases which come from outside.

4 He saw a man lying under the weight of a severe illness, for he carried a great burden of sins, and the suffering brought on by his illness had been protracted. Jesus' question to him somehow expressed what he had been longing to hear: 'Do you want to be healed?' That was all he said, and broke off in the middle of the

question. For the question had two meanings: the disease was of the soul as well as of the body, as is shown by Jesus' following remark: 'See, you have been cured, sin no more lest something worse befall you.' That is why he asked him: 'Do you want to be healed?' Observe the healer's great skill, in that he makes the cure depend upon the desire. It is because salvation comes from faith that the man was asked 'Do you want?', so that the desire might prepare the way for the miracle. No one but Jesus spoke in this way, not even the best of earthly doctors. For doctors who treat earthly diseases cannot say 'Do you want to be healed?' to all their patients; but Jesus gives even the desire; he accepts the faith and grants the favour without a fee.

5 Once our Saviour was walking along the road where two blind men were sitting. However while physically they were blind, their minds still enjoyed the power of vision; for though the scribes did not recognize Jesus, the blind men's cries pointed him out. For though the Pharisees had learnt the law and practised it from childhood to old age, they had become unteachable in their advanced years, and declared: 'We don't know where he comes from' (Jn 9.29); for 'he came into his own and his own did not accept him' (Jn 1.11). The blind, on the other hand, cried out: 'Son of David, have pity on us' (cf. Mk 10.47). The one whom the learned lawyers did not recognize was recognized by those who had no eyes to read with.

The Saviour went up to them and said: 'Do you believe that I can do this?' (Mt 9.28). 'What do you want me to do for you?' (Mt 20.32). He did not say: 'What do you want me to say to you?' but: 'What do you want me to do for you?' For he was the Creator and the giver of life; his creative power was not something new. His Father is always at work (cf. Jn 5.17), and he works alongside his Father; he was Creator of all things by his Father's decree. He who is the Only-begotten of the Only God without intermediary asks the blind men: 'What do you want me to do for you?' Not that he didn't know what they wanted (for the truth was plain to see), but he intended the gift to follow from their own words, so that by their own words they might be justified. It is not to be supposed that the one who knows hearts doesn't know what they would say, but by waiting for them to speak, he let their request elicit the miracle.

6 So Jesus approached the sick man; uninvited, the doctor visited the patient. It should not surprise us that he visited the man lying by the pool, since he came down to us uninvited from heaven.

'Do you want to be cured?', he asked him. By means of this question he led him on to knowledge and aroused him to question in his turn. This was a great and gracious gift. He could not pay the fee, so he had a voluntary healer. 'Yes, Lord', he replied. 'My protracted sufferings have made me long for health. I do long for it, but I have no man.'

Do not be downcast, my friend, because you have no man. You have God standing beside you, who is in one respect[1] man, in another God, for we must profess both truths. To acknowledge his humanity without acknowledging his divinity is useless, or rather brings a curse, for 'Cursed is he who places his hope in a man' (Jer 17.5). So if we place our hope even in Jesus as a man without involving his divinity in our hope, we incur a curse. But as it is, we acknowledge him to be both God and man, and both in literal truth. As the one begotten of a true Father, and as a man born in truth and not in mere appearance, we adore him and look forward to a true salvation.

7 'I want to be cured, but I have no man.' Can't you see that at the very point where the remedy is lacking, he has given you the miracle? For while most of the sick had houses, and relations and perhaps other people too, he suffered complete and utter poverty; and when he had no help from outside to support him, and was left totally to his own resources, God's Only-begotten Son came to his help. 'Do you want to be healed?' 'Yes, Lord, but I have no man to put me into the pool when the water is disturbed.' You have the fountain, for 'with you is the fountain of life' (Ps 35.10 (36.9)), the fountain which is the source of all fountains. 'If anyone drinks from this water, rivers will flow from his belly' (Jn 7.38), not water that flows downwards, but water that 'springs up' (Jn 4.14) – for Jesus' water does not make us leap down from above but leap up from earthly things to heavenly – water that 'springs up to eternal life'. For Jesus is the source of blessings.

8 Why do you linger round a pool? You have the one who walked on the waters, who rebuked the winds, who controlled the sea, the one beneath whom the sea was spread like a floor, and who gave Peter the same power to walk on it. When there was no glimmer in the night, the Light was there unrecognized. For as he walked on the waters no one recognized him by glimpsing his face, but the familiar voice revealed his presence. Thinking they saw a ghost they were terror-struck. But Jesus said to them: 'It is I. Do not be afraid.' 'If you are the one I know', Peter replied, 'or rather the one whom the Father has revealed to me, tell me to come to you

across the waters.' 'Come', said Jesus, unstinting in sharing his gifts.

9 So the one who controlled and created the waters was there beside the water of the pool. 'I have no man', the paralytic said to him, 'to put me into the pool when the water is disturbed.' 'Why are you waiting for the waters to be disturbed?', the Saviour said to him. 'Do not be disturbed; be healed. Why are you waiting for a visible movement? The word of command is swifter than thought. Simply look at the power of the spring and recognize God appearing in the flesh. Do not judge by his appearance, but by the work which he accomplishes through the appearance.[2] 'I have no man to put me into the pool when the water is disturbed.' 'Why do you wait for what is trivial?', Jesus said to him. Why look for healing in the waters? Rise up, the Resurrection has told you. For the Saviour is everything for everyone everywhere: bread for the hungry, water for the thirsty, resurrection for the dead, a physician for the sick, redemption for the sinner.

10 Stand up, pick up your mattress and walk. But first stand up; first cast off your disease. Then recover the sinew of faith. First lean on the mattress which is supporting you, then learn to use a wooden frame to carry the things which have long carried you.[3] This same Saviour ordered you to carry the wooden litter of which it is said: 'The king has made for himself a litter of wood from Lebanon. He has made its posts of silver and its seat of purple, and its interior is paved with stones' (Cant 3.9–10 (LXX adjusted)). Symbols of the Passion are hidden away in these songs, which are bridal, sober and chaste. Do not interpret these words obtusely as many have done, taking them to be passionate love songs. They are bridal words, full of modesty.

However, if you are not familiar with the Canticle, turn to the Proverbs, and make your way up to the Canticle gradually. 'Wisdom has built for herself a house' (the text speaks of Wisdom as a woman) 'and sent out her servants' (Prov 9.1, 3). In another place it says: 'Love her, and she will protect you' (Prov 4.6). This is not love of a woman, but of wisdom, which drives out carnal passion, for where wisdom is gained passion is banished. Passions do not accord with wisdom, but wise thoughts do. Passion makes men like lusting stallions; their craving knows no reason. So if you hear the Canticle apparently speaking of a bridegroom and a bride, do not descend to understanding the words in an erotic sense, but exercise yourself in passionless thoughts as a means of transforming your passions.

11 Meditate then on the sacred lessons of the Canticle, for they are expressions of chastity and tell of Christ's Passion. They reveal the details of his Passion. They tell us the place: 'He has come into the garden' (cf. Cant 5.1), for that is where he was buried. They recalled the spices: 'He has taken the fullness of my myrrh' (cf. Cant 5.5 (LXX)); for his human life[4] has been completed. And after the resurrection he said: 'I have eaten my bread with my honey' (Cant 5.1 (LXX)); for 'they gave him a piece of honeycomb' (Lk 24.42 variant). The Canticle spoke also of the wine mixed with myrrh: 'I shall give you spiced wine to drink' (Cant 8.2). In another passage they spoke of the myrrh which was poured on his head: 'While the king was on his couch, my nard gave out its perfume' (Cant 1.12), for 'as he sat at table in the house of Simon the Leper, a woman came in and broke open an alabaster jar of very costly ointment of pure nard and poured it on his head' (Mk 14.3).

So too with regard to the cross. The 'litter' refers to the wood of the cross on which he was carried. 'He has made its posts of silver': the beginning of the cross is of silver, namely the betrayal. Just as a luxurious house is crowned with a golden roof and has pillars to support the whole edifice, so too silver was the beginning of his crucifixion and resurrection; for if Judas had not betrayed him, he would not have been crucified. For this reason he made his pillars of silver as the beginning of his renowned Passion.

12 'Its seat of purple.' And so they dressed him in purple, partly in mockery, partly prophetically, for he was a king. Though they were acting mainly for their own amusement, still they did it, and it was a sign of his royal dignity. And though his crown was of thorns, it was a crown, and one woven by soldiers, for kings are proclaimed by their soldiers. 'Its seat of purple, its interior paved with stones.' Well instructed members of the Church know of Lithostrotos,[5] also called Gabbatha, in Pilate's house.

13 In explaining this I have digressed from the mattress to the litter. Well then, Jesus said to the man: 'Stand up, pick up your mattress and walk.' The disease had been protracted, but the treatment was instantaneous; for years the sinews had been paralysed, instantaneously they were restored. For the very creator of the sinews was here, the one who contrived various cures for the blind, who used a salve of mud to dispense a miraculous remedy. For if mud is applied to a man who can see, it impedes his vision; but Jesus used mud to give sight to the blind. In other cases Jesus used other means to exercise his healing power; in this case by the words: 'Stand up, pick up your mattress and walk.'

Imagine the onlookers' amazement. Yet however wonderful the sight, their lack of faith was strange. The years-old disease was cured, but the protracted incredulity was not. The Jews remained ill, and had no desire to be cured.

14 If they should have marvelled at the event, they should have also worshipped the healer of souls and bodies. But they grumbled, for grumbling ran in their family; they inverted good and evil, calling bitter sweet and sweet bitter.

With full deliberation Jesus used to work on the Sabbath, doing works that transcended the Sabbath in order to teach a lesson by the very act of working. Since one argument defeats another but action is invincible, he used to give an object-lesson by healing on the Sabbath, not pitting argument against argument, but using the work to persuade the onlookers.

15 'It is the Sabbath', they said. 'It is not lawful for you to carry your mattress.' Although the Lawgiver himself was present, he was not the one who said: 'It is not lawful.' The text 'Appoint, O Lord, a lawgiver against them' (Ps 9.21 (20) (LXX)) refers to the Saviour. They were at once answered by the man who had just been healed in soul and body. Wisdom lent him wise words; though unable to answer in legal terms, his reply was concise.

'You are all aware', he said, 'how long I have been ill, how many years I have been bed-ridden and how helpless my case has been. Not one of you ever did me the service of lifting me up and putting me first in the pool to be cured. So when you have done nothing to help me, why do you now act like lawyers and say: "It is not lawful for you to carry your mattress on the Sabbath"?

'I can answer you very briefly: the man who cured me told me to do it. You may think nothing of me, but the event should leave you dumbfounded. He put no ointment on me; he employed no medical techniques or aids. He simply spoke, and the effect followed. He gave me an order, and I am obeying it. I trust his command, because his command healed me. If the man who gave me the order hadn't the power to heal me by his orders, it would not be right for me to obey them. But since my illness, which for many years has been plain to see, has ceased at his command, it is right for me to listen to him, seeing that my illness has listened to him and departed. It was the man who restored my health who said to me: "Pick up your mattress."'

16 The man who was healed did not know who his Healer was. We can see how far our Saviour was from vainglory. Having worked the cure, he slipped away, not wanting to receive credit for the cure.

We do just the opposite. If we ever experience dreams, or perform works of healing with our hands, or drive away demons by an invocation, we are so far from hiding our success that we boast of it even before we are questioned. Jesus teaches us by his own example not to speak about ourselves. Once the cure was provided, he slipped away so as not to receive the credit. He withdrew at the right time, and came back at the right time. In order to set healing of the soul alongside the physical cure, he came once the crowd had dispersed, and said: 'See, you are cured. Do not sin any more.'

17 What a versatile healer! Sometimes he heals the soul before the body, sometimes vice versa. 'Do not sin any more, in case something worse happen to you.' This one example contains a general lesson, for the words apply not only to that one man, but to us all. If ever we suffer illness or grief or hardship, we should not blame God. 'For God cannot be tempted with evil, nor does he himself tempt anyone' (Jas 1.13). Each of us is 'caught in the ropes of his own sin' (Prov 5.22) and scourged.

'Do not sin any more, in case something worse happen to you.' Let all mankind attend to these words. Now let the fornicator set aside his lust; now let the miser turn almsgiver; now let the thief heed the words: 'Do not sin any more.'

God's forgiveness is great, his grace generous. But do not let the vastness of his mercy lead you to presumption, or make his forbearance a reason for sin. Rather let your carnal passions in future be healed, and make your own the words of the reading which suit your case so well: 'For while we were in the flesh, our sinful passions which came through the law were active in our members' (Rom 7.5). When the apostle said: 'While we were in the flesh', he was not speaking of the flesh which clothes us but of our carnal actions; for when he said: 'While we were in the flesh', he was still clothed in flesh himself. But just as God said before bringing about the Flood: 'My spirit shall not remain in these people because they are flesh' (Gen 6.3) (for the spirit had been transformed into carnal desire), in the same sense the Apostle says 'While we were in the flesh' in this passage.

18 So no one should be in the flesh, or rather, while in the flesh we should not 'walk according to the flesh' (Rom 8.4). For the apostle doesn't want us to withdraw completely from the world in order to avoid doing evil, but while remaining in the flesh to enslave the flesh and not be led by it. We should be leaders not slaves. We should take food in moderation, and instead of being carried away by gluttony we should restrain our bellies in order to control

our lower parts. Let the body be led by the soul instead of the soul being carried away by carnal pleasures.

'Do not sin any more, in case something worse happen to you.' These words contain a message for us all; I only wish everyone had ears to hear them. For when words reach the hearing of the flesh they are not always admitted to the mind. This is what the Saviour implied when he said: 'he that has ears to hear, let him hear' (Mt 11.15), for he was speaking to people who had the ears of the flesh.

19 So let everyone listen to Jesus and avoid sin in future, running instead to the one who forgives our sins. If we are ill, let us seek refuge with him; if our spirits are afflicted, let us have recourse to the doctor of knowledge; if we are hungry, let us accept his bread; if we are dead, let us share his resurrection; if we have grown old in ignorance, let us ask Wisdom to grant us wisdom.

20 My thoughts have led me into speaking for too long; perhaps this has impeded our Father's teaching.[6] The hour calls us to hear greater words; may they enable us to perform greater works through which to praise God, to whom is the glory now and always and for ever and ever. Amen.

PROCATECHESIS

or Prologue to the Catecheses[1]

1 Already, dear candidates for enlightenment, the scent of blessedness has come upon you; already you are gathering spiritual flowers to weave into heavenly crowns; already the perfume of the Holy Spirit has breathed over you. You are already outside the outer hall of the palace; I pray that the king may lead you inside. The blossom can now be seen on the trees; I pray that the fruit may follow. So far your enrolment has taken place; and your call to military service. We have had the bridesmaids' lamps, a yearning for the heavenly city, good intentions and the hope which accompanies them; for he who said 'for those who love God everything works together for good', does not lie (Rom 8.28). For God is a generous benefactor, but he waits for each one's decision. This is why the Apostle went on to say: 'to those who are called according to their purpose'. It is a true purpose which makes you one of the called; for if you are here in body but not in mind, you gain nothing.

2 Once upon a time Simon Magus came to the font. He was baptized but not enlightened; he dipped his body in the water, but did not enlighten his heart with the Spirit. As far as his body was concerned, he went down into the water and came up from it; but his soul was not buried with Christ or raised with him. I give you examples of falls to save you from falling. For these things 'happened to them as a type, and are recorded as a warning' (1 Cor 10.11) to those who come forward to this day.[2] May none of you be found to tempt grace; may no root of bitterness spring up to trouble you. Let no one come here saying: 'Come on, let's see what the Faithful do.[3] Let me go in and watch, so as to learn what goes on.' Do you expect to see without being seen? Do you think that you can be curious about what is going on without God being curious about your heart?

3 There once was a man in the Gospels (Mt 22.8ff) who was curious about the wedding. He went in without a proper garment and sat down and ate, because the bridegroom allowed him to do so. But having seen that everyone else was wearing white, he should have dressed in the same way himself. He had an equal share of the food; but he was not equal in his dress or in his disposition. Now, though the bridegroom was generous, he was not undiscriminating. As he made a tour of inspection round each of the guests, he was not concerned with what they were eating but with their behaviour. When he saw a stranger without a wedding-garment, he said to him: 'Friend, how did you get in here, in a garment of that colour and in that frame of mind? I realize the doorkeeper did not keep you out, because of the host's generosity. I realize you didn't know what you should be wearing for the banquet. But when you came in, you could see the guests' robes shining like lightning. Shouldn't you have learnt from what was before your eyes? Shouldn't you have gone out while there was still time so as to come back when the time was right? As it is, you have made a disorderly entrance only to suffer a disorderly ejection.' And he gives orders to his servants: 'Bind his feet which presumed to enter, bind his hands which didn't know how to put on a white garment, and throw him out into the darkness outside, for he doesn't deserve the wedding-torches.' You see what happened to the man in the story; put your own affairs in order.

4 We are the servants of Christ. We welcomed you. We had the responsibility of doorkeepers, but we left the door open. Perhaps you came in with your soul spattered with the mud of your sins and with your intentions soiled. You came in; you were admitted; your name was recorded. Can you see the solemn arrangement of this assembly? Can you take to heart its order and its discipline, the reading of the Scriptures, the presence of the clergy, the programme of instruction? The very place should put you to shame;[4] be taught by what you can see. Leave now in good order, and come back tomorrow in better. If your soul is dressed in avarice, change your clothes before you come in; take the garment off; don't cover it up. Take off fornication and impurity, and put on the shining white garment of chastity. I am giving you a warning, before Jesus, the bridegroom of souls, comes in and sees what you are wearing. You have ample notice. You have forty days for repentance; you have plenty of time to take your clothes off and wash them and come back properly dressed. But if you persist in your ill will, the preacher is not to blame. Don't expect to receive grace. The water will re-

ceive you, but the Spirit will not. If anyone is aware of a wound, he should put ointment on it. If anyone has fallen, he should pick himself up. Let there be no Simon[5] among you, no hypocrisy, no idle curiosity about what is going on.

5 Perhaps you have another reason for coming. Perhaps some man among you has come because he wants to win the approval of his girl-friend; the same can apply to women too. Perhaps a slave has wanted to please his master or someone has wanted to please a friend. I accept this as bait for my hook and let you in. You may have had the wrong reason for coming, but I have good hope that you will be saved. Perhaps you didn't know where you were going or recognize the net waiting to catch you. You have swum into the Church's net. Allow yourself to be caught; don't try to escape. Jesus is fishing for you, not to kill you but to give you life once you have been killed. For you have to die and rise again. You have heard the Apostle say: 'dead to sin, alive to righteousness'.[6] Die to your sins and live to righteousness. Make today the first day of your life.

6 Consider the honour that Jesus is bestowing on you. Up till now you have been called a catechumen,[7] one who hears from the outside. You heard hope, but you didn't know it. You heard mysteries, but you didn't understand them.[8] You heard the Scriptures, but you didn't understand their depth.[9] But now you are not hearing a sound outside you but one within, for now the Spirit lives in you and makes your mind God's home. When you hear what is written about the mysteries, then you will understand things which you didn't know. And don't imagine that you are to receive something trivial: pitiful human being that you are, you are to receive one of God's own titles.[10] Listen to what Paul says: 'God is faithful.' And listen to another text: 'God is faithful and just' (1 Cor 1.9; 1 Jn 1.9). It was with foreknowledge of this, since human beings are destined to receive one of God's own titles, that the Psalmist, speaking for God, declared: 'I said you are all Gods and sons of the Most High' (Ps 81 (82).6). So take care not to have the title 'faithful' but an unfaithful disposition. You have entered the contest: keep going for the whole race. You won't have another opportunity like this. If your wedding-days were approaching, wouldn't you drop everything else and concentrate on preparations for the celebration? Well then, as you are shortly to make your soul holy for your heavenly Bridegroom, won't you take a rest from material things for the sake of gaining spiritual ones?

7 You are not allowed to receive baptism twice or three times; in that case you could say: 'If I fail once, I can succeed the second

time.' But if you fail once, you can't put matters right. There is 'one Lord, one faith, one baptism' (Eph 4.5). The only people who are rebaptized are some heretics, and only because their first baptism wasn't a baptism at all.[11]

8 For God requires nothing more of us than a good intention. Don't say: 'How can my sins be wiped off?' I will tell you: by desire, by faith. How could I put it more simply than that? But if your lips declare your desire but your heart says the opposite, your Judge can read hearts. From today give up every unworthy occupation. Don't let your tongue speak any unholy words; don't let your eye go astray and rove after unwholesome sights.

9 Be eager to attend the catechetical classes. Be earnest in submitting to the exorcisms. If you are blown upon[12] and exorcised, the process brings you salvation. Imagine an unworked lump of gold that is adulterated and combined with a variety of other substances, like bronze, tin, iron and lead. We are trying to get pure gold. Can the impurities be removed from it without fire? In the same way, the soul can't be purified without exorcisms. They are sacred, for they have been taken from holy Scripture. Your face is veiled to leave your mind at rest, to prevent a wandering gaze from making your heart wander too. Though your eyes are veiled, your ears are free to receive salvation. As goldsmiths achieve their effect by directing their breath into the fire through narrow pipes and blowing on the gold hidden in the retort and stimulating the flame underneath, so too the exorcists inspire fear[13] through the Holy Spirit and, so to speak, rekindle the soul inside the retort of the body. Our enemy the devil departs, but salvation and the hope of eternal life remain. Purified of its sins, the soul henceforth possesses salvation. So, brethren, let us persevere in hope, and offer ourselves, and be hopeful, so that the God of all things, seeing our intentions, may cleanse us of our sins, inspire us with good hope of our welfare and give us the repentance which leads to salvation. God has called; you have been called.

10 Persevere with the catechetical classes. If we have a lot to say, don't relax your attention. You are being given weapons to use against the powers ranged against you, weapons against heresies, against Jews and Samaritans and pagans. You have many enemies; take a good supply of weapons, for you have to shoot against many adversaries. You must learn how to shoot down the Greek, how to fight against the heretic, the Jew and the Samaritan. Your arms are ready, above all the sword of the Spirit. You must stretch out your right hand for the good cause to fight the Lord's fight, to conquer

the powers ranged against you, and to become invincible to any heretical force.

11 Let this be your order of the day: learn what you are told and keep it for ever. Do not imagine that these are ordinary homilies, which are good and deserve credence, but if we do neglect them today, we have tomorrow to learn. But the instructions on the font of rebirth are given in sequence; if they are neglected today, when will the loss be made good? Imagine it is the season for planting trees. If we haven't dug deep, when else can the tree that has once been badly planted be planted properly? Think of catechesis as if it were a house. If we don't use clamps in the right order to hold the structure together and to prevent gaps appearing so that the building becomes unsound, even our earlier efforts will be wasted. Stone must follow stone and corner fit corner in the right order. We must smooth away irregularities if the building is to rise. In the same way we bring you, so to speak, stones of knowledge. You must learn about the living God; you must learn about judgment; you must learn about Christ; you must learn about the resurrection. I shall have many things to say in order: first I must explain them point by point, and only later in their mutual connections. If you don't join them together into a single whole, remembering what comes first and what second, I will have performed my task of building, but the structure you have will be unsound.

12 When an instruction is given, if one of the catechumens asks you what the teachers have said, say nothing to the outsider. We are entrusting you with a mystery and the hope of the life to come. Keep the mystery safe for the One who will reward you. Be warned in case someone says to you: 'What harm does it do if I get to know as well?' The sick are like that when they ask for wine. If it is given when it is bad for them, it makes them delirious and has two harmful results: the patient dies and the doctor is blamed. It is like that with the catechumen if he learns from one of the Faithful. The catechumen is delirious because he doesn't understand what he has heard; he criticizes the subject-matter and despises what he is told; while the Faithful is condemned for betraying the secret. You are standing now between two frontiers.[14] Make sure that you don't talk carelessly, not because what you are told isn't fit to talk about, but because your listener isn't fit to hear it. You used to be a catechumen yourself, and I didn't explain to you then what the future had in store. When you learn from experience how sublime the teaching is, then you will understand that catechumens are not fit to hear it.

13 Now that you have been enrolled you have become sons and daughters of the same mother. When you enter the church before the time of the exorcisms, you should only talk about things that are conducive to devotion. If one of you is missing, go to look for him. If you had been invited to a dinner-party, wouldn't you wait for your fellow-guest? If you had a brother, wouldn't you look for what was good for him? Don't gossip any more about unprofitable subjects, – 'What has happened in the city?' 'What has happened in the village?' 'What has the Emperor been doing?' 'What has the bishop been doing?' 'What has the priest been doing?' Fix your thoughts upwards; that is what your moment of opportunity requires. 'Be still and know that I am God' (Ps 45 (46).10). If you see the Faithful taking part in the service in an off-hand way, they are safe, they know what they have received, they possess the grace. But you are still in the balance: are you to receive or not receive? Don't imitate those slack people. Try to experience a reverent awe.

14 When the exorcism takes place, while you are waiting for the others to arrive for their exorcism, the men and the women are kept apart. At this point I could do with Noah's ark, to separate Noah and his sons from his wife and his sons' wives.[15] There was only one ark, and the door was shut, but things were arranged decently. So too, although the church is closed and you are all inside, there are separate places, the men all together and the women all together, to prevent a means of salvation turning into an occasion for damnation. Even though there may be a good reason for sitting together, it is better to keep the passions at a distance. So let the men sit together and have a good book; one man can read and the rest listen. If there isn't a book available, one man might pray, and another speak a few helpful words. The unmarried women should be kept together in the same way, either singing or reading silently, so that their lips move inaudibly, 'for I do not allow a woman to speak in church'.[16] Married women should observe the same practice, praying and moving their lips silently, so that Samuel can come and your barren soul can conceive salvation, for God will hear you, which is what the name Samuel means.[17]

15 I shall observe each man's earnestness and each woman's devotion. Your mind should be ardent in devotion, your soul wrought like bronze, the hardness of your unbelief hammered out; let the scales fall away from the iron and leave the metal clean; let the rust fall away and leave the metal pure. Soon God will show you that night, the darkness which is as bright as day which Scripture speaks of: 'The darkness will not be dark for you, and the night will be

made as bright as the day' (Ps 138 (139).12). Then for each man and woman among you may the gate of paradise be opened. Then may you enjoy the Christ-bearing waters in all their fragrance.[18] Then may you receive the name of Christ,[19] and the power of things that are divine. Even now, I urge you, turn your mind's eye upwards: picture the choirs of the angels, and God, the Lord of all things, seated there, and his Only-begotten Son seated there with him at his right hand, and the Spirit there with them,[20] and the Thrones and Dominations celebrating the heavenly liturgy, and each one of you, men and women, who is to be saved. Even now let your ears seem to ring with that glorious sound which the angels will raise when you gain salvation. 'Blessed are those whose sins are forgiven' (Ps 31 (32).1), when, like the stars of the Church, you will come in with your bodies shining and your souls radiant.[21]

16 The baptism which lies before you is a matter of great importance. For prisoners it means ransom; for sins forgiveness; the death of sin; new birth for the soul; a shining garment; a holy, indelible seal; a chariot to heaven; the food of paradise; the grant of royalty; the grace of adoption.[22] Nevertheless a serpent is on the lookout for those who take this road; do not let him bite you and infect you with unbelief. He sees so many people being saved and 'seeks someone to devour' (1 Pet 5.8). You are approaching the Father of spirits, but you have to pass that serpent; how will you get past? Let your feet be shod in readiness with the gospel of peace, so that even if you are bitten, you will come to no harm. Have faith living within you, and sturdy hope like a strong shoe, so that you can get past your enemy and reach the Lord (cf. Eph 6.15). Prepare your heart to welcome your instruction and to share in the holy mysteries. Pray more frequently, that God may choose you to receive the heavenly, immortal mysteries. Do not be idle by day or by night. As soon as sleep falls from your eyes, let your mind be intent on prayer. If you notice any shameful thought coming to the surface of your mind, remember judgment and salvation. Concentrate your mind on receiving instruction, so as to forget unworthy thoughts. If you meet anyone who says: 'So you are going to go down into the water? Aren't there baths in the city any more?', imagine that this is the sea-serpent plotting against you. Pay attention not to what the man is saying but to what God is doing. Guard your soul so as not to be caught, but to remain in hope and become an heir to eternal salvation.

17 These, my friends, are my orders and instructions. Do not make your house of hay and straw and chaff, in case your handiwork

burns down and we incur the loss. Make your work rather of gold and silver and precious stones. It is for me to say this, for you to undertake it, and for God to bring the work to completion (cf. 1 Cor 3.12–15; 3.6). So let us tighten the sinews of our minds, tense our souls, prepare our hearts. For the prize we are running for is our soul; we have our hopes set on heavenly things. God reads your hearts, he knows who is sincere and who is a hypocrite; he has the power to protect the sincere and give faith to the hypocrite. God has power even to give faith to the unbeliever, if only the unbeliever gives his heart. May he cancel the bond in force against you (cf. Col 2.14), grant you an amnesty for your past offences, plant you in the Church, enlist you in his army and put on you the 'armour of righteousness' (2 Cor 6.7). May he endow you with the heavenly realities of the new covenant and give you the indelible seal of the Holy Spirit for all eternity, in Jesus Christ our Lord, to whom is the glory for ever and ever. Amen.

CATECHESES

The MSS give the following titles to these Lenten pre-baptismal instructions:

1 Introduction
2 Concerning repentance, the remission of sins and the Adversary
3 Concerning baptism
4 On the Ten Dogmas
5 Concerning faith (this instruction begins with an account of the virtue of faith, and ends with the rite of the Presentation of the Faith, i.e. the Creed; the remaining thirteen instructions are explanations of the articles of the Creed)
6 Concerning the unity of God's rule, on 'I believe in one God' and concerning heresies
7 On 'the Father'
8 On 'Almighty'
9 On 'Maker of heaven and earth, of all things seen and unseen'
10 On 'and in one Lord, Jesus Christ'
11 On 'the Only-begotten Son of God who was born of the Father as true God before all ages, through whom all things were made'
12 On 'who became incarnate and became a human being'
13 On 'who was crucified and buried'
14 On 'and he rose from the dead on the third day, and ascended into heaven, and is seated at the right hand of the Father'
15 On 'Who will come in glory to judge the living and the dead, of whose kingdom there will be no end'
16 On 'and in one Holy Spirit, the Paraclete, who spoke in the prophets'
17 What remains concerning the Holy Spirit

18 On 'and in one holy catholic church, and in the resurrection of the flesh, and in everlasting life' (N. 22 shows that this clause was preceded by the words: 'and in one baptism of repentance for the forgiveness of sins')

It can be seen that the baptismal Creed in use in Jerusalem was similar to the Nicene Creed, though without the anti-Arian formulas. Some MSS insert the Nicene Creed itself at the end of 18.12; but this is probably a scribal addition.

Cyril gives an overview of all his teaching in Catechesis 4. From the rest of the series we have concentrated especially on addresses concerning Christ because of their relevance to the setting in Jerusalem.

CATECHESIS 3

For candidates for baptism
Concerning baptism

Reading: Rom 6.3ff: 'Or are you unaware that all of us who were baptized into Christ Jesus were baptized into his death? So we were baptized with him through baptism . . .'

1 'Exult, you heavens, and rejoice, you earth' (Is 49.13), for those who are to be sprinkled with hyssop, and purified with spiritual hyssop by the power of the one who in his passion was given a drink on hyssop and the reed. Let the heavenly powers rejoice, and let the souls soon to be joined to their heavenly Bridegroom make ready. For there is 'a voice of one crying in the wilderness: "Prepare the way of the Lord."' (Is 40.3). For this is no small matter; this is not the customary, injudicious embrace of bodies, but election in faith by the Spirit who 'searches all things' (1 Cor 2.10). For in the world marriages and engagements are not generally made judiciously, but the Bridegroom is quick to give his consent where wealth or beauty are to be found; but here it is given not where there is bodily beauty, but where there is an irreproachable conscience in the soul; not where there is condemned mammon, but where there are the godly riches of the soul.

2 So, my children of righteousness, do what John urges you to do when he says: 'Prepare the way of the Lord.' Remove every obstacle, every stone that makes you stumble, so as to have a level journey to eternal life. Through sincere faith make the vessels of your soul clean and ready for receiving the Holy Spirit. Begin to wash your garments through repentance, so that you may be found clean when you are invited into the bridal chamber. For the Bridegroom invites all alike, since his grace is generous; the loud voice of the heralds is gathering everyone together; later he will himself sort out those who have come in.[1] May none of the enrolled now hear the words: 'Friend, how did you get in without a wedding-garment?'

(Mt 22.12). May you all rather hear the words: 'Well done, good and faithful servant. You were faithful over a few things; I shall set you over many. Enter into the joy of your Lord' (Mt 25.21). Up till now you have been standing outside the door; may you all be able to say: 'The king has brought me into his storehouse' (Cant 1.4). 'Rejoice, my soul, in the Lord, for he has dressed me in the robe of salvation and the tunic of joy; he has bound on me the diadem of a bridegroom, and adorned me with jewels as a bride' (Is 61.10 (LXX)). So may all your souls be found to be without spot or stain or the like. I do not mean, before you receive grace, but that, when grace is given, your conscience, being found without reproach, may correspond with the grace.

3 This is truly a great matter, brethren; approach it attentively. Each one of you is to be presented before God in the presence of myriads of angelic hosts; the Holy Spirit is to seal your souls; you are to enlist in the army of the great king. So get ready; prepare yourselves – not by dressing in shining robes, but by clothing your souls in piety and a good conscience. Do not think of the baptismal bath as ordinary water; think of the spiritual grace which is given with the water. Just as the invocation of idols pollutes the food which is offered on pagan altars, even though in itself it is ordinary food, so too by contrast when ordinary water receives the invocation of the Holy Spirit and Christ and the Father, it acquires the power of holiness.[2]

4 For since human beings have a double nature and are composed of soul and body, the purification is twofold also: immaterial for the immaterial, and bodily for the body. The water cleanses the body, and the Spirit seals the soul, so that we can approach God with hearts sprinkled and bodies washed in pure water (cf. Heb 10.22). So when the time comes for you to go down into the water, do not attend to its common nature; welcome your salvation by the power of the Holy Spirit; for you need both[3] in order to be made perfect. These are not my words; no, the Lord Jesus, who possesses the authority in this matter, says: 'Unless one is born of water and Spirit, one cannot enter the kingdom of God' (Jn 3.5). Even if you are baptized in water, you don't possess the fullness of grace if you have not been granted the Spirit; even if your deeds have made you virtuous, you won't enter the kingdom of heaven if through the water you have not received the seal.[4] This is a bold saying, but it is not mine; it was revealed by Jesus, and I will give you the proof from holy Scripture for what I am saying. Cornelius was a righteous man and was granted a vision of angels; he had set up his prayers

and almsdeeds like a noble monument before God in heaven. Peter came, they believed, the Holy Spirit was poured out on them, and they spoke in strange tongues and prophesied (Acts 10.44–6). The Scripture says that after they had received the grace of the Spirit, Peter ordered them to be baptized in the name of Jesus Christ, so that after their souls had been reborn through faith, their bodies also might share the grace through the water.

5 If anyone wishes to know why the grace is given through water and not through some other element, they will find the answer if they take up the holy Scriptures. For water is an important thing, the noblest of the four elements we observe in the world. Heaven is the abode of the angels; but the heavens are made of water. Earth is the abode of water, but the earth is made of water; and before any of the six days of creation, 'the Spirit of God moved over the waters' (Gen 1.2). Water was the beginning of the universe, and the Jordan was the beginning of the gospels. Israel gained its freedom from Pharaoh through the sea, and the world gained its freedom from its sins through 'the bath of water in the word' of God (Eph 5.26). Wherever a covenant is made with anyone, water is to be found there. After the Flood, a covenant was made with Noah; a covenant was made with Israel on Mount Sinai – but 'with water, and scarlet wool and hyssop' (Heb 9.19). Elijah was taken up to heaven – but not without water; for before going up to heaven in the chariot he crossed the Jordan. The high priest bathes before offering incense; for Aaron bathed before being made high priest. For how could he pray for others if he had not yet been cleansed in water? Again, the basin placed inside the Tabernacle stood as a symbol of baptism.

6 Baptism is the end of the Old Testament and the beginning of the New. For John was the precursor, and there was no one greater 'among those born of woman' (Mt 11.11). He was the end of the prophets, 'for all the prophets and the law' lasted 'up to John' (Mt 11.13). He was also the beginning of the age of the gospels. For the passage: 'the beginning of the gospel of Jesus Christ' continues 'John appeared in the desert baptizing' (Mk 1.1, 4). You may point to Elijah, who was taken up to heaven, but he is not greater than John. Enoch was transported, but he is not greater than John. Moses the Law-giver was very great, and so were all the prophets, but they were not greater than John. I don't presume to compare prophet with prophet; but their Master and ours, the Lord Jesus Christ, declared: 'No greater has arisen among those born of women' (Mt 11.11). He doesn't say: 'among those born of virgins', but 'of women'.

One can compare the greatest slave with his fellow slaves; but in the case of a son and servants, the pre-eminence and the privileges of the former rule out comparison. You see the sort of man God chose to be the precursor of this grace? A man with no property who was a lover of solitude rather than a hater of mankind; one who ate locusts and grew wings for his soul; who fed on honey, and whose words were sweeter and more wholesome than honey; who wore a garment of camel's hair, and served as a model of the ascetic life; who was sanctified by the Holy Spirit while still carried in his mother's womb. Jeremiah was sanctified in the womb too, but he did not prophesy there (cf. Jer 1.5). John was the only one to leap for joy in the womb; and though he could not see with the eyes of the body, he recognized his Master in the Spirit. For the greatness of the grace of baptism called for a great man to dispense it.

7 He was baptizing in the Jordan, and the whole of Jerusalem went out to him (cf. Mt 3.5) to enjoy the beginnings of baptism; for Jerusalem holds precedence in all blessings. But notice, people of Jerusalem, how they were baptized by him when they came out: 'confessing their sins' (Mt 3.6). First they showed their wounds, then he applied the remedies, and he conferred redemption from eternal fire to those who believed. If you want to be convinced of this, that John's baptism was redemption from the threat of fire, listen to what he says: 'Offspring of vipers, who taught you how to escape from the wrath to come?' (Mt 3.7). Don't be a viper any longer, he says: though you were once the offspring of a viper, lay aside the nature of your former sinful life. For all snakes go into narrow places to slough off their old age, squeezing out of their former state and restoring youth to their bodies. In the same way you have to enter through the narrow and constricting doorway (cf. Mt 7.13, 14); squeeze yourself by fasting and force out your corruption. 'Take off the old man with his deeds', and make your own the words of the Canticle: 'I have taken off my tunic. How shall I put it on again?' (Col 3.9; Cant 5.3). But perhaps there is among you a hypocrite and a toady, who goes through the motions of piety without believing in his heart, and follows the hypocrisy of Simon Magus; he doesn't come in order to share the grace, but because he is curious about what is given. Let such a one attend to John's words: 'Now the axe is laid to the root of the trees; so every tree that does not bear sound fruit will be cut down and thrown into the fire' (Mt 3.10). The Judge is inexorable; so get rid of hypocrisy.

8 So what is to be done? What are the fruits of repentance? 'Let him who has two tunics give to him who has none.' The teacher

deserves to be believed, for he first practised what he taught; and he was not afraid to speak, for there was nothing on his conscience to restrain his tongue.[5] 'And let him who has food do likewise' (Lk 3.11). Do you want to enjoy the grace of the Holy Spirit, while not deigning to give material food to the poor? You aspire to the great things while refusing to share the small? Even if you are a tax-collector or a fornicator, you may hope for salvation. 'Tax-collectors and harlots will enter the kingdom of God ahead of you' (Mt 21.31). Paul is our witness when he says: 'Neither fornicators nor idolators' nor the others he lists 'will inherit the kingdom of God. And some of you were such; but you have washed; you have been sanctified' (1 Cor 6.9–11). He didn't say: 'some of you are', but: 'some of you were such'. Sin committed in ignorance is pardoned; but persistent evil is condemned.

9 The proudest boast of baptism for you is the Only-begotten Son of God himself. Why should I speak any more about a man? John was a great man, but what was he compared with the Lord? The voice was powerful, but what was he compared with the Word? The herald was most noble, but what was he compared with the king? The one who baptized in water was noble, but what was he compared with him who baptizes 'with the Holy Spirit and fire' (Mt 3.11). The Saviour baptized the apostles with the Holy Spirit and fire when 'suddenly there was a sound from heaven like that of the blowing of a violent wind, and it filled the whole house where they were sitting. And there appeared to them separate tongues, as of fire, and it settled on each one of them, and they were all filled with the Holy Spirit' (Acts 2.2–4).

10 The unbaptized do not receive salvation, with the single exception of martyrs who receive the kingdom without the water. For when the Saviour was redeeming the world through the cross and his side was pierced, he shed blood and water, for this purpose, that some in times of peace might be baptized in water, others during persecutions in their own blood. For the Saviour could call martyrdom 'baptism', when he said: 'Can you drink the cup which I drink, and can you be baptized with the baptism with which I am baptized?' (Mk 10.38). The martyrs profess their faith, becoming 'a spectacle to the world, to angels and to men' (1 Cor 4.9); and you too will make your profession. But it is not yet the time for you to learn about these things.[6]

11 Jesus made baptism holy when he was baptized himself. If the Son of God was baptized, can anyone now belittle baptism without blaspheming? He was not baptized in order to receive pardon

for his sins, for he was sinless;[7] but, sinless though he was, he was baptized in order to confer divine grace and dignity[8] on the baptized. For 'since the children share flesh and blood, he shared them too' (Heb 2.14), so that by sharing in his incarnate life among us, we might share also in his divine grace; in the same way Jesus was baptized so that by sharing with him we might recover both salvation and dignity. The serpent was in the waters, according to Job, the serpent who receives the Jordan in his eye (cf. Job 40.23 (LXX)); so since he was destined to crush the serpent's heads, Jesus went down into the water and bound the strong one, so that we might receive 'power to tread on snakes and scorpions' (Lk 10.19). It was no small beast, but a fearful one. For 'no fishing-boat could withstand one scale of his tail . . . and before him ran destruction, devastating all who met it' (cf. Job 40.31; 41.14 (LXX)). But life charged against it, so that death might henceforth be muzzled, and we, the saved, might all say: 'Death, where is your victory? Hell, where is your sting?' (cf. 1 Cor 15.55). Death's sting is abolished by baptism.

12 For when you go down into the water you are carrying your sins; but when the invocation of the grace has sealed your soul, it allows you no longer to be swallowed up by the terrible serpent. Dead in your sins when you go down, you come up revived in righteousness. For if you are planted with the Saviour in the likeness of his death, you will also be held worthy of his resurrection. For just as Jesus took on himself the sins of the world, and died to put sin to death and rise in righteousness, so too, when you have gone down into the water and have, so to speak, been buried in the waters, as he was buried in the rock, you will be raised again to 'walk in newness of life' (Rom 6.4).

13 Then once you are granted the grace, it gives you strength to wrestle against the powers that oppose you. For Jesus after his baptism was tempted for forty days – not because he was unable before then to prevail, but because he wished to follow the proper order in everything; so you too, though not daring to wrestle against your adversaries before your baptism, once you have received the grace may take courage to fight with the arms of righteousness, and, if you wish, to preach the gospel.

14 Jesus Christ was the Son of God, but he did not preach the gospel before his baptism. So if even the Master chose the time for this in the proper order, should we servants presume to act out of order? Jesus began his preaching only after 'the Holy Spirit descended on him, in bodily form like a dove' (Lk 3.22) – not that

Jesus wished to see the Spirit first, for he knew the Spirit even before he came in bodily form;[9] what he wanted was that John, who was baptizing him, should see. For, John said, 'I did not know him; but he who sent me to baptize in water told me: The one on whom you see the Spirit descending and remaining on him' (Jn 1.33), that is he. If your devotion is genuine, the Holy Spirit will descend on you too, and the Father's voice will resound over you; but it will not say 'This person is my Son', but 'This person has now become my son.' Over Jesus 'is', because 'in the beginning was the Word, and the Word was with God, and the Word was God (Jn 1.1); over him 'is', because he has always been the Son of God. But over you 'has now become', because you do not possess sonship by nature, but receive it by adoption. He is eternal; you receive the grace as an advancement.

15 So get your soul ready like a jar, to become a son of God, 'God's heir' and 'Christ's fellow-heir' (Rom 8.17) – provided you get yourself ready to receive; provided you approach in faith so as to become one of the Faithful; provided you lay aside the old man in earnest. For all your misdeeds will be forgiven, even fornication, adultery or any other form of licentiousness. What sin is greater than crucifying Christ? Yet even this can be washed away by baptism. For when the three thousand who had crucified the Lord came to Peter and asked him: 'What shall we do, brothers?' (Acts 2.37), for their wound was severe, Peter gave them an answer. You have charged us, Peter, with our fall, saying: 'You have killed the Author of life' (Acts 3.15). What salve is there for so grave a wound? What cleansing for so bad a stain? What salvation for such damnation? 'Repent', he says, 'and be baptized, each of you, in the name of Jesus Christ our Lord for the remission of sins, and you will receive the gift of the Holy Spirit' (Acts 2.38). How inexplicable God's love for mankind! They do not hope to be saved, and they are judged fit to receive the Holy Spirit. You observe the power of baptism. If any of you has crucified Christ by blasphemous words; if any of you has denied him before men in ignorance; if anyone has provoked blasphemy against Christ's teaching by their evil deeds, repent and be of good hope, for the same grace is now offered to you.

16 Take heart, Jerusalem; the Lord will take away all your sins (cf. Zeph 3.14–15). The Lord will wash away the dirt from his sons and daughters in the 'spirit of judgment and the spirit of burning' (Is 4.4). He will 'sprinkle you with pure water and you will be cleansed of all your sin' (Ezek 36.25). The angels will dance around you saying: 'Who is she who comes up clothed in white and leaning

on her kinsman?' (Cant 8.5 (LXX)). For the soul that was once a slave has now called her master her kinsman; and he, accepting her sincere intentions, will address her thus: 'See you are fair, my companion, you are fair . . . Your teeth are like flocks of shorn ewes' because of your sincere confession. He continues: 'all of the ewes bearing twins' (Cant 4.1–2), because of the twofold grace – I mean the grace conferred by water and the Spirit; or else the grace proclaimed by the Old Testament and the New. May you all complete the course of fasting, remember what I have told you, and bring in a harvest of good deeds, so that you may stand without reproach before your spiritual Bridegroom and receive from God the remission of your sins in the same Christ Jesus our Lord, to whom be the glory for ever and ever. Amen.

CATECHESIS 4

For candidates for baptism
On the Ten Dogmas

Reading: Col 2.8ff: 'See that no one carries you off through philosophy and empty trickery, according to human tradition, according to the elements of the world . . .'

1 Vice imitates virtue, and cockle strives to be taken for wheat; but though it looks like wheat, it is betrayed to the discerning by its taste. The devil too changes his appearance to that of an angel of light (cf. 2 Cor 11.14) – not in order to return to the place he came from, but to snare those who live like angels with a blind darkness and a pestilential condition of unbelief. Many wolves go around in sheep's clothing (cf. Mt 7.15); their clothing is that of sheep, but not their claws and their teeth. As they wear the fleece of tame animals, their appearance can deceive the innocent, but their fangs drip with the venom of their impiety. Therefore we need divine grace and a sober mind and seeing eyes, lest, taking cockle for wheat, we eat it in ignorance and come to harm; or mistaking the wolf for a sheep, we become his prey; or assuming the malignant devil to be a good angel, we be devoured. For 'he goes around like a roaring lion, seeking whom he can devour', as Scripture says (1 Pet 5.8). This is the reason for the Church's warnings, for the present instructions, and for the readings which take place.

2 Two things make up a devout way of life: holy dogmas and good works. Just as dogmas without good works are not pleasing to God, so too God does not accept works performed without holy doctrines. For what use is it to have a fine knowledge of the dogmas about God and to be a shameless fornicator? Conversely, what use is the most admirable self-control, if one is an impious blasphemer? Therefore knowledge of the dogmas is a great treasure; it requires a sober mind, for there are many who try to 'carry you off though philosophy and empty trickery' (Col 2.8). The Greeks lead one

astray by rhetoric, for honey drips from the lips of a harlot; the people of circumcision, on the other hand, deceive their followers by false interpretations of Scripture, which they practise from childhood to old age, growing old in their ignorance. The disciples of the heretics deceive the hearts of the innocent by clever talk and rhetoric; they use the name of Christ like honey to disguise, as it were, the poisoned darts of their impious doctrines. The Lord's words apply to all of these alike: 'See that no one leads you astray' (Mt 24.4). This is why you are taught the Creed and have it explained to you.

3 However, before our presentation concerning the Creed,[1] it seems to me a good idea now to provide a concise summary of the necessary dogmas, in case the length of my instructions and the intervening days of holy Lent should lead the simpler-minded among you to forget them. Nevertheless, while we sow the seed thinly in a summary fashion now, we must not lose sight of these teachings when we cultivate them more widely later. At the same time we ask those in the congregation who are more advanced in disposition and whose instincts are already trained to discern right from wrong, to be patient when they hear an introductory talk about more childish things which is like milk for babies. In this way those who need instruction will receive what they need, while those who know these things already will be able to rekindle the memory of what they have already learnt.

ON GOD

4 So to begin with, let your soul have the dogma concerning God as its foundation. There is one God, who is unique, unbegotten, without beginning or change or alteration. He was not begotten by another, and has no one who will succeed to his life. He did not begin his life in time, nor will he ever end it. He is good and just. So if you ever hear a heretic saying that one God is just and another good,[2] you will immediately remember what I say and recognize the poisoned dart. For some people have presumed in their blasphemous teaching to divide the one God: some have distinguished between two Lords and creators, of the soul and bodies respectively – a foolish and irreverent doctrine. For how can one person become the servant of two masters, when the Lord says in the gospels: 'No one can serve two masters' (Mt 6.24)? God is therefore one and unique, the Maker of both souls and bodies. The one Creator of heaven and earth is also the Maker of angels and archangels. Though Creator of

many beings, he is the eternal Father of one alone, his one, Only-begotten Son, our Lord Jesus Christ, through whom he made all things, both visible and invisible.

5 He is the Father of our Lord Jesus Christ. He is not circumscribed in space or smaller than the sky. No, the heavens are the work of his fingers, and he holds the whole earth in his grasp (cf. Ps 8.4 (8.3); Is 40.12). He is in everything and outside everything. Do not imagine he is smaller than the sun or its equal; for the one who made the sun ought rather to be, in the first place, incomparably greater and brighter. He foresees the future and is more powerful than anything; he knows everything and acts as he will; he is not subject to the succession of things, or to generation or chance or fate. In everything he is complete, and he contains equally every form of perfection. He does not grow lesser or greater, but is always identical and the same. He has prepared punishment for sinners and rewards for the righteous.

6 Many have strayed away from the one God in various ways: some have made God out to be the sun, so that when the sun sets, they remain godless throughout the night; others have made him out to be the moon, so that they have no God by day; some the other parts of the universe; some the arts; some foods; some pleasures. Some in their lust for women set up on high the statue of a naked woman calling it Aphrodite,[3] and worshipped passion under this visible form. Others have been so smitten by the brightness of gold that they have made a god of it and of other substances. However, if from the beginning you set the teaching about God's undivided power as a foundation in your heart and believe it, you will cut out at a stroke all the corrupting evils of idolatry and heretical error. So in faith set this first doctrine of religion in your soul as a foundation.

ON CHRIST

7 Believe too in God's one and only Son, our Lord Jesus Christ, who is God begotten by God, Life begotten by Life, Light begotten by Light, like in everything to the one who begot him.[4] He did not begin to be in time, but was begotten by the Father before all ages, eternally and inconceivably.[5] He is God's Wisdom and Power and Justice in substantial form. He has been seated at the Father's right hand before all ages. He was not crowned after his Passion, as some have imagined, as if he received from God the throne at his right hand because of what he endured;[6] he has held the royal dignity

throughout his existence. He is seated alongside the Father as God and Wisdom and Power, as we have said. He shares the Father's reign, and is the Creator of all things for the sake of the Father. He suffers no diminution in his divine dignity, and knows the one who begot him just as he is known by his Begetter.[7] In short, recall the words of the gospels: 'No one knows the Son except the Father, and no one knows the Father except the Son' (Mt 11.27; cf. Jn 10.15).

8 Do not separate the Son from the Father, or construct a compound and believe in a Son-Father. Believe rather that the one God has one Only-begotten Son, who before all ages is God the Word: not an uttered word[8] which is dispersed in the air, or like insubstantial words, but God the Son, the maker of rational[9] beings, the Word who hears his Father and speaks himself. In due time, God willing, we shall explain this to you more fully, for we have not forgotten our intention of providing you now with a summary introduction to the Creed.

ON THE VIRGIN BIRTH

9 You must believe too that this Only-begotten Son of God came down from heaven to earth because of our sins, assumed a humanity subject to the same feelings as ours, and was born of the holy Virgin and the Holy Spirit. The humanity he assumed was not an appearance only or an illusion, but true. He did not pass through the virgin as if through a pipe, but truly took flesh from her and was truly nourished by her milk.[10] For if the Incarnation was an illusion, so too was our salvation. Christ was twofold: man in appearance, and God, but not in appearance. As man he ate truly as we do, for he had the same fleshly feelings as ourselves; but it was as God that he fed the five thousand from five loaves.[11] As man he truly died; but it was as God that he raised the dead body to life after four days.[12] As man he truly slept on the boat; but it was as God that he walked on the waters.

ON THE CROSS

10 He was truly crucified for our sins. For even if you would like to deny it, the place visibly refutes you, this blessed place of Golgotha where we are now congregated because of the one who was crucified here. Besides, the whole world has since been filled with the wood of the cross, piece by piece.[13] It was not for his own sins that he was crucified, but that we might be freed from our sins. As man he was

despised then by men and beaten; but he was acknowledged as God by the whole of creation. For when the sun saw its Master dishonoured, it trembled and was eclipsed, because it could not bear the sight.

ON THE BURIAL

11 He was truly placed in the rock tomb as man, but because of him the rocks in terror were split asunder. He went down into the underworld to rescue the just from there. For tell me, would you want the living to enjoy grace, even though the majority are not holy, while those from Adam down who had long been confined should never regain their freedom? The prophet Isaiah shouted aloud and proclaimed so many truths about him; wouldn't you want the king to go down to rescue his herald? David was there, and Samuel, and all the prophets, and even John who asked through his messengers: 'Are you the one to come, or should we look for another?' (Mt 11.3). Wouldn't you want Jesus to go down to rescue such men as these?

ON THE RESURRECTION

12 However the one who went down to the underworld came up again; on the third day the buried Jesus truly rose again. If the Jews ever taunt you, confront them at once with this question: 'Jonah emerged from the whale on the third day; couldn't Christ be raised from the earth on the third day? The dead man rose again after touching the bones of Elisha (cf. 2 Kings 13.21); wasn't it much easier for the maker of mankind to be raised by his Father's power?' So he truly rose again, and having risen he was seen again by the disciples. The twelve disciples are witnesses to his resurrection, though they did not use flattering words to give their evidence; they fought for the truth of the resurrection to the point of torture and death. Finally, Scripture says that 'by the mouth of two or three witnesses any saying shall be held valid' (Deut 19.15; cf. Mt 18.16); there are twelve witnesses to Christ's resurrection; will you still refuse to believe in the resurrection?

ON THE ASCENSION

13 When Jesus completed his course of endurance, and had redeemed mankind from their sins, a cloud received him and he returned to heaven. Angels stood by as he ascended while the apostles

looked on. If anyone does not believe what I say, let them believe the very power of what now lies before their eyes. In general when kings die, their authority is extinguished along with their life; but the crucified Christ is worshipped throughout the world. We proclaim the Crucified, and demons tremble. In the course of history many men have been crucified; but has there ever been another crucified man who has put demons to flight when he is invoked?

14 Let us not be ashamed of Christ's cross. No, even if others hide it, you place it openly as a seal on your forehead, so that demons may see the royal sign and run far away in terror. Make this sign when you eat and when you drink; when you sit down, when you go to bed, when you get up; when you talk, when you walk – in a word, on every occasion. For the one who was crucified here is in heaven above. For if after his crucifixion and burial he had remained in the grave, we would have reason to be ashamed; but as it is, the one who was crucified here on Golgotha ascended into heaven from the Mount of Olives, which lies to the east. For after he had descended into hell and come up again to us, it was from there that he departed from us and went back to heaven, while his Father spoke to him these words: 'Sit on my right until I make your enemies your footstool' (Ps 109 (110).1).

ON THE FUTURE JUDGMENT

15 This same Jesus Christ who ascended into heaven will come again, not from the earth, but from heaven. I said not from the earth; for many antichrists are now destined to come from the earth. Already, as you have seen, many have begun to say: 'I am the Christ' (Mt 24.5); and it still remains for the 'abomination of desolation' (Mt 24.15) to come, assuming the false name of Christ. But I ask you to wait for the true Christ, God's Only-begotten Son, who will come again not from the earth, but from heaven. He will appear, brighter than any lightning or flashing light and escorted by angels, to judge the living and the dead, and to exercise a heavenly, eternal and everlasting reign. I urge you to be certain about this, because there are many who say that Christ's reign will come to an end.

ON THE HOLY SPIRIT

16 Believe also in the Holy Spirit, and understand him correctly, for there are many who are at variance with the Holy Spirit and teach blasphemous doctrines about him. You have to learn that

the Holy Spirit is one, indivisible, and endowed with many powers; his operations are many, but he himself is undivided; he knows the mysteries, he 'searches all things' (1 Cor 2.10), even the depths of God. He came down on the Lord Jesus Christ in the form of a dove; he worked through the law and the prophets; now he will seal your soul at the time of baptism. Every rational nature needs the holiness that comes from him. If anyone presumes to blaspheme against him, he will not be forgiven either in this life or in the life to come (cf. Mt 12.32). He receives the honour due to his rank together with the Father and the Son. Thrones and Dominations, Principalities and Powers have need of him. For there is one God, the Father of Christ; and one Lord Jesus Christ, the Only-begotten Son of the only God; and one Holy Spirit, who sanctifies and deifies all, who has spoken through the law and the prophets, the Old Testament and the New.

17 So keep always in your mind the seal of which we have now spoken to you summarily, touching on the most important points. However, if the Lord allows it, I shall speak about this later as best I can and give scriptural proof. For where the divine and holy mysteries of the Creed are concerned, one must not teach even minor points without reference to the sacred Scriptures, or be led astray lightly by persuasive and elaborate arguments. Do not simply take my word when I tell you these things, unless you are given proof for my teaching from holy Scripture. For this is the guarantee of our Creed, not clever argument, but proof based on Scripture.

ON HUMAN NATURE

On the soul

18 Now that you have learnt about this sacred, glorious and holy Creed, it remains for you to learn about yourself: that a human being is twofold by nature, consisting of both soul and body; that the same God, as I explained just now, is the Creator of both soul and body. You should know too that you have a self-determining soul, which is God's fairest work, formed in the image of its Maker; it is immortal, because God endowed it with immortality; a living, rational, incorruptible being, because of him who gave it these gifts; with power to do what it chooses. For you are not a sinner by birth or a fornicator by chance; nor, as some say in their madness, do the conjunctions of the stars compel you to devote yourself to wantonness. Why do you avoid acknowledging your own evil deeds,

and cast the blame on the innocent stars? I implore you, do not attend any more to astrologers. Holy Scripture says this about them: 'Let the astrologers of the heavens stand and save you.' And further on: 'See, they will all be burnt up in the fire like faggots, and they shall never rescue their soul from the flames' (Is 47.14).

19 I would have you know this too, that before the soul enters this world, it has committed no sin;[14] but though we arrive sinless, now we sin by choice. Please don't pay attention to anyone misinterpreting the text: 'If I do what I do not want' (Rom 7.16); remember the one who says: 'If you are willing and obey me, you may eat the good things of the land; but if you are not willing and do not obey me, a sword will eat you, etc.' (Is 1.19–20). And again: 'Just as you have delivered your bodies as slaves to impurity, and to sin upon sin, so now deliver your bodies as slaves to the righteousness that leads to holiness' (Rom 6.19). Remember too the text: 'And since they did not think fit to pay recognition to God' (Rom 1.28); and: 'What can be known about God is clear to them' (Rom 1.19); and: 'They have closed their eyes' (Mat 13.15). Remember too how God accuses them again, saying: 'I planted you to be a fruitful vine, true through and through; how did you turn to sourness and become a wild vine?' (Jer 2.21 (LXX)).

20 The soul is immortal. All souls are alike, both of men and women; it is only the bodily parts which are different. There is not one class of souls which are by nature sinners, and another of those which by nature live justly. Both are a matter of choice; since for all the structure of the soul is uniform and similar. I realize I have a lot to say, and I have been speaking for a long time; but what is more precious than salvation? Aren't you willing to take the trouble to acquire provisions for facing the heretics? Don't you want to learn the wrong turnings along the way, so as not to be led in ignorance over the edge of a precipice? If your teachers think it no small gain if you learn these truths, shouldn't learners like you put up gladly with the length of my address?

21 The soul determines its own state. Though the devil can tempt you, he can't force you against your will, for he has not power to do so. He represents to you the thought of fornication; if you choose, you consent; if you don't choose, you don't consent. For if you were a fornicator by necessity, why did God prepare hell? If you lived justly by nature and not by choice, why has God prepared indescribable rewards? A sheep is gentle, but it is never rewarded for its gentleness, for it possesses its gentleness not by choice but by nature.

On the body

22 Dearly beloved, you now know as much about the soul as time allows. Listen now as well as you can to the facts concerning your body. Do not allow anyone to say that this body of ours has nothing in common with God.[15] For those who believe the body is something alien, live in it as if in an alien container which they readily abuse by fornication. Why have they found fault with this admirable body of ours? Is it lacking in dignity in any way? Is there anything badly designed in its constitution? Shouldn't they have considered the brilliant construction of the eyes? How the ears, being set at an angle, provide unobstructed hearing? How the sense of smell distinguishes and receives various scents? How the tongue serves two purposes, the sense of taste and the power of speech? How the lungs, though lying hidden, ceaselessly breathe the air? Who installed the ceaseless beating of the heart? Who divided the system into so many veins and arteries? Who strung the bones together with sinews so cleverly? Who devoted part of our food to build up the body and set aside part for decent excretion, concealing the unbecoming members in the more decent places? When human nature was likely to become extinct, who devised intercourse as an easy means for its survival?

23 Don't tell me that the body shares the blame for sin. For if sin is due to the body, why doesn't a corpse sin? Place a sword in the right hand of a man who has just died; no murder will take place. Whatever forms of beauty are displayed before a young man who has just died, no desire of fornication will be felt. Why not? Because the body by itself does not sin; the soul sins through the body. The body is the soul's instrument and, so to say, its clothing and its attire. If the body is given up to fornication by the soul, it becomes unclean; but if it co-exists with a holy soul, it becomes the temple of the Holy Spirit. These are not my words, but those of the apostle Paul: 'Do you not know', he said, 'that your bodies are the temple of the Holy Spirit within you?' (1 Cor 6.19). So respect your body, because it is the temple of the Holy Spirit. Do not pollute your flesh by fornication; do not soil this fairest of robes. But if you have soiled it, wash it now through repentance, for this is the time for washing.

24 Our teaching about chastity should be heeded above all by the order of celibates and virgins, who while in the world live like the angels. A great reward is in store for you, my brothers and sisters; do not forfeit your great glory for the sake of a little pleasure.

Listen to the words of the Apostle: 'Let no one be a fornicator, or profane like Esau, who sold his birthright for one meal' (Heb 12.16). Once you have been enrolled in the angelic register for your vow of chastity, see that your name is not subsequently removed for practising fornication.

25 On the other hand, if you are observing chastity, do not give yourselves airs at the expense of those who have entered into marriage. For 'let marriage be held in honour and the marriage-bed kept unstained' (Heb 13.4), as the Apostle says. You have preserved your virginity; but weren't your parents married? Don't despise silver because you have a store of gold. No, those who are married and fulfil their marriage lawfully should live in good hope – those who have made their marriage virtuous and not self-indulgent in unrestrained licence; who know periods of abstinence so that they can give themselves to prayer; who bring clean bodies as well as clean clothes to services in church; who were led into marriage by the desire of children rather than of pleasure.

26 Those who have married only once should not despise those who are living in a second marriage. For continence is a beautiful and admirable thing; but one should be tolerant to those who marry a second time lest their weakness betray them into fornication. For 'it is good for them if they remain as I am', said the Apostle. 'But if they cannot remain continent, let them marry; for it is better to marry than to burn' (1 Cor 7.8–9). But everything else should be driven far away: fornication, adultery, and every form of self-indulgence. Keep your body pure for the Lord, to make it fit for his eyes.

On food

27 Your body should be given food for nourishment in order to keep it alive and fit for service, not to indulge it with luxuries. With regard to meals, keep these rules, for many trip up where food is concerned. Some indiscriminately make use of food that has been offered to idols; others practise restraint, but despise those who eat (cf. Rom 14.3). People's souls can become soft in various ways in the matter of food, if they do not know the appropriate reasons when to eat and when not. For we abstain from wine and give up meat not because we abhor them as abominations, but because we look for a reward; so that through making little of material food we may enjoy a spiritual and immaterial table; so that if we 'sow in tears' we may 'reap in joy' in the next life (Ps 125 (126).5). So don't

despise those who eat and take food because of bodily infirmity. Don't find fault with people who take a little wine for the sake of their digestion or because of frequent illnesses (cf. 1 Tim 5.23); do not condemn them as sinners. Do not condemn meat as something alien: for the Apostle's words show that he knew some such people: 'They forbid marriage and enjoin abstinence from food, which God created for the Faithful to share with thanksgiving' (1 Tim 4.3). Therefore if you abstain from such things, do not do so as if they were abominable, for then you would have no reward; yet excellent as they are, hold them of little account for the sake of the nobler, spiritual things you are promised.

28 Make a firm resolution never to eat anything which has been offered to idols. I know I am not the only one to be concerned with what you eat; the apostles and James the bishop of this church were concerned before me. The apostles and the elders wrote a general letter to all the gentiles, instructing them above all to abstain from food offered to idols, and then from blood and animals that had been strangled (cf. Acts 15.29). For there are many savage people who live like dogs, lap up blood in imitation of the wildest animals, and eat lavish quantities of strangled meat. But you are one of Christ's servants; when you eat, be sure to eat reverently. I have now said enough about food.

On clothing

29 Wear clothes that are plain, for the sake of necessary covering rather than adornment. Don't choose them out of vanity, but to provide warmth in winter and covering for the unseemly parts of the body. But do not, on the pretext of concealing these parts, fall into another form of unseemliness by adopting excessive ornamentation.

On resurrection

30 I beg you, treat your body with respect, in the knowledge that you will rise from the dead with this body to face judgment. If a sceptical thought occurs to you suggesting that this is impossible, let your own case cast light on these hidden truths. Tell me, you yourself, where were you a hundred or more years ago? Think it out. Again, how very small and insignificant was the material from which you grew to your present stature and comeliness. So why can't the one who brought the non-existent into existence also raise up again something which has once existed but has perished? Every year he

raises up the wheat which dies once it is sown for our use; why should he be reluctant to raise us up ourselves, for whose sake the wheat was raised? You can see how the trees have remained now without fruit or leaves for so many months; but once the winter is over, they revive intact as if from the dead. Is it not much more to be expected, is it not easier, that we should be restored to life? By God's design Moses' rod was changed and assumed a nature that was not its own, the nature of a snake; cannot a human being who has succumbed to death be restored again to himself?

31 Do not listen to those who say that this body does not rise again. For it does rise, as Isaiah testifies: 'The dead will be raised', he says, 'and those in their tombs will rise again' (Is 26.19 (LXX)). And according to Daniel: 'Many of those who are sleeping in the dust of the earth will rise up, some to eternal life, and others to eternal shame' (Dan 12.2 (adjusted)). Yet, while rising again is the lot of every human being, their resurrection takes different forms. For though we shall all be given everlasting bodies, they will not all be alike: the just will be given bodies for dancing eternally with the angels, sinners for suffering eternal torment for their sins.

On baptism

32 The Lord foresaw this and so in his mercy gave us baptism as a means of repentance, to enable us to throw off the great, indeed the whole, burden of our sins, and to inherit eternal life by receiving the seal through the Holy Spirit. However, as we said enough about baptism the day before yesterday,[16] let me now go on to the remaining introductory doctrines.

ON THE HOLY SCRIPTURES

33 This is what the inspired Scriptures of the Old and New Testaments teach us. For there is one God of both testaments, who in the Old Testament foretold the Christ who appeared in the New, and led us to him like children through the law and the prophets.[17] For 'before the faith came, we were kept in custody under the law'; and 'the law became our tutor leading us to Christ' (Gal 3.23, 24). So if you ever hear any heretic blaspheming against the law or the prophets, raise this victory cry against them: 'Jesus did not come to abolish the law but to fulfil it' (cf. Mt 5.17). Be a good student and learn from the Church which the books of the Old Testament and

the New are. Please do not read any of the apocrypha; for if you don't know the works which are universally accepted, why do you waste effort over the disputed ones? Read the holy Scriptures, the twenty-two books of the Old Testament which were translated by the seventy-two translators.

34 When Alexander the King of Macedon had died, his empire was divided into the four kingdoms of Babylon, Macedon, Asia and Egypt. Now one of the kings of Egypt, Ptolemy Philadelphus, who was a very scholarly king and had gathered together books from every part of the world, learnt from his librarian Demetrius of Phaleron about the holy Scriptures of the law and the prophets. He decided it was much better not to force people against their will to provide him with books but rather to win the owners over with gifts and friendship; he realized too that what is given perforce and involuntarily is often corrupted, while what is offered voluntarily is an authentic gift. So he sent many presents to Eleazer, who was High Priest at the time, in the Temple here in Jerusalem, and induced him to send him six men from each of the twelve tribes of Israel to serve as translators.[18] Then, wishing to test whether or not the books were inspired, and suspecting that the members of the panel might copy from one another, he allotted to each of the translators who had come a separate room in the island called Pharos which lies off Alexandria, and instructed each of them to translate the whole of the Scriptures. When they had completed their task after seventy-two days, the king compared all the translations, which they had made each in his own room without access to one another, and found they agreed not only in content but even verbally. This was not due to their facility with words or the product of human skills; the holy Scriptures had been dictated by the Holy Spirit and through the Holy Spirit their translation was accomplished.

35 Read the twenty-two books of these Scriptures, and have nothing to do with the apocrypha.[19] Give careful study to these books and to these only; these are the ones in which we have confidence for reading in church. The apostles and the ancient bishops who presided over the Church were much wiser and more devout than we are, and they handed these books on to us. You are a child of the Church; so don't falsify the Church's laws. Study the twenty-two books of the Old Testament, as I say, and, if you are studiously inclined, take the trouble to memorize their names when I tell you them. The books of the law are the first five books of Moses, namely Genesis, Exodus, Leviticus, Numbers, Deuteronomy; then Joshua

and the book of Judges, including Ruth, which is the seventh book. Of the remaining historical books, the first and second books of Kings are treated by the Hebrews as a single book; the same is true of the third and fourth books.[20] In the same way they take first and second Chronicles to be a single book, and first and second Esdras also count as one. The twelfth book is Esther. These are the historical books. There are also five books written in verse: Job, the book of Psalms, Proverbs, Ecclesiastes, and the Song of Songs, which is the seventeenth book. Next come the five prophetical books: one book consisting of the twelve prophets; one of Isaiah; one of Jeremiah, including Baruch, Lamentations and the Letter;[21] one of Ezekiel; and one of Daniel, which is the twenty-second book of the Old Testament.

36 In the New Testament there are four gospels, and only four; any others are spurious and harmful. The Manichees wrote another, the Gospel of Thomas,[22] which, being scented and painted with the name of gospel, corrupts the souls of the simple. You should also accept the Acts of the twelve apostles, and in addition the seven catholic epistles of James, Peter, John and Jude; and finally, to set the seal on them all, the fourteen epistles of Paul, which form the last work of the disciples. Treat any other books as secondary. Those which are not read in churches you should not read privately either, as you have already been told. This is all that needs to be said on this subject.

37 Keep away from all the works of the devil. Don't believe the rebellious serpent, who by his own choice was transformed from his good state. He is able to win over those who consent, but he can't force anyone. Pay no attention to horoscopes, auguries or omens, or to the oracles of the Greeks which are based on myths. As for potions, spells and the evil practices of mediums, do not allow them even to be talked about. Avoid every kind of indulgence; don't be a glutton or a hedonist; and don't descend to any kind of avarice or usury. Don't take part in pagan gatherings and shows, and never use amulets when you are ill. Refuse to frequent degrading taverns. Don't desert to the Samaritans or the Jews, for Jesus Christ has redeemed you for ever. Avoid all sabbath observance or describing harmless food as common or unclean. Above all hold all wicked heretical assemblies in abhorrence. Take every means to safeguard your soul by fasting, prayer, almsgiving and the reading of Scripture, so that after living the rest of your earthly lives in temperance and holy beliefs, you may enjoy the one salvation which comes

through baptism. In this way you will be enrolled by God the Father in the heavenly armies and rewarded with a heavenly crown in Jesus Christ our Lord, to whom is the glory for ever and ever. Amen.

CATECHESIS 5

For the candidates for baptism
Concerning faith

Reading: Heb 11.1ff: 'Faith is the substance of things hoped for, the proof of things which are not seen . . .'

1 How great is the honour the Lord is conferring on you, when he transfers you from the rank of the catechumens to that of the Faithful![1] The Apostle Paul stands as a witness and says: 'God is Faithful, through whom you were called into the fellowship of his Son Jesus Christ' (1 Cor 1.9). For since 'Faithful' is God's name, you should take it as a great honour to be given the same name. For God is called 'Faithful', just as he is called 'Good', 'Righteous', 'Almighty' and 'Creator of the Universe'. So consider the dignity to which you are being raised, since you are soon to share God's title.

. . .

10 Although there is a single word 'faith', it is applied in two ways. One kind of faith concerns doctrines, and involves the soul's assent to some truth. It benefits the soul, as the Lord says: 'The one who listens to my words and believes him who sent me has eternal life, and does not come to judgment' (Jn 5.24). And again: 'The one who believes in the Son is not judged' (Jn 3.18), 'but has passed from death to life' (5.24). How great is God's love for mankind! The righteous earned God's approval over many years; but what they obtained by earning his approval over many years Jesus now bestows on you in a single hour. For if you believe that Jesus Christ is the Lord and that God raised him from the dead, you will be saved and transported to Paradise by the one who admitted the thief into Paradise. Don't doubt whether it is possible. For the one who saved the thief here at holy Golgotha for the faith of a single hour will save you too if you believe.

11 Here is a second kind of faith, which is given by Christ as a grace. 'For to one it is given to speak wisdom through the Spirit, to

another to speak knowledge according to the same Spirit, to another in the same Spirit faith, and to another gifts of healing' (1 Cor 12.8–9). Consequently this faith, which is given by the Spirit as a grace, doesn't only concern doctrines, but can produce effects which transcend human powers. For anyone who has faith of this kind 'will say to this mountain: "Move from here to there", and it will move' (Mt 17.20). For when anyone says this with faith and believes it will happen, and 'does not hesitate in their heart' (Mk 11.23), then they receive the grace. It is to this kind of faith that the saying: 'If you have faith like a mustard-seed' (Mt 17.20) refers. For a mustard-seed is small in size but is fiery in power; it is sown in a tiny area, but comprises great branches, and when it grows it can provide shelter for the birds; so too faith in the briefest instant can produce great results in the soul. For when enlightened by faith, the soul forms an image of God and contemplates him, in so far as that is possible. It circles the boundaries of the world, and before the fulfilment of this age it already beholds the judgment and the promised rewards. So maintain the faith which comes from yourself and is directed towards him, so that you may receive from him the faith which can accomplish works transcending human powers.

12 Learn the faith and profess it; receive it and keep it – but only the Creed[2] which the Church will now deliver to you, the Creed which is firmly based on the whole of Scripture. For since not everyone is able to read the Scriptures, but some are prevented from learning them by illiteracy, others by lack of time, we summarize the whole teaching of the faith in a few lines, so that ignorance will not lead you to lose your souls. I want you to memorize it word for word, and to recite it very carefully among yourselves.[3] Do not write it down on paper, but inscribe it in your memories and in your hearts. But when you repeat it, make sure that none of the catechumens overhears the words that have been handed on to you. Keep it as food for your journey at every moment of your life, and never accept another Creed apart from it, even if we ourselves change our minds and contradict what we are teaching now, even if a hostile angel is 'transfigured into an angel of light' (2 Cor 11.14) and tries to lead you astray. For 'if we or an angel from heaven preach to you a gospel which is opposed to what you have been taught, let him be accursed' (Gal 1.8). So for now, listen to the Creed and memorize it word for word, and in due time you will be taught the proof from the holy Scriptures for each point it contains. For the articles of the Creed were not put together according to human choice; the most important doctrines were collected from

the whole of Scripture to make up a single exposition of the faith. Just as the mustard-seed contains its many branches in a tiny grain, so too this Creed embraces in a few words all the religious knowledge contained in the Old and New Testaments. So see to it, brethren, and 'hold fast to the traditions' (2 Thess 2.15) which will now be entrusted to you; and engrave them 'on the tablet of your heart' (Prov 7.3).

13 Guard them religiously, in case the Enemy should try to rob any of you who grow slack. Do not let any heretic pervert any of the traditions. For faith is like money entrusted to the banker; God requires you to submit accounts of the deposit. I charge you, in the words of the Apostle, 'before the God who gives life to every creature, and before Christ Jesus who testified under Pontius Pilate and made the good confession', to 'preserve uncorrupted' this Creed which has been entrusted to you, 'until the appearance of our Lord Jesus Christ' (1 Tim 6.13–14). The treasure of life has now been entrusted to you; the Master will demand his deposit at his appearing, 'which will be revealed at the proper time by the one blessed Sovereign, the King of kings and Lord of lords, who alone possesses immortality and dwells in unapproachable light, whom no human being has seen or can see' (1 Tim 6.15–16). To him is the glory, honour and power for ever and ever. Amen.

CATECHESIS 6

For candidates for baptism
Concerning the unity of God's rule, on 'I believe in one God'; and concerning heresies

Reading: Is 45.17ff (LXX): 'Be renewed for me, you islands. Israel is saved by the Lord with an eternal salvation . . .'

1 'Blessed is the God and Father of our Lord Jesus Christ' (2 Cor 1.3). One should not think of God without thinking of him as Father, to make the glory paid to the Father, the Son and the Holy Spirit complete and inseparable. For the Father's glory is not different from the Son's, but one and the same. Since the Son is the Father's Only-begotten, he shares the Father's glory when the Father is glorified; for glory accrues to the Son from honour paid to the Father, while glory paid to the Son is greatly to the honour of the Father of one who is so excellent.

2 Though the intellect is very swift in its understanding, the tongue needs the medium of words and long verbal formulas. In the same way the eye encompasses a large number of the host of the stars, but if you want to indicate them one by one, which is the Morning and which the Evening star, and each of the others, you have to use many words. In a similar way again the intellect encompasses land and sea and all the ends of the world in the briefest moment; but it needs many words to explain what it has grasped in an instant. These comparisons are significant, but they are still weak and feeble. For we do not say as much as needs to be said about God, but as much as human nature can grasp and our weakness can bear. We do not explain what God is; we admit with a good grace that we do not know the exact truth about him. For in what concerns God the height of knowledge is to admit one's ignorance. So 'magnify the Lord with me, and let us exalt his name together, all

as one' (Ps 33.4 (34.3)). For singly we are incapable; or rather, even if we all join our voices, it will still be beyond us to do what we ought. I am not just speaking about all of you present; for even if all the Church's offspring throughout the whole world, both now and in the future, were to join voices, they would be incapable of singing their shepherd's praises as he deserves.

3 Abraham was a great and honoured man; but great only in comparison with other men. But once he was admitted to God's presence, he declared truthfully and with a good grace: 'I am earth and ashes' (Gen 18.27). He didn't say 'I am earth' and leave it there, not wishing to give himself the name of the great element; he added: 'and ashes', to indicate his corruptible and defective side. Is there anything, he means, that is finer and lighter than ash? Compare, he means, ash with a house, a house with a city, a city with a province, a province with the Roman Empire, the Roman Empire with the whole world and all its confines, the whole world with the heavens which embrace it – the world which is to the heavens what the hub of a wheel is to the whole circumference; and bear in mind that this visible first heaven is smaller than the second, and the second than the third; and when you have conceived in your mind all the heavens, even these heavens will not be able to praise God as he is, even if they speak louder than the thunder. If these great vaults of the heavens cannot sing the praise of God as he deserves, when will earth and ashes, the smallest and least of all beings, be able to raise a hymn that is worthy of God, 'who holds together the circle of the earth and views its inhabitants as locusts' (Is 40.22 (LXX))?

4 If anyone will undertake to speak about God, let him first give an account of the boundaries of the earth. You live on earth, but you do not know the ends of the earth, which is your own dwelling; how can you form an adequate concept of its Maker? You gaze at the stars, but you cannot gaze at their Creator. First count what you can see, and then explain the One you cannot see, who 'numbers the hosts of the stars and calls each one of them by name' (Ps 146 (147).4). Not long ago there was a violent downpour and the raindrops all but killed us. Calculate the number of the raindrops that fell on this city alone; calculate, if you can, the number that fell in a single hour, I won't say on the whole city, but on your own house; then, if you can't, you will realize your own inadequacy. This shows you the extent of God's power. For 'he numbers the raindrops' (Job 36.27 (LXX)) which pour down over the whole earth – not only today but ever. The sun is God's creation; it is vast, but compared with the whole sky it is very small. First gaze at the sun, and then

speculate about its Lord. 'Do not inquire into what is too deep for you, or examine what is too strong for you; ponder on what has been assigned to you' (Sir 3.21–2).

5 Perhaps someone will say: 'If the divine substance is incomprehensible, why do you discuss these things yourself?' But since I can't drink up a whole river, does this mean that I can't take as much as is good for me? Since the construction of my eyes doesn't allow me to take in the whole sun, does this mean that I can't see enough for my own needs? Or if I enter a great garden and can't eat all the produce of the fruit-trees, do you want me to leave totally famished? I praise and glorify our Maker, for the divine command tells us: 'Let every breath give praise to the Lord' (Ps 150.6). My purpose now is to glorify the Lord, not to explain him, knowing that I shall fall short of glorifying him worthily, but regarding it as a work of devotion simply to make the attempt. For the words of the Lord Jesus console me in my weakness: 'No one has ever seen God' (Jn 1.18).

6 'What?', someone will say. 'Doesn't Scripture say that the angels of the little ones "always behold the face of my Father in heaven"' (Mt 18.10)? But the angels see God not as he is, but according to their capacity. For Jesus himself said: 'Not that anyone has seen the Father, except the one who is from God, he has seen the Father' (Jn 6.46). The angels see according to their capacity, and the archangels according to their ability; the Thrones and Dominations more than the first, but still fail to do him justice. Only the Holy Spirit, together with the Son, can see adequately. 'For the Spirit searches everything, even the depths of God' (1 Cor 2.10), just as the Only-begotten Son, together with the Holy Spirit, knows the Father adequately. For Jesus says that 'no one knows the Father except the Son and those to whom the Son reveals him' (Mt 11.27). For he sees God as he needs to see him and reveals him through the Spirit according to each one's receptivity; for the Only-begotten Son shares in the Father's godhead together with the Holy Spirit. The Begotten knows his Begetter, and the Begetter knows the one he has begotten. Therefore since angels are ignorant (for the Only-begotten reveals according to each one's power through the Holy Spirit, as we have said), let no human be ashamed to confess his ignorance. I am speaking now, as everyone speaks when occasion offers; but how we speak, we cannot say. How then can I give an account of the one who gives me the power of speech? I have a soul, but I cannot list its properties; how will I be able to give a full account of the one who gave me my soul?

7 There is only one thing that religion will require us to know, and that is that we have a God: a God who is one, a God who exists, who exists eternally, who is always like himself, who has no other as his father, who has no one stronger than himself, whom no successor can expel from his kingdom, who is many-named, all-powerful and uniform in substance. For the fact that he is called good and just and all-sovereign and Sabaoth does not make him subject to difference and diversity; remaining one and the same, he radiates myriad divine energies. He is not more developed on one side and less on another; in everything he is like himself. He is not great only in love of mankind and small in wisdom; he is equally powerful in wisdom and love of mankind. He is not endowed with sight in one part of his being and deprived of it in another; he is all eye and all hearing and all mind. He is not endowed with thought in one part of his being and without consciousness in another, as we are; that would be a blasphemous idea and unworthy of the divine substance. He has foreknowledge of all that is; he is holy and all-sovereign; he is more excellent and greater and wiser than any being. We shall never be able to ascribe to him shape or form. 'His voice you have never heard; his form you have never seen' (Jn 5.37), says Scripture. So too Moses told the Israelites: 'Keep it firmly in your hearts that you have seen no likeness of him' (Deut 4.15 (LXX)). For if it is impossible for his general likeness to be manifested, will thought come close to his substance?

CATECHESIS 10

For candidates for baptism
On 'and in one Lord, Jesus Christ'

Reading: 1 Cor 8.5ff: 'Yet although there are so-called 'gods' in heaven or on earth, for us there is one God, the Father, from whom all things exist and for whom we exist, and one Lord Jesus Christ, through whom all things exist, and we too exist through him . . .'

1 Those who have been taught to believe 'in one God the Father Almighty' ought also to believe 'in his Only-begotten Son'. For one cannot both deny the Son and have the Father. 'I am the Door', Jesus says. 'No one comes to the Father except through me' (Jn 10.9); if you deny the door, you are shut off from knowledge of the Father. 'No one knows the Father except the Son and those to whom the Son reveals him' (Mt 11.27); if you deny the revealer, you remain in ignorance. There is a saying in the Gospels: 'the one who does not believe in the Son will not have life, but God's anger rests upon him' (Jn 3.36); for God is angry when his Son is slighted. A king regards it as a serious offence if even one of his soldiers is dishonoured, and if a bodyguard or a friend is dishonoured his anger is all the greater; but if it is the king's only son who is insulted, who will appease the father's anger at this?

2 So if you wish to show reverence for God, you should adore his Son, or else the Father will not accept your worship. For the Father proclaimed from heaven: 'This is my beloved Son in whom I am well pleased' (Mt 3.17). The Father took pleasure in his Son, and if you do not do the same, you do not have life. Do not be led astray like the Jews, who say craftily: 'There is one God alone.' No, besides knowing that there is one God, you must know too that he has an Only-begotten Son. I am not the first to say this: the Psalmist speaking for the Son says: 'The Lord said to me: "You are my Son" ' (Ps 2.7). Pay attention then, not to what the Jews say, but to what

the prophets say. Are you surprised that the people who stoned the prophets disregard what they say?

3 So believe 'in one Lord Jesus Christ, the Only-begotten Son of God'. We say that Jesus Christ is one Lord to preserve our belief that he is the Only-begotten Son. We say he is one in case anyone might suppose that he is a second Lord. We say he is one to prevent the many names by which his power is described leading you to an impious belief in many sons.[1] For he is called the Door; but don't imagine the title refers to a wooden door; it refers rather to a spiritual, living door which determines who may enter. He is called the Way: not a way that is walked on, but one that leads to our Father in heaven. He is called a Sheep (Is 53.7; Acts 8.32): not a dumb animal, but the one who purified the world from its sins with his precious blood, the one who was led to the shearer and knew when to be silent. But conversely this sheep is called the Shepherd, who said, 'I am the Good Shepherd' (Jn 10.11): sheep in his humanity, shepherd by the mercy of the godhead. Do you need proof that there can be sheep in the spiritual sense? He says to the apostles: 'See, I am sending you out like sheep amid wolves' (Mt 10.16). Again he is called Lion, though not a man-eating one, signifying by this name his royal, strong and resolute character. He is given this title in contrast with our enemy the roaring lion who swallows the victims it has tricked (1 Pet 5.8). For when the Saviour came, he did not change the gentle side of his nature, but as the powerful lion of the tribe of Judah he saved believers and trod the enemy under foot. He is called Stone: not the inanimate stone which men have quarried, but the Corner-stone, by whom the 'believer . . . will not be put to shame' (1 Pet 2.4, 6).

4 He is called Christ: yet he was not anointed by human hands; he was anointed by the Father to an eternal, superhuman priesthood. He is called the Dead one (Apoc 1.18): yet he did not remain among the dead like all the rest in the Underworld; he alone was 'free among the dead' (Ps 87.6 (LXX) (88.5)). He is called 'Son of Man'; yet he did not derive his origin like each of us from the earth, but he will come on the clouds of heaven to judge the living and the dead (Dan 7.13–14; Mt 24.30). He is called Lord, though not in the loose sense, like lords among men. His proper name was Jesus, a title derived from the saving art of the healer.[2] He is called Son, not by an act of adoption but by natural birth. Our Saviour thus has many titles; and so to prevent this multiplicity of titles leading you to think there are many sons, and because of the errors of the heretics who say among other things that Christ, Jesus, the

Door, etc. are not one and the same, the Creed takes the precaution of giving you its precise formulation: 'in one Lord Jesus Christ'. For although there are many titles, they belong to a single individual.

5 The Saviour provides for our needs, for each in a different way. For those who lack joy, he is the Vine; for those who need to enter, he is the Door; for those who need to pray, he is the Mediator and the High Priest. Again, for those who are sinners, he becomes the Sheep to be slain on their behalf. He becomes 'all things for all men' (1 Cor 9.22), while remaining what he is by nature. For while continuing to hold the unchangeable dignity of Son, he adapts to our weaknesses like a skilled doctor or a sympathetic teacher. He is Lord literally; he did not gain the rank of lord by advancement but possesses it by nature.[3] He is not called Lord in the loose sense as we are, but he is literally Lord, because he rules over his own handiwork by his Father's decree. The lordship we exercise is over human beings who share our rank and our feelings, even over our elders, for often a young ruler has authority over those who are old. But the lordship of our Lord Jesus Christ is not like this, for he was Creator before becoming Lord. First he made everything according to his Father's will, and only then is Lord of the things he made.

6 Though born in David's city, he is Christ the Lord. Do you need proof that before he became man he was Christ the Lord with his Father, so as not only to accept what we say on faith, but to have the evidence of the Old Testament? Go to the first book, Genesis. God says: 'Let us make man', not 'according to my image' but 'our image'. And after the creation of Adam it says: 'And God made the man; in the image of God he made him' (Gen 1.26–7). The text does not restrict the divine dignity to the Father alone, but included the Son, to show that man is not only the work of God but also of our Lord Jesus Christ.[4] This Lord who works with the Father did so also at Sodom, according to the text: 'And the Lord rained fire and brimstone on Sodom and Gomorrha from the Lord out of heaven' (Gen 19.24). Again, the same Lord was seen by Moses in so far as he was able (cf. Exod 3.2, 6; 33.20). For the Lord is gracious, and always adapts to our weaknesses.

7 To prove to you that it was he whom Moses saw,[5] listen to the evidence of Paul's words: 'For they drank from the prophetic rock which followed them, and the rock was Christ' (1 Cor 10.4). And again: 'By faith Moses left Egypt' (Heb 11.27). And a little further on:[6] 'He considered abuse suffered for Christ greater wealth than the treasures of the Egyptians.' It was Moses too who said to him: 'Show yourself to me' (Exod 33.13 (LXX)). Do you notice that the prophets

saw Christ in their own day, but each according to his capacity? 'Show yourself to me so that I may recognize you.' 'No one shall see my face', he replied, 'and live' (Exod 33.20). So because no one could see the face of the godhead and live, he assumed the face of manhood, so that we might see it and live. When he did choose to reveal even this with some little degree of majesty so that his face shone like the sun, his disciples fell to the ground in terror (cf. Mt 17.6). Although the brightness of his bodily face was proportionate to the disciples' capacity and not to his energy and power, it terrified them and they could not bear it; how then could anyone gaze at the majesty of his godhead? What you desire, Moses, the Lord says to him, is something great. I acknowledge your longing. Although your desire cannot be fulfilled, 'I will do for you what you ask' (Exod 33.17), only according to your capacity. 'See, I will set you in the cleft of the rock' (Exod 33.22). Since you are small, you will remain in a small space.

8 Please understand clearly what I now have to say because of the Jews. I intend to prove that the Lord Jesus Christ was with the Father. Thus the Lord says to Moses: 'I shall pass before you in my glory, and in your presence I shall call upon the name of the Lord' (Exod 33.19). Lord that he is, what does it mean to call upon the name of the Lord? Observe how he was hinting at the sacred doctrine concerning the Father and the Son. Again, in the subsequent verses it says explicitly: 'And the Lord came down in a cloud and stood before him there, and called upon the name of the Lord. And the Lord passed before his face saying: 'The Lord, the Lord, merciful and compassionate, slow to anger, rich in mercy and true, observing justice and doing deeds of mercy for thousands, taking away wickedness and injustice and sin' (Exod 34.5–7). Moses then bowed down to the ground and worshipped before the Lord who had called upon the Father; 'Walk alongside us, Lord', he said (Exod 34.8–9).

9 This then is the first proof; let me give you another clear one. 'The Lord said to my Lord: "Sit at my right hand"' (Ps 109 (110).1). The Lord says this to the Lord, not to a slave: to the Lord of all, who is his Son to whom he has given authority over all things. 'It is clear that all this does not include the One who had given him the authority over all things . . . that God may be all things to everyone' (1 Cor 15.27–8). The Only-begotten Son is Lord of all things; he is the Father's obedient Son, who did not usurp his lordship but received it by nature from the one who gave it freely. The Son did not usurp it; nor was the Father grudging in sharing it. For the Son himself said: 'All things have been handed over to me by my Father'

(Lk 10.22). To say they have been handed over to me does not mean that I did not possess them before. I have the right to keep them; I am not robbing the one who handed them over.

10 Thus the Son of God is the Lord. The child born in Bethlehem of Judaea is the Lord, as the angel told the shepherds: 'I bring you good tidings of great joy . . . today Christ the Lord is born to you in David's city' (Lk 2.10–11). In another passage one of the apostles has this to say on the subject: 'the message which he sent to the sons of Israel, proclaiming the good news of peace through Jesus Christ; he is the Lord of all' (Acts 10.36). When the text says 'of all', do not subtract anything from his lordship. Angels and archangels, principalities and powers, every creature named by the apostles, all fall under the Son's lordship (cf. Col 1.16). He is lord of the angels, as you read in the gospels: 'then the devil left him, and the angels came and served him' (Mt 4.11). It does not say 'they assisted him', but 'they served him', which is the function of a slave. When the Virgin was about to conceive him, Gabriel acted as a servant, taking this service to be his proper privilege. When Jesus was about to travel to Egypt to overthrow the gods of Egypt made by human hands,[7] the angel appeared once more to Joseph in a dream. After the crucifixion and the resurrection, an angel announced the good news, and like a true servant told the women: 'Go and tell his disciples that he is risen, and is going ahead of you into Galilee. See, this is my message to you' (Mt 28.7). It was as if he said: 'I have not disobeyed my orders. I ask you to testify that I have told you. If you ignore my message, I shall not be to blame, but you will be for your negligence.'

It follows that he is the one Lord Jesus Christ, about whom today's reading says: 'Although there are so-called "gods" in heaven or on earth . . . for us there is one God, the Father, from whom all things exist and for whom we exist, and one Lord Jesus Christ, through whom all things exist, and we too exist through him.'

11 Jesus Christ has two names: he is called Jesus because he saves, Christ because he is the Priest. Realizing this, Moses, the most inspired of all the prophets, gave these two titles to the two most specially chosen men. He changed the name of his own successor in authority from Auses [Hoshea] to Jesus [Joshua] (Num 13.16); and he gave his own brother Aaron the added name of Christ. Thus through two specially chosen men he signified the priestly and royal prerogatives of the one Jesus Christ who was to come. For Christ is the High Priest like Aaron, since he 'did not take upon himself the glory of becoming High Priest, but it was given him by the one

who said to him: "You are a priest for ever according to the order of Melchizedek"' (Heb 5.5–6; cf. Ps 109 (110).4). Jesus the son of Nave [Joshua the son of Nun] also prefigured him in many ways.[8] His rule over the people began at the Jordan, where Christ began to preach the good news after his baptism. The son of Nave appointed twelve men to divide the people's inheritance; Jesus sent out twelve apostles throughout the world to be heralds of the truth. The first Jesus saved the harlot Rahab because she believed; the true Jesus said: 'See, the tax-gatherers and the harlots enter the kingdom of heaven before you' (Mt 21.31). Under the Jesus who was a type a shout was enough to bring down the walls of Jericho (Jos 6.20); because Jesus said: 'A stone will not be left upon a stone', down fell the Jewish Temple which stood facing us.[9] This is not to say that it was his prediction caused the downfall of the Temple; it was rather the sin of the evil people.

12 There is one Lord Jesus Christ – a glorious name which the prophets proclaimed indirectly in advance. The prophet Isaiah said: 'See, the Saviour is coming with his reward' (Is 62.11 (LXX)). The Hebrew name 'Jesus' means 'Saviour'; but the inspired prophet concealed the name because he foresaw that the Jews would seek to murder the Lord, and did not want direct knowledge of his name to prepare them for their conspiracy. He was given the name Jesus openly not by human choice but by the angel, who did not come on his own authority but was sent by the power of God. 'Do not be afraid to take Mary as your wife', the angel said to Joseph, 'for what is conceived in her is of the Holy Spirit. She will give birth to a son, and you shall give him the name Jesus.' The angel at once gave the reason for the name: 'He will save his people from their sins' (Mt 1.20–1). Consider, how can one who is not yet born have a people, if he did not exist before he was born? Again, the prophet says in his person: 'While I was still in my mother's womb he gave me my name', referring to the angel's prediction that he would be called Jesus. He goes on to refer to Herod's plot, saying: 'He has hidden me under the shadow of his hand' (Is 49.1–2).

13 So Jesus' name in Hebrew means 'Saviour', but in Greek it means 'Healer'.[10] For he is the physician of bodies and the healer of spirits. He cures physical blindness and gives light to people's minds. He heals visible lameness and guides the steps of sinners towards repentance, saying to the paralytic both 'Do not sin any more' and 'Pick up your mattress and walk' (Jn 5.14, 12). Since it was the sin of his soul which caused the paralysis of his body, he first healed the soul to prepare for the healing of the body. So if you are sick in soul

through sin, you have a physician. If there is anyone here of little faith, let him say to Jesus: 'Help my unbelief' (Mk 9.24). If anyone is suffering from bodily illness, do not be without faith, but come forward (he heals these illnesses too) and acknowledge that Christ is Jesus.

14 The Jews accept that he is Jesus, but do not yet accept that he is Christ. That is the point of the Apostle's words: 'Who is a liar, if not one who denies that Jesus is the Christ?' (1 Jn 2.22). Christ is the High Priest who 'holds an inviolable priesthood' (Heb 7.24); his priesthood had no beginning in time, nor will another succeed him in it, as you heard me say last Sunday at the Eucharist when I was preaching on the text: 'according to the order of Melchizedek' (Ps 109 (110).4; Heb 7.17). He did not receive the high priesthood through physical succession or an anointing with man-made oil,[11] but from his Father before time began; and he is greater than other priests in so far as he was appointed with an oath. 'Whereas others became priests without an oath, he did so with an oath through the one who said: "The Lord has sworn and will not repent of his oath"' (Heb 7.21). The Father's will by itself was guarantee enough for him, but he has a double reason for assurance, since the Father's will is accompanied by an oath, 'so that through two unchangeable things in which it is impossible for God to lie, we' who accept Jesus Christ the Son of God 'might have strong encouragement' for faith (Heb 6.18).

15 When this Christ came, though the Jews denied him, the demons acknowledged him. However his ancestor David was not unaware of him when he said: 'I have prepared a lamp for my Anointed' (Ps 131 (132).17). Some people have interpreted the 'lamp' as the shining light of prophecy, others as the flesh he took from the Virgin, according to the Apostle's saying: 'We have this treasure in earthenware vessels' (2 Cor 4.7). The prophet was not unaware of him when he said: 'and announcing his Anointed to mankind' (Amos 4.13 (LXX)). Moses knew him, Isaiah knew him, Jeremiah knew him; there was not one of the prophets who did not know him. Even the demons recognized him, for when he rebuked them, the text says, 'they knew him to be the Christ' (Lk 4.41). The high priests did not know him, but the demons acknowledged him. The high priests did not know him, but the Samaritan woman proclaimed him, saying: 'Come and see the man who has told me everything I have done. Surely he is the Christ?' (Jn 4.29).

16 This is Jesus Christ, who 'appeared as the High Priest of the good things to come' (Heb 9.11), who with divine generosity allowed

us to share his own title. Although human kings cannot share with other men the title of king which they hold, Jesus Christ the Son of God allowed us to be called Christians. However someone may say: 'Christian is a new name without precedent, and what is unfamiliar is often opposed because of its strangeness.' The prophet forearmed us with an answer to this objection when he said: 'My servants will be given a new name which shall be a blessing over the earth' (Is 65.15–16 (LXX)). Let us question the Jews: 'Do you serve the Lord or not? Show us then your new name. For you were called Jews and Israelites at the time of Moses and the other prophets, after the return from Babylon and up to the present time. So where is your new name? Because we serve the Lord we have a new name – new, it is true, but the "new name" which shall be a blessing over the earth.' This name has taken hold of the whole world. The Jews have spread within a certain area, but Christians within the confines of the whole world, for it is the name of the Only-begotten Son of God which is proclaimed.

17 Do you want proof that the apostles knew Christ's name and proclaimed it, or rather had Christ himself within them? Paul says to his listeners: 'Are you looking for proof that Christ is speaking in me?' (2 Cor 13.3). Paul proclaims Christ. Who is Paul? The one who had persecuted him (cf. Acts 9.5). How amazing! The former persecutor proclaims Christ. Why? Was he bribed to do so? But there was no one to bribe him. Was it because he saw Christ in person and was overawed by him? But he had already been taken up into heaven. He went out bent on persecution, and after three days in Damascus the persecutor had become the herald. What is the significance of his evidence? Any other person would call friends as witnesses in his cause; I have called before you a former enemy as a witness. Are you still unconvinced? The evidence of Peter and John is impressive, but it is open to suspicion because they were friends. But who will doubt the truth of the former enemy who then gave his life?

18 While I am on the subject, I am truly amazed at the dealings of the Holy Spirit. Why did he determine that the other apostles should write so few letters, while he allowed Paul, the former persecutor, to write fourteen? It cannot be true that he restricted the grace granted to Peter or John because they were not so great. Rather it was to make the lesson unmistakable that the former enemy and persecutor was allowed to write more for the sake of our faith. 'They were all astonished at Paul and said: "Isn't this the former persecutor? Didn't he come here to put us in chains and take

us to Jerusalem?" ' (cf. Acts 9.21) 'Don't be astonished', Paul says, 'I know that it causes me pain to kick against the goad. I know that I am not fit to be called an apostle, because in my ignorance I persecuted God's church. I thought that to proclaim Christ was to overthrow the law. I didn't know that he came to fulfil the law, not to overthrow it. But God's grace in me was superabundant' (cf. Acts 26.14; 1 Cor 15.9; Mt 5.17; 1 Tim 1.14).

19 Dearly beloved, there are many true testimonies concerning Christ. The Father bears witness to his Son from heaven. The Holy Spirit bears witness descending in bodily form as a dove. The archangel Gabriel bears witness announcing the good news to Mary. The Virgin Mother of God bears witness. The blessed place of the manger bears witness. Egypt bears witness, which gave a home to its master when he was still young in body. Simeon bears witness, who took him in his arms and said: 'Now, Master, you let your servant depart according to your word in peace. For my eyes have seen your salvation' (Lk 2.29–30). The prophetess Anna, the austere and most devout ascetic, bears witness to him (cf. Lk 2.36–8). John the Baptist bears witness to him, John, the greatest of the prophets, the herald of the new covenant, who so to speak joined in his own person the two covenants, the old and the new. The River Jordan bears witness. Of all seas the Sea of Tiberias bears witness. The blind bear witness, the lame bear witness, the dead restored to life bear witness. The demons bear witness saying: 'What have you to do with us, Jesus? We know who you are, God's Holy One' (Mk 1.24). The winds, which were muzzled at his command, bear witness. The five loaves multiplied for the five thousand bear witness. The holy wood of the cross, still to be seen among us today, bears witness; its fragments were taken from here by the Faithful and now virtually fill the whole earth.[12] The palm-tree in the valley[13] bears witness, which provided the palms for the children who greeted Christ there. Gethsemani bears witness, which all but reveals Judas to the mind's eye. Holy Golgotha, which rises above us here, bears witness. The Holy Sepulchre and the stone still lying there bear witness. The sun bears witness, shining today, but at the moment of the saving passion suffering eclipse. The darkness which fell there from the sixth to the ninth hours bears witness. The light which shone from the ninth hour till evening bears witness. The holy Mount of Olives from which he ascended to the Father bears witness. The rain-clouds which received the Master bear witness. The gates of heaven bear witness, according to the Psalmist's words: 'Raise your gates, you rulers, lift yourselves up, you eternal gates,

and the king of glory will enter' (Ps 23 (24).7 (LXX)). His enemies bear witness, including blessed Paul, for a short time his enemy, for long his servant. The twelve apostles bear witness, proclaiming the truth not only by their words but by their torture and death. Peter's shadow bears witness, which healed the sick in Christ's name (Acts 5.15). The handkerchiefs and aprons bear witness, which likewise through Paul healed the sick by Christ's power (Acts 19.12). The Persians and the Goths and all the gentiles bear witness, who died for him though they had not seen him with the eyes of the body. The demons driven out by the Faithful bear witness to this day.

20 With such a great number and variety of witnesses (and there are even more who could be mentioned) can anyone now fail to believe in the Christ whom their testimony supports? Let those who have so far been lacking in faith believe now; let those who already believe grow in faith, believing in our Lord Jesus Christ and understanding who it is they are named after. You have been given the name of Christian; take good care of that name. Do not give grounds for blasphemy against our Lord Jesus Christ, the Son of God. Let your good works shine out more brightly before men, so that those who see them may give glory in Jesus Christ our Lord to our heavenly Father (cf. Mt 5.16), to whom is the glory now and for ever, world without end. Amen.

CATECHESIS 11

For the candidates for baptism On 'The Only-begotten Son of God who was born of the Father as true God before all ages, through whom all things were made'

Reading: Heb 1.1ff: 'In many and various ways God spoke of old to our fathers through the prophets, but in these the last days he has spoken to us through his Son . . .'

1 In our instruction yesterday we gave to the best of our ability sufficient explanation of the meaning of hope in Jesus Christ. But we are not required simply to believe in Jesus Christ, or accept him as if he were one of the many who are given the name of 'christs' in the loose sense. For these were 'christs' as prefigurations;[1] he is the true Christ. He did not attain priesthood from among men by promotion;[2] he possessed the priestly dignity from his Father from all eternity. This is why the Creed prevents us from taking him to be one of these ordinary 'christs' by expanding the clause in the Creed so that it states that we believe 'in one Lord Jesus Christ, the Only-begotten Son of God'.

2 Again, when you hear him described as 'Son', do not conceive him to be adopted, for he is the Son by nature, the Only-begotten Son, without any brother. The reason why he is called 'Only-begotten' is that he has no brother in his divine rank or in his birth from the Father. We do not call him Son of God on our own authority, but because the Father himself named him Christ his Son. The name which parents give their children is the true one.

3 Our Lord Jesus Christ became man then, though most people did not recognize him. The disciples did not understand this truth; so, wishing to teach it to them, he gathered them together and asked them: 'Who do people say that the Son of Man is?' (Mt 16.13). He asked this, not out of vainglory, but out of the desire to

show them the truth, in case their familiarity with God's divine and Only-begotten Son might lead them to belittle him as an ordinary man. When they told him that some said he was Elijah, others Jeremiah, he replied: 'They can be excused, for they know no better; but you are the apostles, who in my name cleansed lepers, cast out demons and raised the dead. You ought not to be ignorant about the one through whom you work these miracles.' When all the rest remained silent, because the teaching was beyond human understanding, it was Peter, the leader of the apostles and the chief herald of the Church, who answered, not out of fluency of speech or conviction based on human reason, but because his understanding had been enlightened by his Father. 'You are the Christ', he answered, and added: 'the Son of the living God' (Mt 16.16). This declaration led to a blessing – for it truly was beyond human reason – and to seal his affirmation he was told that it had been revealed by the Father. For the Saviour declared: 'You are blessed, Simon Bar-Jonah, for flesh and blood did not reveal this to you, but my Father in heaven' (Mt 16.17). It follows that anyone who recognizes our Lord Jesus Christ to be the Son of God shares in this blessing, but anyone who denies the Son of God is wretched and unfortunate.

4 Once more, when I tell you that he is the Son, do not take this statement to be a mere figure of speech, but understand that he is the Son truly, Son by nature, without beginning, not promoted from the state of slave to that of son, but eternally begotten as Son by an inscrutable and incomprehensible birth. Similarly when I tell you that he is the Firstborn, do not understand this to mean he was the firstborn among men. For in human families the firstborn have brothers. Thus the Bible somewhere speaks of 'Israel my firstborn Son' (Exod 4.22). However, like Reuben, Israel forfeited his position as firstborn: Reuben for getting into his father's bed, Israel for driving the Father's Son out of the vineyard and crucifying him (Gen 49.4; Mt 21.39). Scripture says also with regard to other men: 'You are sons of the Lord your God.' And in another place: 'I said, "You are all gods and sons of the Most High"' (Gen 49.4; Mt 21.39). 'I said', not 'I begot'. They received adoption when God spoke, and did not enjoy it before. But Christ did not first exist in one form before being begotten in another, but he was begotten as Son from the beginning, Son of the Father in every way like his Begetter,[3] Light begotten from Light, Truth from Truth, Wisdom from Wisdom, King from the King, God from God, and Power from Power.

5 So when you hear the Gospel saying: 'the book of the genealogy of Jesus Christ, the Son of David, the Son of Abraham' (Mt 1.1), you must understand that this is said about his humanity. For though he became Son of David 'at the end of the ages' (Heb 9.26), he was Son of God before all ages. The former title he assumed as something not previously possessed; the latter he possessed eternally, being begotten by the Father. He has two fathers: the first is David according to the flesh, the second God the Father according to his divinity. His Davidic sonship was subject to time, was 'touched by hand' (cf. 1 Jn 1.1) and its 'genealogy traced' (cf. Heb 7.3); his divine sonship, however, was not subject to time or place or genealogy, for 'who will recount his genealogy?' (Is 53.8 (LXX)). 'God is Spirit' (Jn 4.24), and being Spirit and incorporeal, he begot spiritually, by an inscrutable and incomprehensible generation. The Son himself says of the Father: 'The Lord said to me, "You are my Son, today I have begotten you"' (Ps 2.7). This 'today' is not recent but eternal; this 'today' is timeless, before all ages. 'From the womb before the morning star I begot you' (Ps 109 (110).3 (LXX)).

6 So believe in Jesus Christ, the Son of the living God. He is the 'Only-begotten Son', according to the words of the Gospel: 'For God so loved the world that he gave his Only-begotten Son, so that they who believe in him may not perish, but may have eternal life' (Jn 3.16). Again: 'Whoever believes in the Son is not judged' (Jn 3.18), 'but has passed from death to life' (Jn 5.24). 'Whoever does not believe in the Son will not see life, but the wrath of God remains on him' (Jn 3.36), because he has not believed in the Only-begotten Son of God (cf. Jn 3.18). John witnessed to this saying: 'And we saw his glory, the glory as of the Only-begotten from the Father, full of grace and truth' (Jn 1.14). Trembling before him the demons said: 'Leave us alone! What have you to do with us, Jesus, Son of the living God?' (cf. Lk 4.34; Mk 5.7).

7 So he is the Son of God by nature and not by adoption, being begotten of the Father. 'Those who love the Begetter also love the One he begot' (1 Jn 5.1); and those who despise the Begotten direct their pride against the Begetter. However, when you hear me speak of God as the Begetter, do not lower your thoughts to bodily things or conceive of corruptible generation; to do so would be blasphemous. Since 'God is Spirit' (Jn 4.24), his begetting is spiritual, for bodies beget bodies; moreover the generation of bodies requires the intervention of time, and no time intervenes for the generation of the Son from the Father. In this world a being is begotten in an

imperfect state; but the Son was already perfect when begotten by the Father. He was begotten from the beginning, just as he is now. In our begetting, we change from the ignorance of a child to rationality. Your own generation was imperfect, my friend, for your development requires gradual advance. But do not imagine that it was the same with the Son, or attribute any weakness to his Begetter. If he had begotten something imperfect which acquired perfection only in the course of time, you might well attribute weakness to the Begetter, in so far as the Begetter did not grant from the beginning what according to you he granted only at a later time.[4]

8 So do not conceive the begetting anthropomorphically, as for example Abraham begot Isaac. For when Abraham begot Isaac, he did not beget what he chose but what was granted him by another. But when God the Father is the Begetter, there is neither uncertainty nor intervening deliberation. To say that he did not know what was being begotten would be the greatest blasphemy; and to say that he became Father only after spending time in deliberation is equally blasphemous. For God was not originally childless before becoming a father. He always had his Son, for he begot him not after the human fashion, but in a unique way before all ages, begetting him as 'true God'.[5]

9 For the Father, who is 'true God', begot a Son who is 'true God' like himself – not as teachers beget pupils, in the way Paul writes to certain people: 'I begot you in Christ Jesus through the Gospel' (1 Cor 4.15). For in Paul's case one who is not a son by nature became a son through being a pupil; but Christ is Son by nature, a true son. This is not the sense in which you candidates for baptism are now in the process of becoming sons of God; for you are becoming sons by grace and adoption, according to the scriptural statement: 'As many as received him, he gave power to become children of God, to those who believe in his name, who were begotten not of blood or the will of the flesh or the will of man, but of God' (Jn 1.12–13); we are begotten of water and Spirit (cf. Jn 3.5). But the begetting of Christ by the Father was not like this. For when the Father addressed him at the moment of his baptism, saying: 'This is my Son', he did not say, 'This has now become my Son', but 'This is my Son', because he wanted to show that he was already the Son before he had received the effect of his baptism.

10 The Father did not beget the Son in the way that the human mind begets speech.[6] For the mind has a substantial reality[7] within us, but our speech once uttered is scattered on the air and expires. We know that Christ was begotten not as an uttered[8] word but as

the substantial, living Word, not a word spoken by the lips and scattered, but begotten by the Father eternally, indefinably and substantially. For in the beginning the Word existed, seated at the Father's right hand, the Word who knew the Father's will and made all things by the Father's decree. The Word descended and ascended, but the uttered word in being spoken neither descends or ascends. The Word speaks and says: 'What I have seen with my Father, these things I speak' (Jn 8.38). The Word is endowed with authority and universal rule, for the Father has entrusted all things to the Son (cf. Jn 13.3).

11 Thus the Father did not beget the Son in a way a human being can comprehend, but in a way known to himself alone. For we do not undertake to tell you *how* he was begotten, but we will explain how he was *not*. We are not the only ones who don't understand the Son's begetting by the Father; no created nature of any kind understands it. 'Speak to the earth to see if it will teach you' (Job 12.8 (LXX)); but even if you question every creature on the earth, they will not be able to tell you. For the earth cannot explain the being of its own potter who fashioned it. If the earth does not know, neither does the sun. For the sun was created on the fourth day, and so does not know what happened on the three days before it existed. So if the sun does not know what happened on the three days before it existed, it will not be able to explain its maker. The sky will not give an explanation, for 'the heaven was solidified like vapour' (Is 51.6 (LXX)) by Christ at the Father's decree. Nor will the 'heaven of heavens' (cf. Ps 148.4) give an explanation, or the waters above the heavens. Why then does it distress you, my friend, not to know what even the heavens do not know? And it is not only the heavens which do not know the begetting, but even the whole angelic nature. For if you were to ascend to the first heaven (were that possible) and behold the angels arrayed there, and if you approached them and asked how God begot his own Son, they would probably say: 'We have greater beings above us; ask them.' So ascend to the second or the third heaven, make your way if you can to the Thrones and Dominations, the Principalities and Powers. Even if you were to reach them (which is impossible), they too would deny you an explanation, for they do not know the answer.

12 I never cease to be amazed at the presumption of those bold thinkers who in their reputed reverence decline into profanity. For although they have no knowledge of Thrones and Dominations, or of Principalities and Powers, which were created by Christ, they embark on speculations concerning the Creator. Tell me first, my

brave friend, the difference between a Throne and a Domination, before you speculate about Christ. Tell me what a Principality is, or a Power or a Virtue or an Angel, before you speculate about their Maker, for everything was made through him. Nor will you wish to question Thrones or Dominations; indeed, you could not. What else is there which knows 'God's depths' except the Holy Spirit who spoke the sacred Scriptures (cf. 1 Cor 2.10)? But even the Holy Spirit has not spoken in the Scriptures about the Son's generation from the Father. So why do you speculate about matters which even the Holy Spirit has not written of in the Scriptures? If you are ignorant of what is written there, will you speculate about what is not written? The sacred Scriptures raise many questions; so if we do not understand what is written, why do we meddle with matters which are not? It is enough for us to know that God begot the one Son alone.

13 Do not be afraid to admit your ignorance, since you share it with the angels. It is only the Begetter who knows the Begotten, and only the one he begot who knows his Begetter (cf. Mt 11.27). The Begetter knows why he begot, and the Scriptures bear witness that the Begotten is God. 'For just as the Father has life in himself, so he has granted the Son also to have life in himself' (Jn 5.26), 'so that all may honour the Son just as they honour the Father' (Jn 5.23). 'Just as the Father gives life to those whom he chooses, so the Son also gives life to those whom he chooses' (cf. Jn 5.21). There is no defect in the Begetter, and nothing lacking to the Begotten. (I know I have said this often, but I have done so for your own protection.) The Begetter has no father, and the Begotten has no brother. The Begetter was not transformed into the Son, nor did the Begotten become the Father. There is one Only-begotten Son of the one and only Father. There are not two Unbegotten or two Only-begotten: there is one unbegotten Father (for to be unbegotten is to have no father), and one Son eternally begotten by the Father, not begotten in time but begotten before all ages, not one who grew and developed, but begotten as he is now.

14 So we believe 'in the Only-begotten Son of God, who was begotten from the Father, true God'. For, as we have explained, the true God does not beget a false one, nor did he deliberate before begetting. He begot from eternity, much more rapidly than our words or our thoughts. For we speak in time, and our words take time to utter, but where God's power is concerned, the begetting is outside time. As I have often said, he did not lead the Son from non-being to being, or bring a non-existent being to adoption. The

eternal Father eternally and ineffably begot his one and only Son who has no brother. Nor are there two principles; the Father is the Head of the Son, a single principle.[9] For the Father begot his Son as the 'true God', who was given the name Emmanuel, and Emmanuel means 'God with us'.

15 Do you want proof that the one who was begotten of the Father and subsequently incarnate is God? Listen to the words of the prophet: 'He is our God, no other will be numbered beside him. He has discovered every way of knowledge and given it to Jacob his servant and to Israel his beloved. After this he was seen on earth and consorted with mankind' (Baruch 3.36–8 (LXX)). Do you notice that God became man after Moses gave the law?[10] Listen to a second testimony concerning Christ's deity, which we have just heard read: 'Your throne, O God, lasts for ever and ever.'[11] To prevent his bodily presence in the world leading us to think that he advanced to deity later, the psalm says explicitly: 'Therefore God, your God, has anointed you with the oil of gladness beyond your fellows.'[12] Do you notice that Christ is God, anointed by God his Father?

16 Would you like to hear a third piece of evidence in support of Christ's deity? Listen to Isaiah's words: 'Egypt and the stores of the Ethiopians toiled'; and a little later: 'They will make their petitions in your name because God is in you, and there is no other god but you. For you are God, and we did not know it, the God, the Saviour of Israel' (Is 45.14–15 (LXX)). Did you notice God the Son, with God the Father within him, saying in effect what he says in the Gospels: 'The Father in me and I in the Father' (cf. Jn 14.11; 17.21)? He did not say: 'I am the Father', but 'The Father in me and I in the Father.' Again, he did not say: 'I and the Father am one', but: 'I and the Father are one' (Jn 10.30), to prevent us either separating them or constructing a compound Son–Father.[13] They are one in respect of the dignity of godhead, since God begot God. They are one in respect of kingship, since the Father and the Son do not have different subjects, as if the Son, like Absalom, was his Father's rival; the Father's subjects are the same as the Son's. They are one because there is no disharmony or disagreement between them, for the Father's wishes are not different from the Son's. They are one because Christ's creations are not distinct from the Father's, because there is a single act of creation of all things, performed by the Father through the Son, according to the Psalmist's words: 'he spoke, and they were made; he gave the command, and they were created' (Ps 148.5 (LXX)). For to speak implies a hearer, and to command implies a partner.

17 So the Son is true God, and has the Father within himself without being changed into the Father; for it was not the Father but the Son who became man, as we can declare with confidence. The Father did not suffer for us; he sent the one who suffered for us. We should not say: 'There was when the Son was not',[14] or accept a Son–Father; let us walk along the royal road without straying either to left or to right.[15] We should never imagine that we honour the Son if we proclaim him as the Father, or imagine that we honour the Father by suspecting that the Son is numbered among created things. The one Father should be worshipped through the one Son, and the worship should not be divided. The one Son should be proclaimed, who has been seated before all ages at the Father's right hand; that he is seated with his Father is not something he acquired in time by advancement, but an eternal possession.

18 'He who has seen the Son has seen the Father' (Jn 14.9). For the Son is in everything like the Father.[16] He was begotten as life from life, light from light, power from power, God from God. The characteristics of the godhead are unchanged in the Son. Anyone who is allowed to see the Son's godhead enters into the enjoyment of the Begetter. These are not my words but the Only-begotten Son's: 'Have I been with you so long, and you do not know me, Philip? He who has seen me has seen the Father' (Jn 14.9). To make the point more precisely, we must not separate, we must not make a compound. Nor should you say that the Son was ever alien to the Father, or listen to those who say that the Father is at one time Father, at another Son.[17] These teachings are outlandish and blasphemous, and not the teachings of the Church. When the Father begot the Son, he remained the Father and was not changed. In begetting Wisdom, he did not cease to be wise himself; in begetting Power, he did not himself become weak; in begetting God, he did not forfeit godhead himself. He lost nothing; he was in no way diminished or changed. Nor is the Begotten in any way deficient. The Begetter is perfect, the Begotten is perfect; the Begetter is God, the Begotten is also God: God of all things, yet describing his Father as his God. For he is not ashamed to say: 'I am ascending to my Father and your Father, to my God and your God' (Jn 20.17).

19 Lest you might imagine that he is Father of the Son and of creatures in the same sense, Christ went on to draw a distinction. He didn't say: 'I am ascending to our Father', in case creatures might seem to have something in common with the Only-begotten. Instead, he said; 'My Father and your Father'. He is my Father in one way, by nature; he is your Father in a different way, by adoption.

Again: 'To my God and your God'. He is my God in one way, in so far as I am the true and Only-begotten Son; he is your God in a different way, in so far as you are creatures. The Son of God, then, is true God, ineffably begotten before all ages; I tell you this repeatedly, in order to impress it upon your minds. That God has a Son, you must believe, but do not speculate how, for however much you look for an answer, you will not find one. Don't climb too high, lest you fall. What you are required to believe, keep in mind – that but no more. First tell me who the Begetter is, and then learn what he begot. If you can't grasp the nature of the Begetter, don't speculate about the mode of the Begotten.

20 For piety it is enough for you to know, as we have said, that God has one only Son, one begotten by nature. His existence does not begin with his birth in Bethlehem but was 'before all ages'. Listen to the words of the prophet Micah: 'And you, Bethlehem, home of Ephrathah, are very small to be among the thousands of Judah. From you will come my leader who will be the shepherd of my people, Israel. His origin is from the beginning, from the days of eternity' (Micah 5.2 (LXX) adjusted). So don't think of the one who is now from Bethlehem, but adore the one begotten by the Father from all eternity.[18] Don't attend to anyone who says that the Son's origin was in time; understand that his origin in the Father was outside time. For the Son's origin is timeless, incomprehensible, itself without origin, namely the Father. For the Father is the source of the Only-begotten who is the river of righteousness, and he alone knows how he begot him. Do you want proof that our Lord Jesus Christ is the eternal King? Hear once more what he says: 'Abraham delighted to see my day; he saw it and rejoiced' (Jn 8.56). When the Jews found this saying hard to accept, he then added words which they found even harder: 'Before Abraham came to be, I am' (Jn 8.58). Again, he said to the Father: 'And now, Father, glorify me in your presence with the glory which I had in your presence before the world existed' (Jn 17.5). For he was clearly implying: 'Before the world came into existence, I had glory in your presence.' Again, when he said: 'You loved me before the foundation of the world' (Jn 17.24), he was clearly implying: 'The glory I have in your presence is eternal.'

21 So let us believe 'in one Lord Jesus Christ, the Only-begotten Son of God, begotten of the Father, true God, before all ages, through whom all things were made'. Whether Thrones or Dominations, whether Principalities or Powers, all things were made through him; nothing that is made is excluded from his power. Let every

heresy which introduces different creators and makers of the universe be silent;[19] silent every heresy which blasphemes against Christ the Son of God; silent those who say Christ is the sun, for he is the sun's maker, not the visible sun itself; silent those who say that the world is the work of angels, wishing to rob the Only-begotten of his prerogative. For whether visible or invisible, whether Thrones or Dominations, or anything that can be named, everything was made through Christ (cf. Col 1.16; Eph 1.21). He reigns over the things he made; he did not capture them as booty from another; he reigns over what his own work produced. As John the Evangelist said: 'All things were made through him, and without him nothing was made' (Jn 1.3). All things were made through him, as the Father worked through the Son.

22 I would like to put before you an illustration of what I am saying, but I realize it is feeble; for what visible thing can provide an illustration of the divine power? Nevertheless, allow me to propose it, feeble though it is – the feeble speaking to the feeble. Imagine a king, with a king for a son, desiring to found a city and proposing a plan for its foundation to the son who shares his royal authority; the son accepts the plan and puts his father's intention into effect. In some such way, when the Father decided to create the universe, the Son made everything according to his Father's decree. In this way the Father's decree maintained his proper authority, while the Son retained authority over his own workmanship; thus the Father was not excluded from lordship over his own creation, nor did the Son rule over beings made by another but over those he had made himself. For, as we have said, the world was not made by angels, but by the Only-begotten Son who was begotten before all ages, according to the text: 'all things were made through him', without exception. By the grace of Christ this concludes what I have to say on this subject.

23 However, to return to the Creed, let us stop at this point. Christ has made all things, whether you speak of Angels and Archangels, or Dominations and Thrones. Not that the Father was too weak to create by his own action; rather he intended the Son to rule over creatures which the Son himself had made, according to the plan of creation given by the Father. For out of respect for his Father the Only-begotten said: 'The Son can do nothing of himself, except what he sees the Father doing; for what the Father does, the Son does also' (Jn 5.19). Again: 'My Father has been working until now, and I work' (Jn 5.17); for there is no lack of harmony between the workers. For 'all mine are yours, and yours are mine', the Lord

says in the Gospels (Jn 17.10). We can discover this clearly in the Old and New Testaments. For the words 'Let us make man in our own image and likeness' (Gen 1.26) were evidently spoken to someone present. Even more explicitly the Psalmist says: 'He spoke and they were made, he commanded and they were created' (Ps 32 (33).9). This implies that the Father commanded and spoke, while the Son made all things by his Father's decree. Job too said figuratively: 'He who alone spread the heavens and walks on the sea as on the dry land',[20] showing us, if we reflect, that the one who in his incarnate life walked on the sea was also the one who before had made the heavens. Again, the Lord says: 'Have you taken clay from the earth and made a living creature?' (Job 38.14 (LXX)). And later: 'And the gates of death open for you in terror' (Job 38.17 (LXX)), showing that the one who out of love for mankind descended to the underworld was also the one who in the beginning formed the man from clay.

24 Thus Christ is the Only-begotten Son of God and the maker of the world. For 'he was in the world, and the world was made through him'; and 'he came to his own' (Jn 1.10, 11), as the Gospel teaches us. By his Father's decree Christ is the maker of things both seen and unseen. For, as the Apostle says, 'In him were all things created in the heavens and on earth, things visible and invisible, whether Thrones or Dominations, whether Principalities or Powers; all things were created through him and for him' (Col 1.16). Even if you speak of the very ages, Jesus Christ is their maker too by the Father's decree. For 'in these last days he has spoken to us in his Son, whom he appointed heir of all things, through whom he also created the ages' (Heb 1.2). To him are glory, honour and power for ever and ever. Amen.

CATECHESIS 12

To the candidates for baptism On 'who became incarnate and became a human being'

Reading: 'And again the Lord spoke to Ahaz: "Ask for yourself a sign . . ."' (Is 7.10ff).

1 My people, nurtured on purity and instructed in chastity, with pure lips let us celebrate the God who was conceived by the Virgin. We have been chosen to share the flesh of the spiritual lamb: let us then partake of the head with the feet, understanding the head as his deity, the feet as his humanity.[1] Since we listen to the holy Gospels, we should accept the words of John the divine; for after stating: 'In the beginning was the Word, and the Word was with God, and the Word was God', he added: 'And the Word was made flesh' (Jn 1.1, 14). For while it is not holy to adore a mere man, it would be blasphemous to say that he was only God without the humanity. For if Christ were God – as indeed he is – but did not assume humanity, we would be debarred from salvation. So while we adore him as God, let us believe him also to have been made man. For just as it does us no good to speak of him as man without the godhead, it does not help our salvation if we do not couple manhood with the godhead. Let us confess the presence of our King and Healer. For our King Jesus, intending to heal us, girded himself with the towel of humanity, and so cured our sickness. The consummate teacher of children became himself a child among children to make the foolish wise. The bread of heaven came down to earth to feed the starving.

2 The children of the Jews spurn the Christ who has come, and wait for one whose coming will bring harm; they rejected the true Christ, and, being deceived, they await the deceiver. Still even in this the Saviour has proved truthful, for he said: 'I have come in my Father's name and you do not receive me; but you will receive another if he comes in his own name' (Jn 5.43).

It would be helpful to put a question to the Jews: When the prophet Isaiah said that Emmanuel would be born of a virgin, was he telling the truth or lying? It would not be surprising if they accused him of lying, for it is their way not only to accuse the prophets of lying but even to stone them. If on the other hand the prophet is telling the truth, show us Emmanuel. Is the Emmanuel who is to come, whom you await, to be born of a virgin or not? If he is not to be born of a virgin, you are accusing the prophet of lying; if however you expect this will be true of the one to come, why do you refuse to accept it when it has already happened?

3 So let the Jews be led astray if that is what they want, and let God's Church be glorified. For we acknowledge God the Word made man in truth, made man not by the will of a man and a woman as the heretics say, but by a virgin and the Holy Spirit according to the Gospel, not in appearance but truth. If you wait for the appropriate point in my exposition, you will learn the proofs of the fact that he truly became man from a virgin. For errors of the heretics take many different forms: some flatly deny that he was born of a virgin; others say that he was born not of a virgin but of a woman living with a man; others again say that Christ was not God made man, but a man who became God.[2] For they have dared to say that he was not the pre-existent Word who became man, a man who was promoted and crowned.

4 Remember what we said yesterday about his divinity. You must accept that, being God's Only-begotten Son, he underwent birth again of the Virgin. Believe John the Evangelist when he says: 'And the Word was made flesh and dwelt among us' (Jn 1.14). For the eternal Word who was begotten by the Father before all ages, in recent times took flesh for our sake.

Many people however deny this, saying: 'What was this great reason which led God to descend to humanity? Is it consistent with God's nature to mingle with human beings in any way? Is it possible for a virgin to conceive without a man?' So because of the strength of this opposition and the many forms the resistance takes, listen, and by Christ's grace and with the help of your prayers I shall answer each of these difficulties.

5 First let us ask why Jesus came down. Do not look for subtle arguments from me, for you might perhaps be led astray by logical tricks. If you don't accept the evidence of the prophets on each point, don't believe what I say. If you don't agree that the holy Scriptures teach about the virgin and the place and the time and the circumstances, don't accept these facts on human testimony. You

might well harbour suspicions about someone coming here and teaching you, but how could anyone with common sense be suspicious about a prophet speaking a thousand and more years ago?

So if you are seeking the reason for Christ's coming, go to the first book of the Bible. God made the universe in six days, but the universe was made for the sake of mankind. For though the sun shines out with the brightest beams, it was made to provide light for human beings. All the animals were made to serve us; plants and trees were created for our enjoyment. All the works of creation are beautiful, but none of them except man is God's image. The sun was made by God's mere command, but human beings were made by the divine hands. 'Let us make man in our own image and likeness' (Gen 1.26). A wooden image of an earthly king is honoured; how much more the rational image of God? He was the greatest of God's creations and danced in Paradise; but his enemy the devil in envy drove him out and exulted over the fall of the object of his jealousy. Would you have wanted our enemy's triumph to last? Since he didn't dare to approach the man because of his strength, he approached the woman, who was the weaker partner, while she was still a virgin; for Adam did not know his wife Eve until after their fall from Paradise.[3]

6 Cain and Abel formed the second generation of the human race; Cain was the first murderer. Later the magnitude of human wickedness led God to unleash the Flood, and because of their sin fire came down from heaven upon the people of Sodom. Later God chose Israel, but even his chosen people was corrupted and wounded. For while Moses was meeting God on the mountain, the people were worshipping the calf instead of God. In the very time of Moses, the Law-giver who said 'You shall not commit adultery', a man dared to enter an alcove and give way to his passions (cf. Num 25.6–8). After Moses prophets were sent to restore the health of Israel. But even the healers bewailed their own subjection to passion; in the words of one of them: Alas that 'the godly have perished from the earth, and there is none among mankind who lives an upright life!' (Micah 7.2). And again: 'All have gone astray, all alike have been corrupted, and there is no one who acts virtuously, no, not one' (Ps 13 (14).3). And again: 'Cursing and theft and adultery and envy have been poured out over the earth' (Hosea 4.2 (LXX adjusted)). 'They sacrificed their sons and their daughters to demons' (Ps 105 (106).37). They practised augury, enchantment and divination. And again: 'They fastened their garments with ropes, and made curtains next to the altar' (Amos 2.8 (LXX)).

7 Thus mankind was grievously wounded. 'From feet to head there was nothing sound in him; there was no place to apply salve or oil or bandages' (Isaiah 1.6 (LXX adjusted)). Then the prophets wept and lamented as they asked: 'Who will give salvation from Zion?' (Ps 13 (14).7 (LXX)). And again: 'Let your hand be upon the man at your right and upon the son of man whom you have made strong for yourself, and we shall never desert you' (Ps 79.18–19 (80.17–18)). Another of the prophets pleaded: 'Lower the heavens, Lord, and come down' (Ps 143 (144).5). Mankind's wounds exceed our powers of healing. 'They have killed your prophets and torn down your altars' (cf. 1 Kings 19.10). We cannot put right our misfortune; we need you to put it right.

8 The Lord listened to the prophets' plea. Our Father did not ignore our doomed race. He sent his Son the Lord from heaven to be our Healer. As one of the prophets says: 'The Lord you seek is coming; suddenly he will come.' Where? 'The Lord will come into his Temple' (Mal 3.1). There you stoned him (cf. Jn 8.59). Hearing these words, another of the prophets said to him: Do you speak softly to announce God's salvation? Do you speak in secret to announce the good news of God's saving presence? 'Go up on to a high mountain, herald of good news to Zion. Say to the cities of Judah . . .' What shall I say? 'See, our God. See, the Lord is coming with strength' (Is 40.9–10).

Again, the Lord himself has said: 'See, I am coming, and I shall dwell in your midst, says the Lord, and many nations will seek refuge with the Lord' (Zech 2.10–11). The Israelites rejected the salvation I offered. 'I am coming to gather together all nations and all tongues.' For 'he came to his own, and his own did not receive him' (Jn 1.11). You come, and what do you offer the nations? 'I come to gather together all nations . . . and I will leave a sign over them' (Is 66.18–19). For from my struggle on the cross I give each of my soldiers a royal seal to carry on their forehead.[4] Another of the prophets said: 'And he lowered the heavens and came down, and darkness lay beneath his feet' (Ps 17.10 (18.9)); for his descent from heaven was hidden from mankind.

9 Later Solomon listened to these words of his father David and built a wonderful house. Looking forward to the one who was to enter it, he marvelled and said: 'Will God truly live on earth' (1 Kings 8.27) among human beings? Yes, says David with foresight in the psalm dedicated to Solomon: 'He will come down like rain falling on a fleece' (Ps 71 (72).6 (LXX)). Like rain, because he is from heaven; on a fleece, because of his humanity. When rain falls

on a fleece, it falls soundlessly, so that the mystery of his birth was hidden, and the Magi had to ask: 'Where is the one who is born King of the Jews?' (Mt 2.2); and Herod in his anxiety had to inquire about the new-born child: 'Where is the Christ to be born?' (Mt 2.4).

10 Who is the one who comes down from heaven? The psalm continues: 'he will last as long as the sun and existed before the moon, from generation to generation' (Ps 71 (72).5 (LXX)). And again another of the prophets says: 'Rejoice greatly, daughter of Zion. Raise a cry, daughter of Jerusalem. See, your King is coming to you, the just saviour' (Zech 9.9 (LXX)). Interpret your words for us, prophet. There are many kings; which one do you speak of? Give us a sign which does not belong to other kings. If you tell us the king will be dressed in purple, others have already assumed the privilege of such apparel. If you tell us he will have a military escort and will sit in a golden chariot, others have already this privilege too. Give us a sign which is unique to the king whose coming you proclaim.

This is how the prophet replies: 'See, your King is coming to you, the just saviour, meek and riding on an ass, a young foal', not in a chariot. There you have a unique sign that the king has come. Alone among kings Jesus sat upon a foal unaccustomed to a burden, and entered Jerusalem amid royal acclamations. And what does the King do when he has entered? 'And in the blood of the covenant you have set your prisoners free from the waterless pit' (Zech 9.11 (LXX)).

11 Still, even his sitting on a foal might be coincidental. Give us rather a sign that will show where the King will stand when he enters; give us a sign not far from the city so that it will be familiar to us. Give us a sign that is nearby and plain to see, so that we can examine the place while we are in the city. The prophet replies again: 'and on that day his feet will stand on the Mount of Olives opposite Jerusalem to the east' (Zech 14.4). Isn't it true that anyone could examine the place while standing inside the city?[5]

12 We have, then, two signs, but we want to hear of a third. Tell us, what does the Lord do when he comes to us? Another prophet tells us: 'See, our God.' And later: 'He will come and save us. Then the eyes of the blind will be opened and the ears of the deaf will hear; then the lame man will leap like a stag, and the tongue of the stammerer will be released' (Is 35.4–6 (adjusted)).

Give us yet another testimony. You tell us, prophet, that the Lord is to come performing great signs, the like of which have never been performed before. What is this other clear sign you speak of? 'The Lord himself is coming to judgment with the elders of the people and its leaders' (Is 3.14). An exceptional sign, the master enduring to be judged by the elders who are his slaves.

13 The Jews read these words, but do not hear them; for they have stopped the ears of their heart in order not to hear. But let us believe in Jesus Christ who came in the flesh and became a human being, because in no other way could we have comprehended him. For since we were unable to look at him or enjoy him as he was, he became what we are, to enable us in this way to become capable of enjoying him. For if we are incapable of looking fully at the sun, which was created on the fourth day, tell me, would we have been able to look at God, its Maker? When the Lord came down on to Mount Sinai in fire, the people could not bear the sight, but said to Moses: 'You speak to us, and we shall listen; do not let God speak to us, lest we die' (Exod 20.19). And again: 'Who is there of all flesh who has heard the voice of the living God speaking from the midst of the fire and will live?' (Deut 5.26). If to hear God's voice when he speaks causes death, surely to see him must bring death too. Even Moses said: 'I tremble with terror' (Heb 12.21; cf. Deut 9.19).

14 Tell me, would you want the one who came for our salvation to become an agent of destruction because humanity could not bear him, or would you want him to temper his grace to our capacity? Daniel could not bear the vision of the angel, and could you take in the sight of the Lord of the angels? Daniel was prostrated when Gabriel appeared. Under what nature did he appear, in what form? 'His face was like lightning', rather than the sun, 'and his eyes were like blazing torches', rather than a fiery furnace, and 'when he spoke his voice was like that of a crowd', rather than twelve legions of angels (Dan 10.6). Nevertheless the prophet was prostrated, and the angel approached him and said: 'Do not be afraid, Daniel. Stand up, take courage: your words have been heard.' 'I stood up', Daniel said, 'trembling'; but he still did not reply until a hand like a man's touched him. Once the vision has changed into the appearance of a man, Daniel was able to speak. And what did he say? 'Lord, when I see you, my guts are twisted within me, my strength will not hold firm within me, and no breath is left in me' (Dan 10.16–17 (adjusted)). If the vision of an angel robbed the prophet of his speech and his strength, would the sight of God have left him with the power to breathe? It was not until 'the appearance of a man touched me' (Dan 10.18), Scripture says, that Daniel took heart. Thus, having

first provided a demonstration of our weakness, the Lord took on what the human race was seeking. For since mankind needed to hear from one who shared their own appearance, the Saviour assumed a share in their feelings, to make it easier for human beings to be instructed.

15 Let me tell you another reason. Christ came to be baptized and to sanctify baptism. He came to perform the miracle of walking on the waters of the sea. So while before the Incarnation 'the sea beheld and fled and the Jordan was bent backwards' (Ps 113 (114).3), the Lord took a body which the sea might behold and be still, and the Jordan receive without fear. That is one reason; there is also a second.

Death came through the virgin Eve. Life had to appear through a virgin, or rather from a virgin, so that just as the first virgin was deceived by the serpent, the second might receive the good news from Gabriel.[6]

Mankind abandoned God and made for themselves wooden images in human form. So since lying adoration had been paid to a god in human form, God became truly human to put an end to the lie.

The devil had used flesh as a weapon against us. Knowing this, Paul says: 'I see another law in my members which does battle against the law of my reason and takes me prisoner' (Rom 7.23), etc. We were saved by the very weapons the devil was using to defeat us. The Lord took on from us a condition like ours, so that our salvation might come through humanity. He took on a condition like ours in order to supply for its defects with a greater grace, and sinful humanity might become a partner of God.[7] 'For where sin was abundant, grace was superabundant' (Rom 5.20).

It was 'necessary' for the Lord to 'suffer' on our behalf (cf. Lk 24.26). Nevertheless the devil would not have dared to approach him if he had known who he was. 'For if they had known, they would not have crucified the Lord of glory' (1 Cor 2.8). His body thus served as a bait for death so that the serpent, instead of swallowing it as he hoped, might be forced to disgorge those whom he had already swallowed.[8] For 'death grew strong and devoured. And God has wiped away again all the tears from every face' (Is 25.8 (LXX)).

16 Did Christ become man in vain? Are our teachings mere speculations and human inventions? Aren't the sacred Scriptures our salvation? And the prophets' predictions? So keep this deposit unshaken and let no one disturb you. Trust God made man. That it

was possible for him to be made man has been proved. But if the Jews still disbelieve, let us put this point to them: What is strange about our proclamation that God became man, when you say that Abraham gave hospitality to the Lord? What is strange about our proclamation, seeing that Jacob said: 'I saw God face to face, and my life has been spared' (Gen 32.30)? The Lord who ate with Abraham is the same Lord who ate with us. So what is strange about our proclamation?

We can also cite two witnesses who stood beside the Lord on Mount Sinai. Moses was in the cleft of the rock, as was Elijah in his day (Exod 33.22; 1 Kings 19.9). They were with the Lord when he was transfigured on Mount Tabor and they told the disciples 'of the departure which he was about to undergo in Jerusalem' (Lk 9.31). However, we have now proved, as we promised, that it was possible for him to become man; the remaining proofs can be left for the studious to read.[9] . . .

33 So God is a witness, and the Holy Spirit joins him as witness, and Christ says: Why 'do you seek to kill me, a man who has told you the truth?' (Jn 8.40). So let heretics who deny his humanity hold their tongues. For they are contradicting the one who said: 'Feel me and see that a spirit does not have flesh and bones, as you see that I have' (Lk 24.39). So let the virgin-born Lord be adored, and let virgins recognize the crown which belongs to their way of life. Let the order of monks also recognize the glory of their chastity, for we are not deprived of the dignity of chastity. For the Saviour spent nine months in the Virgin's womb, but the Lord spent thirty-three years as a man, so that, if a virgin is honoured by the nine months, we are much more honoured by the many years.

34 But let us all run the race of chastity by God's grace, young men and girls, the old and the young, shunning self-indulgence and praising Christ's name. Let us be aware of the glory of chastity, for the crown it brings is angelic, and its achievement is beyond human powers. Let us treat our bodies with respect, for they will shine like the sun. Let us not defile such noble bodies for the sake of a little pleasure. For the sin is small and lasts but an hour, but the shame lasts many years, indeed for ever. Those who practise chastity are angels walking on earth. Virgins share the lot of the Virgin Mary.

Let us banish all embellishment, all harmful glances, all affected gait, all dress and perfume which entice to lust. For perfume let us all be content with the sweet scent of prayer and of good works and the holiness of our bodies, so that the words of the Lord who was born of a virgin may apply to us, chaste men and garlanded women: 'I shall live among them and walk among them; and I shall be their God and they will be my people' (2 Cor 6.16; Lev 26.12; Ezek 37.27). To him is the glory for ever and ever. Amen.

CATECHESIS 13

To candidates for baptism
On 'who was crucified and buried'

Reading: Is 53.1ff (LXX): 'Lord, who believed what we heard? And to whom is the Lord's arm revealed? . . .' Is 53.7ff. (LXX): 'Like a lamb he was led to the slaughter . . .'

1 Jesus' every deed is the boast of the Catholic church, but the boast of all boasts is the cross. Knowing this, Paul said: 'Far be it from me to boast of anything save of the cross of our Lord Jesus Christ' (Gal 6.14). It was marvellous when the man born blind regained his sight at the Pool of Siloam; but what good is this to all the blind throughout the world? It was a great and supernatural event when Lazarus rose again on the fourth day after his death; but the grace affected him alone. What good was this for all those throughout the world who have been killed by sin? It was marvellous when five loaves supplied food for five thousand people; but what good was this to all those throughout the world who are starved for knowledge? It was marvellous when the woman who had been bound by Satan for eighteen years was unbound; but what good is this to all of us who are bound by the ropes of our sins? The crown of the cross brought light to those blinded by ignorance, freed all those constrained by sin, and redeemed the whole of mankind.

2 Do not be surprised that the whole world was redeemed. For the one who gave his life was no ordinary man, but the Only-begotten Son of God. The sin of one man, Adam, had power to bring death to the world. If death gained rule over the world through the sin of one man, will not life even more gain rule through the righteousness of one man (cf. Rom 5.17–18)? If they were expelled from Paradise then because of the fruit of a tree, will it not be easier for believers to enter Paradise now through Jesus' tree?[1] If the first man, whom God fashioned from the earth, introduced death into

the world, cannot the one who created him from the earth introduce eternal life, since he is life himself (cf. Jn 14.6)? If Phinehas in his zeal appeased God's anger by killing the wrong-doer, could not Jesus dispel God's anger against the human race, not by killing another, but by offering himself as a ransom?[2]

3 So we should not be ashamed of the Saviour's cross, but rather make it our boast. For 'the word of the cross' is 'a scandal to the Jews and folly to the gentiles', but to us it is salvation. 'To those who are perishing it is folly, but to us who are being saved it is God's power' (1 Cor 1.18, 23). For the one who gave his life for us, as we have said, was not an ordinary man, but the Son of God, God made man. In Moses' time a lamb drove away the destroyer (Ex 12.23); was not 'the Lamb of God who takes away the sin of the world' (Jn 1.29) much more able to bring release from sins? The blood of a dumb lamb brought safety; will not the blood of the Only-begotten be much more able to save? If any doubt the power of the Crucified, let them ask the demons. If any doubt what they hear, let them believe what they can see. Many men round the world have been crucified, but the demons have not cowered before any of them; but the mere sight of the sign of the cross of Christ who was crucified for us does make the demons cower.[3] For other men have died because of their own sins, whereas he died for the sins of others. For 'he committed no sin, and no guile was found in his mouth'. The words are not Peter's own (1 Pet 2.22), for he would have been open to the suspicion of seeking to please the Master; they are the words of Isaiah (Is 53.9), who, though not present in the flesh, in spirit foresaw Christ's incarnate coming. But why should I only cite a prophet as a witness? Accept the testimony of Pilate, who passed judgment on him in these words: 'I do not find him guilty of any charge' (Lk 23.14). And when he had handed Jesus over, he washed his hands saying: 'I am innocent of the blood of this just man' (Mt 27.24). There is another witness to Jesus' sinlessness, the thief who was the first to enter Paradise, and addressed these words of reproach to his fellow-thief: 'We are receiving a just reward for our deeds, but he has done nothing wrong' (Lk 23.41); for we were both present at his trial.

4 So Jesus truly suffered for all mankind.[4] For the cross was no pretence, for then our redemption would have been a pretence. His death was no illusion, for then our salvation would have been an illusion. If his death had been an illusion, there would have been truth in the words: 'We have remembered that that deceiver said while he was alive: "After three days I shall rise again"' (Mt 27.63).

No, his Passion was real, for he was really crucified; we are not ashamed of the fact. He was crucified; we do not deny it, we boast of it. If I do deny it now, I am given the lie by Golgotha here, beside which we are now gathered. I am given the lie by the wood of the cross, whose fragments have since been distributed all round the world.

I affirm the cross, because I know the resurrection. For if he had remained crucified, perhaps I would not have affirmed the cross; perhaps I would have concealed it, and my Master too. But since the cross was followed by the resurrection, I am not ashamed to affirm it.

5 Christ was crucified in the flesh which he shared with the rest of mankind, for the sake of the sins which he did not share. He was not led to his death because of avarice, for he was a teacher of poverty. He was not convicted of lust, for he said clearly: 'If anyone looks at a woman lustfully, he has already committed adultery with her' (Mt 5.28). It was not for striking and beating others in anger, for he turned the other cheek to the man who struck him. It was not for contempt of the law, for he fulfilled the law. It was not for insulting a prophet, for he was the one whom the prophets proclaimed. It was not for depriving workers of their wages, for he served without wage or fee. It was not for sins of word or deed or thought, for 'he committed no sin, no deceit was found on his lips, when insulted he returned no insults, when suffering made no threats' (1 Pet 2.22–3; Is 53.9), and he was not taken to his Passion against his will but went willingly. If anyone today seeks to dissuade him saying: 'Far be it from you, Lord', he will make the same reply: 'Get behind me, Satan' (Mt 16.22–3).

6 Do you wish to be convinced that he went willingly to his Passion? Others die in ignorance, against their will; he foretold his Passion: 'See, the Son of Man is handed over to be crucified' (Mt 26.2). You know why the Lover of mankind did not try to escape death? So that the whole world should not die for their sins. 'See, we are going up to Jerusalem, and the Son of Man will be handed over . . . and crucified' (Mt 20.18, 19). And again: 'He set his face to walk to Jerusalem' (Lk 9.51).

Do you want a clear indication that for Jesus the cross is glory? Listen to his words, not mine. Judas had become ungrateful to the head of the household (cf. Mt 20.11) and had turned traitor. He had recently left the table; he had drunk the cup of blessing, but in return for the saving drink he wished to shed just blood. He who had eaten his bread lifted his heel against him all the more (cf. Ps 40.10 (41.9)). Scarcely had his hands received the blessings when he plotted Jesus' death for the sake of blood-money. When detected, he heard the words: 'You have said it'; but he went out again. Then Jesus said: 'The hour has come for the Son of Man to be glorified' (Jn 12.23). You observe how he knows the cross to be his special glory? Isaiah had not been dishonoured by being sawn in two; will Christ be dishonoured when he dies for the world? 'Now the Son of Man has been glorified' (Jn 13.31). Not that he did not have glory before, for he was glorified with the glory he possessed before the foundation of the world (cf. Jn 17.5); as God he was glorified eternally, but now he was being glorified and received the crown to wear for his endurance. He was not constrained to give up his life; he was killed not by force but by his own will. Listen to what he says: 'I have power to lay down my life, and I have power to take it up again' (Jn 10.18). I yield to my enemies willingly, for if I had not been willing, it would not have happened. Thus he went to his Passion by choice, rejoicing at its accomplishment, smiling at the crown, with delight at the salvation of mankind, not ashamed of the cross, for he was saving the world. For it was not a common man who suffered, but God made man, competing in the contest of endurance.

7 However an objection is raised by the Jews, who are always ready to contradict and reluctant to believe. This is why the prophet who has just been read says: 'Lord, who believed what we heard?' (Is 53.1). The Persians believe,[5] but the Hebrews do not believe. 'Those who have not been told shall see, and those who have not heard shall understand' (Is 52.15; Rom 15.21), and those who study shall reject what they study. They make this rejoinder to us: 'Does the Lord suffer? Were human hands stronger than his Lordship?' Read the Lamentations: for Jeremiah was lamenting for you when he wrote his Lamentations, and he had plenty to lament about. He saw your destruction, he beheld your fall. His lament was for the Jerusalem of old; there will be no lamentation for the Jerusalem of today. For the former crucified Christ, the latter worships him. This is his lament: 'The breath of our face, the Lord Christ, has been caught in our corruption.' Am I playing with words? You can see, he is testifying that Christ the Lord is to be caught by men. And what will be the consequence of this? Tell me, prophet. He answers: 'He of whom we said: "In his shadow we shall live among the gentiles"' (Lam 4.20 (LXX)). So he is hinting that the grace of life will no longer dwell in Israel, but among the gentiles.

8 Well then, because of the objections which the Jews bring against our position, with the help of your prayers and the grace of

the Lord I shall put before you a few testimonies concerning the Passion in so far as the shortage of time allows. Everything about Christ is included in Scripture; nothing is unclear or unattested. Everything is inscribed, not on tablets of stone, but on the prophetic monuments, written unmistakably by the Holy Spirit . . .[6]

9 So let us look for the testimonies concerning Christ's Passion. For we have gathered here not to perform an allegorical[7] exposition of the Scriptures, but to deepen our faith in things we already believe . . .[8]

. . .

19 . . . However someone will say to me: 'You are speculating. Prove to me the wood of the cross from a prophet. If you can't provide testimony from a prophet, I will not believe.' So hear what Jeremiah has to say, and believe: 'Like an innocent lamb I was led to the slaughter, and did I not know?'[9] (For you must read the text as a question, as I have quoted it; for the one who said: 'You know that after two days it will be the Passover, and the Son of Man will be handed over to be crucified', must have known.) 'Like an innocent lamb I was led to the slaughter, and did I not know?' Why a lamb? Let John the Baptist give the interpretation: 'Behold the Lamb of God who takes away the sin of the world' (Jn 1.29). 'They devised a wicked plot against me, saying . . .' If he knew the plots, was he unaware of the outcome? And what did they say? 'Come, let us put wood into his bread.' Later you will learn,[10] if the Lord thinks fit, that his body bore the form of bread, as the gospel teaches. So, 'let us put wood into his bread and wipe him off from the land of the living'. Life is not wiped off; why waste your efforts? 'And his name will be remembered no more' (Jer 11.19 (LXX)). You plot in vain; for 'his name remains under the sun' (Ps 71 (72).17) in the Church. Again, to prove that it was life which hung on the cross, Moses makes this lament: 'And your life will hang before your eyes, and you will fear by day and by night, and you will not believe your life' (Deut 28.66 (LXX)). Then there is the passage that was read just now: 'Who believed what we heard?'

20 Moses provided a symbol[11] when he fixed the serpent to a cross, so that those who had been bitten by the living serpent might look at the bronze one, believe and be healed. A bronze serpent on a cross saved them then; cannot the incarnate Son of God bring salvation on the cross? Life always comes through wood. In Noah's time life came from the wooden ark. In Moses' time the sea beheld the symbol of the rod and respectfully withdrew from him when he struck it. Moses' rod had this power then; is the Saviour's cross

powerless? There is much that one could say about such symbols, but I shall pass over them for the sake of brevity. In Moses' time the wood sweetened the water, and water flowed from Jesus' side on the wood [of the cross].

21 With Moses blood and water were the first of the signs, and they were the last of all the signs of Jesus. First Moses changed the river into blood (Exod 7.20), and at the last Jesus discharged water with blood from his side (Jn 19.34). This occurred perhaps because of two utterances, one in judgment, the other in outcry; or one for the sake of believers, the other of unbelievers. For Pilate said: 'I am innocent', and washed his hands with water; the others cried out: 'His blood be upon us' (Mt 27.24, 25). So the two things came from his side, the water perhaps for the judge, but for the shouting mob the blood.

But we should consider the events again in another way. The blood was for the Jews, the water for Christians. For the Jews who plotted there was the sentence for bloodshed; for you who believe there is now salvation through water. For nothing happened to no purpose. Our fathers who interpreted the passage gave another reason for the event: in the gospels saving baptism has a twofold power, one granted to the baptized through water, the other for holy martyrs in persecutions through their own blood.[12] For this reason blood and water came from the Saviour's side, and its power confirms the grace of a confession made for Christ whether in baptism or at the moment of martyrdom. There is also another explanation of the side. The woman who was formed from the man's side led the way in sin; but though Jesus came to grant pardon to men and women alike, he was pierced in the side for the sake of women, to do away with their sin.

22 If one were to look, one could find other reasons too. But what I have said so far must suffice, both because of the shortage of time, and so as not to give my listeners too much to digest. All the same, people can never weary of hearing about the Master's crown, especially at this holy place of Golgotha. For while others can only hear, we see and touch. So let no one grow weary; take up your arms against your enemies for the sake of the cross. Set up your faith in the cross as a standard against its opponents. When you are about to discuss Christ's cross with unbelievers, first let them see you make the sign of Christ's cross with your hand, and their objections will be silenced. Do not be ashamed to acknowledge the cross, for angels are proud to say: 'We know whom you are seeking, Jesus the Crucified' (cf. Mt 28.5). Can't you say, angel: 'I know whom you are

seeking: my Master'? 'But', he replies forthrightly, 'the one I know is the Crucified.' For the cross is a crown, not a disgrace.

23 However, for the rest of our time let us return to the demonstration from the prophets which we proposed. The Lord was crucified: you have been given the testimonies. You can see the place of Golgotha. You express your assent with shouts of praise; see that you never deny it in a time of persecution.[13] Do not rejoice in the cross only in times of peace; preserve the same faith even in times of persecution. Don't be Jesus' friend in times of peace, and his enemy in times of war.

You are now to receive the remission of your sins and the graces of the King's spiritual gift. When war comes, fight like a good soldier for your King. The sinless Jesus was crucified for you; will you not endure crucifixion for the one who was crucified for you? You would not be conferring a favour, for one has already been conferred on you. Return the favour and pay your debt to the one who was crucified for you on Golgotha.

'Golgotha' means 'the Place of the Skull'.[14] Who were they then who gave such a prophetic name to this place Golgotha, where Christ the true Head endured the cross? As the Apostle says: 'Who is the image of the unseen God' (Col 1.15); and a little later: 'And he is the head of his body, the church' (Col 1.18); and again: 'The head of every man is Christ' (1 Cor 11.3); and again: 'Who is the head of every principality and power' (Col 2.10). The Head suffered in the Place of the Skull. A great and prophetic name! The very name seems to remind you, saying: Do not consider the Crucified to be a mere man: he is 'the head of every principality and power'. The Crucified was the Head of every power, but the Father is *his* Head. The Head of a man is Christ, and the head of Christ is God.

24 Christ then was crucified for us. He was tried by night when a fire had been laid because it was cold. He was crucified at the third hour, darkness fell from the sixth hour to the ninth, and from the ninth it was light again. Wasn't this in Scripture too? Let us look. Well then, Zechariah says: 'It will happen on that day that there will be no light, and there will be cold and frost for one day' – the cold which led Peter to warm himself – 'and that day is known to the Lord' (Zech 14.6, 7 (LXX)). What? Doesn't he know the other days? There are many days, but this is the day of the Lord's Passion, 'the day which the Lord made' (Ps 117 (118).24); and 'that day is known to the Lord, and it will be neither day nor night' (Zech 14.7). What is this riddle the prophet is speaking? That day is neither day nor night. What shall we call it then? The

gospel account gives the explanation. It was not day, because from the east to the west alike the sun did not shine, but from the sixth to the ninth hour darkness fell in the middle of the day. Thus the darkness was inserted into the day, and God 'called the darkness night' (Gen 1.5). Therefore it was neither day nor night. The day was not wholly light, so as to deserve the name of day, nor wholly darkness, so as to deserve the name of night. No, after the ninth hour the sun shone. The prophet predicts this too. For after saying: 'neither day nor night', he added: 'And towards the evening there will be light.' You observe the prophets' accuracy? You see the truthfulness of the predictions?

25 But are you looking for a clear indication of the time when the sun was eclipsed? Was it the fifth hour or the eighth or the tenth? The Jews are hard of hearing, so tell them exactly when the sun set. Thus the prophet Amos says: 'And it will be on that day, says the Lord God, that the sun will set at midday' – for there was darkness from the sixth hour – 'and by day the light will be darkened over the earth.' What was the occasion, prophet, what day? 'And I will change your feasts into mourning'; for it happened at the Azymes, at the feast of the Passover. He goes on to say: 'And I will make it like the mourning of a loved one, and those with it like a day of grief' (Amos 8.9–10 (LXX)). For on the day of Azymes and at the feast their women beat their breasts and wept, while the apostles grieved in secret. What a remarkable prophecy!

26 But give us another sign, someone will say. What other precise sign is there of the event? Jesus was crucified; he had a single tunic, and wore a single cloak. The soldiers cut the cloak up and divided it into four; but the tunic was not cut up, because it would then have been useless; instead the soldiers cast lots for it. They divided the cloak, but made a lottery for the tunic. Is this in Scripture too? The answer is known to the Church's dedicated singers, who imitate the angelic hosts, and sing unceasing hymns to God. They are privileged to sing here at Golgotha: 'They have divided my clothes among themselves and cast lots for my garment' (Ps 21.19 (22.18)). The 'lots' refer to the lottery.

27 Again, after his trial before Pilate he was dressed in purple, for there they put a scarlet cloak round his shoulders. Is this in Scripture too? Isaiah says: 'Who is this who has come from Edom with purple garments from Bosra?' Who is this who in mockery is made to wear scarlet? (For it is in some such way as this that the Hebrews interpret the word *Bosor.*[15]) 'Why are your garments purple and your clothes as if from treading the wine-press?' (Is 63.1–2).

He answers: 'I stretched out my hands all day to the unbelieving and contradictory people' (Is 65.2 (LXX)).

28 He stretched out his hands on the cross to encompass the ends of the world. For the central point of the earth is Golgotha here. These are not my words, but those of the prophet: 'You have accomplished salvation in the centre of the earth.'[16] He who set the sky in place with his spiritual hands stretched out human hands. They were fastened with nails for this purpose: that when the humanity which bore the sins of mankind had been fastened to the wood and died, sin might die with it, and we might rise again in righteousness. For since death came through one man, life too comes through one man (cf. Rom 5.12–18), the one man who as Saviour voluntarily accepts death. Remember what he said: 'I have power to lay down my life, and I have power to take it up again' (Jn 10.18 adjusted).

29 However, though he came to save us all and endured these sufferings, the people returned evil for good. Jesus says: 'I thirst' (Jn 19.28), though he had brought water out of the sheer rock. He looked for grapes from the vine he had planted, but what did the vine do? This vine, which by nature came from the holy fathers but by choice from Sodom (for 'their vine is from the people of Sodom and their vine-branch from Gomorrha' (Jn 19.28)), offers its thirsty Lord a sponge on a reed, filled with vinegar. 'And they gave me gall for food, and for my thirst they gave me vinegar' (Ps 68.22 (69.21)). You see the clarity of the prophets' prediction? What sort of gall did they give me for food? 'They gave him wine mixed with myrrh' (Mk 15.23). Myrrh is bitter and tastes like gall. Is this the return you make to the Lord? Is this, vine, what you offer your Master? There was justice in Isaiah's prophetic lament for you: 'My beloved had a vineyard on a hill-top, in a fertile place' (Is 5.1 (LXX)). And – not to quote the whole passage – 'I waited', he says, 'for it to produce a bunch of grapes', I thirsted for it to give me wine, 'and it produced thorns' (Is 5.4 (LXX)). You see the crown I am wearing. What decree shall I pass now? 'I shall order the clouds not to drop rain on it' (Is 5.6). For the clouds, that is, the prophets, have been taken away from them; henceforth the prophets are in the Church, as Paul says: 'Let two or three prophets speak and the rest discern' (1 Cor 14.29). And again: God has granted in the Church that 'some should be apostles, others prophets' (Eph 4.11). Agabus, who bound his hands and his feet, was a prophet (cf. Acts 21.10–11).

30 With regard to the thieves who were crucified with him, it is said that 'he was numbered among wrongdoers' (Is 53.12; Mk 15.28).

Beforehand they were both wrongdoers, but one is so no longer. The one who persisted in his wrongdoing would not yield to salvation; though his hands were fixed to the cross, he struck out with his tongue in blasphemy. The Jews as they passed were wagging their heads in mockery of the Crucified, fulfilling the words of Scripture: 'They saw me and wagged their heads' (Ps 108 (109).25). He joined in their taunts. But the other thief rebuked him; it was the end of his life and the beginning of his conversion; he surrendered his life and received a foretaste of salvation. After rebuking the other, he says: 'Remember me, Lord.' I am speaking to you. Pay no attention to him; his mind's eyes are impaired; but remember me. I don't say, remember what I have done, for that frightens me. We all feel for our companions on a journey. We are travelling together to death; remember me, your fellow-traveller. I don't say, remember me now, but: 'when you come into your kingdom' (Lk 23.42).

31 What was the power, thief, that enlightened you? Who taught you to worship your despised companion on the cross? How great the power of the eternal Light to shed light on the benighted! And so the thief deserved to hear the reply: 'Take heart' – not because your present state should lead you to take heart, but the King is here to grant you pardon. The request concerns the distant future; the pardon is most swift. 'Amen, I say to you, today you will be with me in Paradise' (Lk 23.43), for today you have heard my voice and not hardened your heart. Most swift was my condemnation of Adam; most swift is the pardon I grant you. Adam was told: 'On the very day when you eat, you shall die' (Gen 2.17). As for you, today your faith has led to obedience, today is your salvation. Wood caused Adam to fall; wood leads you into Paradise.[17] Don't be afraid of the serpent; he will not cast you out, for he has already fallen from heaven. I do not say to you, 'Today you will depart', but 'Today you will be with me.' Take heart, you will not be cast out. Do not fear the flaming sword; it defers to its Master. How great and inexplicable the pardon! The faithful Abraham had not yet entered, but the thief does. Moses and the prophets had not yet entered, but the lawless thief does. Even before you Paul expressed his wonder: 'Where sin abounded, grace abounded even more' (Rom 5.20). Those who bore the 'heat of the day' had not yet entered, but the one who came about the eleventh hour did. Let no one grumble at the householder, for he says: 'Friend, I do you no wrong. Have I not the right to do what I choose in my own lands?' (Mt 20.12, 13, 15 slightly adjusted). The thief wishes to act justly, but death intervenes. It is not only good works that I look for; I have accepted

faith. I came to 'pasture my flock among the lilies', I came to pasture it 'in the gardens' (cf. Cant 6.2–3). I have found my sheep; it was lost, but I take it on my shoulders. For he believes, since he said himself: 'I have strayed like a lost sheep' (Ps 118 (119).176). 'Remember me, Lord, when you come into your kingdom.'

32 In the Canticle I have already sung to my bride about this garden. This is what I said to her. 'I have come into my garden, my sister, my bride' (Cant 5.1 (LXX)). 'In the place where he was crucified there was a garden' (Jn 19.41). And what do you take from there? 'I gathered my myrrh' (Cant 5.1 (LXX)), drinking wine mixed with myrrh, and vinegar; and when I had taken them, I said: 'It is finished' (Jn 19.30). For the mystery is fulfilled, Scripture is fulfilled, sins are redeemed.

For 'when Christ appeared as High Priest of the good things to come, he entered once for all into the Holy Place through the greater and more perfect tent not made by hands, that is, not of this creation, not through the blood of goats and calves, but through his own blood, and obtained eternal redemption. For if the blood of bulls and goats and the ash of a heifer sprinkles the profaned and sanctifies them for the purification of the flesh, how much more the blood of Christ?' (Heb 9.11–14). And again: 'So, brethren, having confidence to enter the Holy Place in the blood of Jesus through the new and living way which he opened for us through the veil, the veil of his flesh' (Heb 10.19–20). And since the flesh which was his veil had been dishonoured, this was the reason why the symbolic[18] veil of the Temple was rent asunder, as Scripture records: 'And behold, the veil of the Temple was split in two from top to bottom' (Mt 27.51); for not even a small piece of it was left intact. For since the Master said: 'Behold, your house is left empty' (Mt 23.38), the house was destroyed.

33 The Saviour endured these things, 'having made peace through the blood of the cross' for 'things in heaven and things on earth' (cf. Col 1.20). For we were God's enemies through sin, and God had decreed that the sinless one should die. For one of two things had to happen, either that God in his truthfulness would destroy the whole race, or that in his loving kindness he would cancel their condemnation.

But observe God's wisdom. He maintained both the truth of the condemnation and the power of his loving-kindness. Christ 'took our sins in his body on the wood, so that' through his death 'we might die to sins and live to righteousness' (1 Pet 2.24). The one who died for us was not insignificant. He was not a visible sheep, he was not a mere man, he was not only an angel; he was God made man. The lawlessness of sinners was not as great as the righteousness of the one who died for them. The sins we committed were not as great as the justice he wrought when he laid down his life for us, laying it down when he chose and taking it up again when he chose (cf. Jn 10.18).

Are you looking for proof that he did not yield his life to force, or give up his spirit involuntarily? He addressed these words to his Father: 'Father, into your hands I commit my spirit.' I commit it, so as to take it up again. 'And so saying, he gave up his spirit' (Lk 23.46), but not for long, for soon he rose again from the dead.

34 The sun was eclipsed, because of the Sun of justice. The rocks were split, because of the spiritual Rock (cf. 1 Cor 10.4). The tombs were opened and the dead rose again, because of the one who was 'free among the dead' (Ps 87 (88).5 (LXX)). He has 'released' his 'prisoners from the waterless pit' (Zech 9.11 (LXX)). So do not be ashamed of the crucified, but boldly make your own the words: 'He bears our sins and suffers for us', and 'by his bruises we have been healed' (Is 53.4, 5. (LXX)). Let us not be ungrateful to our benefactor. And again: 'Because of my people's sins he was led to death, and I shall give the wicked in return for his burial and the rich in return for his death' (Is 53.8–9 (LXX)). For this reason Paul says clearly: 'that Christ died for our sins according to the Scriptures, and that he was buried and rose on the third day according to the Scriptures' (1 Cor 15.3–4).

35 But we are looking for a clear indication of the place of his burial.[19] Was the tomb man-made? Is it raised above the ground like royal tombs? Was the tomb made of piled stones? And what was set over it? Give us, prophets, the precise facts about the grave: where is it, and where shall we look for it? They reply: 'Look upon the solid rock which you have quarried' (Is 51.1 (LXX)), look upon it and see. You have in the gospels: 'In a carved tomb' (Lk 23.53), where the rock had been quarried. And what happened? What was the door of the tomb like? Again, another prophet tells us: 'They killed my life in the pit, and placed a stone over me' (Lam 3.53 (LXX)). I, the chosen, precious corner-stone, I, the stone to trip up the Jews and bring salvation to believers, I lie for a short time within the stone (cf. Is 28.16; 8.14; 1 Pet 2.6, 8). Thus the tree of life was planted in the earth, so that the cursed earth might enjoy the blessing, and the dead be redeemed.

36 So we should not be afraid to acknowledge the Crucified. We should boldly trace the cross with our fingers as a seal on our

forehead and over everything: over the bread we eat, the cups we drink, when we come in and when we go out, before we go to sleep, when we go to bed and when we get up, on journeys and at rest. It is a powerful protection; to suit the poor, it costs nothing; to suit the weak, it costs no labour, since it comes as a gift from God; it is a sign for the Faithful and a terror to demons. For 'in it he triumphed over them', 'openly making an example of them' (Col 2.15 adjusted). For when they see the cross, they remember the Crucified; they fear the one who crushed the dragon's heads (cf. Ps 73.14 (74.13)). Do not despise the seal because it is a free gift; no, honour the Benefactor all the more because of it.

37 If you ever get into a controversy and have no arguments to put forward, let your faith remain unshaken. Turn polymath, and use the prophets to silence the Jews, and their own myths to silence the Greeks. The Greeks worship people who were struck by thunderbolts. A thunderbolt does not come from heaven at random. If they are not ashamed to worship those whom God abhors and strikes, should you be ashamed to worship God's beloved Son who was crucified for you?

It would embarrass me to speak about these so-called gods; besides, time compels me to pass over this subject and leave it to experts. But as for heretics, let them be silenced. If anyone says that the cross was a fantasy, turn away from him. Hold in abhorrence anyone who says that the crucifixion was an illusion.[20] For if the crucifixion was an illusion, and salvation comes from the cross, then our salvation is illusory too. 'But if Christ is not risen, we are still in our sins' (1 Cor 15.17 adjusted). If the cross is an illusion, the ascension is also an illusion; and if the ascension is an illusion, so is the second coming, and everything in the end is unfounded.

38 So first take the cross as an indestructible foundation on which to build the rest of the faith. Do not deny the Crucified. For if you do deny him, you will find many to give you the lie. The traitor Judas will be the first to give you the lie; for the betrayer knows that he was condemned to death by high priests and elders. The thirty pieces of silver testify. Gethsemani, where the betrayal took place, testifies. I shall not yet mention the Mount of Olives, where they used to go by night to pray.[21] The moon gives its testimony by night. So do the day and the sun which suffered eclipse, because it could not bear to see the conspirators' crime. You are given the lie by the fire by which Peter stood to warm himself; if you deny the cross, the eternal fire is waiting for you. I speak hard words, lest you experience a hard fate. Remember the swords

approaching him in Gethsemani, lest you experience an eternal sword. You will be given the lie by the house of Caiaphas, which in its present abandonment shows the power of the one who was once condemned there.[22]

On Judgment Day Caiaphas himself will stand against you. The servant who gave Jesus the blow will stand against you; so will those who bound him and led him away. Herod and Pilate will stand against you, saying in effect: 'Why do you deny the one who was falsely accused before us by the Jews, though we knew he had done nothing wrong? For I, Pilate, washed my hands that day.' The perjured witnesses will stand against you, together with the soldiers who dressed him in the purple garment and crowned him with thorns and crucified him on Golgotha and cast lots for his tunic. You will be given the lie by Simon of Cyrene, who carried the cross behind Jesus.

39 Of all the stars the sun in its eclipse will give you the lie; of all things on earth the wine mixed with myrrh, of all reeds the reed, of all plants the hyssop, of all sea-creatures the sponge, of all trees the wood of the cross. You will be given the lie, as I have said, by the soldiers who nailed him to the cross and cast lots for his garments; by the soldier who opened his side with the spear; by the women who were present that day; by the veil of the Temple which was torn in two that day; by Pilate's praetorium, now abandoned through the power of the one who was crucified that day; by holy Golgotha here, the pre-eminent,[23] which is still visible today and still shows how the rocks were split because of Christ that day; by the grave nearby, where he was laid; by the stone which was placed over the door and still lies next to the tomb today; by the angels who were there that day; by the women who adored him after the resurrection; by Peter and John, who ran to the tomb, and Thomas, who put his hand into Christ's side and his fingers into the prints of the nails. For it was for our sake that he felt them so carefully; by God's providence he was there to seek what you were to seek though you were not there.

40 As witnesses of the cross you have the twelve apostles, the whole earth and the world of humanity which believes in the Crucified. The very fact that you are here today should convince you of the power of the Crucified. For who brought you together today? Where are the soldiers? Where are the chains which constrained you? What was the sentence which compelled you? It was the saving standard of Jesus, the cross, which brought you all together. It enslaved the Persians and tamed the Scythians; to the Egyptians,

instead of cats and dogs and many forms of error, it brought knowledge of God. To this very day it cures diseases; to this very day it drives out demons, and overthrows the tricks of potions and spells.

41 The cross is destined to come again with Jesus from heaven. The King's standard will lead the way, so that the Jews may 'look on him whom they pierced' (Jn 19.37 adjusted), and recognizing by his cross the one they had dishonoured, may repent and lament. Tribe by tribe they will lament, for when they do repent it will no longer be the time for repentance. But let us boast of the cross and take pride in it, adoring the Lord who was sent and crucified for us, and adoring too God the Father who sent him, together with the Holy Spirit, to whom is the glory for ever and ever. Amen.

CATECHESIS 14

For the candidates for baptism
On 'and he rose from the dead on the third day, and ascended into heaven, and is seated at the right hand of the Father'

Reading: 1 Cor 15.1ff: 'I remind you, brethren, of the gospel which I proclaimed to you . . .'

1 'Rejoice, Jerusalem, and hold festival' (Jn 19.37 adjusted), all you who love Jesus, for he is risen! Be joyful, all you who once lamented when you heard of the presumptuous wickedness of the Jews; for the victim of their violence here has risen again. And just as it was in a way painful for you to hear about the cross, let the good news of the resurrection fill all those present here with joy. Let mourning change to gladness and lamentation to joy; let joy and gladness be on your lips because of the Risen one who said: 'Rejoice' (Mt 28.9). I realize the pain which you who love Christ have been feeling these days; and since my last address stopped at the death and burial and did not include the good news of the resurrection, your minds have been kept in suspense until you heard what you were longing for. So, the one who was dead has risen, he who was 'free among the dead' (Ps 87 (88).5 (LXX)) and their liberator. The one who endured the ignominy of being crowned with thorns has risen and now wears a wreath for his victory over death.

2 We have already set before you the testimonies regarding his cross; we shall now, if you are willing, show you the force of the proofs concerning the resurrection.[1]

. . .

5 Do you want an indication also of the place? It says again in the Song of Songs: 'I went down to the nut-garden' (Cant 6.11). For it was in a garden that he was crucified. For although it has been largely decorated with royal gifts, it was once a garden, and the

signs and remains of it are still present. 'A garden enclosed . . . a spring sealed' by the Jews, who said: 'We have remembered that that deceiver said while he was still alive: "after three days I shall rise". So give orders for the tomb to be made safe.' And later: 'They went and made the tomb safe with the guard, sealing the stone' (Mt 27.63–6). There is a saying which applies to them neatly: 'You will judge them to your rest' (Job 7.18 (LXX adjusted). What is the sealed spring? What is the meaning of the 'spring of the well of living water' (Cant 4.15 adjusted)? It is the Saviour himself, about whom Scripture says: 'With you is the spring of life' (Ps 35 (36).9).

6 But what does Zephaniah say to the disciples speaking in the person of Christ? 'Make ready, rise at daybreak, for all their grapes for the gleaning are destroyed' (Zeph 3.7 (LXX)) – obviously the grapes of the Jews, for whom there remains no grape-cluster of salvation, not even the foliage, for their vine has been cut down. Notice how he says to the disciples: 'Make ready, rise at daybreak.' Expect the resurrection at daybreak.

The same passage of Scripture goes on to say: 'Therefore wait for me, says the Lord, on the day of my resurrection in the Martyrium' (Zeph 3.8 (LXX)). You notice how the prophet foresaw even the place of the resurrection, which was to be called the Martyrium? For why were this site of Golgotha and the resurrection not called a church like other churches, but the Martyrium?[2] Perhaps it was because of the prophet's words: 'On the day of my resurrection in the Martyrium'

. . .

9 And from where did the Saviour rise? It says in the Song of Songs: 'Arise, come, my kinswoman'; and further on: 'in the shelter of the rock' (Cant 2.10, 14 (LXX)). The phrase 'shelter of the rock' refers to the shelter which at that time stood in front of the door to the Saviour's tomb, and had been hollowed from the very rock in the way that was customary here in front of tombs. It is no longer visible because the front chamber was then cut away to give the tomb the decoration it has today. For before the Emperor had set this magnificent structure over the tomb, there was a shelter in front of the rock.[3]

But where is the rock with its shelter? Is it near the centre of the city or at the outskirts, near the walls? Does it lie within the ancient walls or the outer fortifications which were constructed later? It says in the Song of Songs: 'In the shelter of the rock, near the outer fortification' (Cant 2.14 (LXX))

. . .

22 There are many witnesses to the Saviour's resurrection: the night and the light of the full moon, for it was the fifteenth night; the rock of the Tomb, which received the body, and the stone will refute the Jews to their face, for it saw the Lord; and this stone which was rolled away then still lies here today to witness to the resurrection; God's angels were present to witness the resurrection of the Only-begotten; Peter, John and Thomas and all the other apostles; some of whom ran to the tomb and saw the burial-clothes in which he had once been wrapped lying here after the resurrection, while others felt his hands and his feet and inspected the marks of the nails, while all of them together felt the Saviour's breath and were authorized to forgive sins in the power of the Holy Spirit; the women who held on to his feet and observed the force of the earthquake and the shining presence of the angel; the grave-clothes wound round him, which he left behind when he rose again; the soldiers, and the money they were given; the very place, which is still visible, and this building of the holy church, which the Emperor Constantine of happy memory out of his love of Christ undertook to erect and to adorn with the splendour which is before your eyes.

23 There is another witness to Jesus' resurrection: Tabitha, who was raised from the dead in his name. For how can one fail to believe in Christ's resurrection when his very name could raise the dead? The sea was a witness to Jesus' resurrection, as you have already heard.[4] The catch of fish is a witness, and the charcoal fire lying ready, and the food that was placed on it. Peter was another witness, when after denying Jesus he professed his faith in him three times and was told to be the shepherd of his spiritual sheep. To this very day the Mount of Olives stands, all but displaying to the eyes of the Faithful even today the one who ascended on the cloud[5] and the heavenly gate of his ascension. For he came down from heaven to Bethlehem and he ascended into heaven from the Mount of Olives; at Bethlehem he began his struggles for mankind, for which on the Mount of Olives he received a crown. So you have many witnesses: you have the place of the resurrection here; you have also the place of the ascension to the east of us. You have other witnesses too: the angels who testified there, the cloud he mounted, and the disciples who came down from the mountain.

CATECHESIS 18

For the candidates for baptism On 'and in one holy catholic church, and in the resurrection of the flesh, and in everlasting life'

Reading: Ezek 37.1: 'And the hand of the Lord came upon me, and he led me out in the Holy Spirit, and set me in the middle of the plain, and it was full of bones . . .'

32 Beloved brothers and sisters, the remaining part of this instruction will be devoted to encouraging you to prepare your souls to receive the heavenly graces. By the Lord's grace over the past days of Lent I have given you as many catechetical addresses as I could concerning the holy apostolic Creed which was delivered to you for your profession.[1] Not that these were the only things we needed to tell you; there are many matters which we have passed over or which have been developed at greater length by those who are perhaps better teachers. But when the holy day of Easter comes, the day when your charity will be enlightened[2] in Christ through the 'washing of rebirth' (Tit 3.5), you will receive, God willing, the further teaching you will need: concerning the devotion and order with which the called should enter; the purpose of each of the holy mysteries of baptism; the devotion and order with which you should proceed from baptism to God's holy altar, and enjoy there the spiritual, heavenly mysteries. In this way your soul will be enlightened in advance through instruction on every point, and you will learn how sublime the graces are which you will receive from God.[3]

33 After the holy and saving day of Easter, starting on Monday every day of the following week,[4] after the assembly you will enter the holy place of the resurrection, where, God willing, you will hear further catechetical instructions. You will receive further teaching about the reasons for everything that is done, and you will receive

proofs from the Old and New Testaments: first concerning what is done immediately before baptism; then how the Lord purifies you from your sins 'by the bath of water in the word' (Eph 5.26); how like priests you began to share Christ's name, and you were given the seal of the 'fellowship of the Holy Spirit' (Eph 5.26); concerning the mysteries which take place on the altar of the new covenant and which were instituted here, the teachings which the holy Scriptures have passed on to us, the power of these mysteries, how and when you should approach them, and how you should hold them; and finally how in future you ought to behave in deed and word so as to be worthy of the grace and gain eternal life. These things, God willing, will be explained to you.[5] . . .

MYSTAGOGIC CATECHESIS 1

To the newly baptized

Reading: 1 Peter 5.8–11: 'Be sober and wakeful . . .'

1 True-born and longed for children of the Church, for some time I have been looking forward to the day when I would explain to you these spiritual and heavenly mysteries. But since I saw clearly that seeing is much more convincing than hearing, I waited until the present moment, until this night had made you more receptive to what I was going to say, so that I could lead you into the brighter and more fragrant meadow here in Paradise. Besides, you are now able to understand the more divine mysteries concerning baptism, the divine source of life.[1] Since then it remains for me to spread before you a feast of more perfect instruction, listen and I shall explain these things for you in greater detail. In this way you will be able to learn the meaning for you of what happened on that night of your baptism.

2 You began by entering the outer hall of the baptistery. Standing with your face to the west, you heard a voice instructing you to stretch out your hand, and you renounced Satan as though he stood there before you. You ought to know that the symbolic meaning[2] of these events is to be found in the Old Testament. For when the cruel tyrant Pharaoh in his anger was oppressing the free and noble Hebrew people,[3] God sent Moses to rescue them from their sufferings as the Egyptians' slaves. The doorposts were smeared with the lamb's blood to make the destroyer avoid the houses bearing the sign, and miraculously the Hebrew people were set free. After their release Pharaoh[4] pursued them, and when he saw that the sea parted miraculously for them, he still pressed on, following in their footsteps, until suddenly he was submerged to be drowned in the Red Sea.

3 I invite you now to turn your attention from the old to the new, from symbol to reality. There Moses was sent by God to

Egypt; here Christ is sent from the Father into the world; there to lead his oppressed people out of Egypt, here Christ is sent to rescue his people in the world who are afflicted by sin; there the blood of the lamb warded off the destroyer, here the blood of the spotless Lamb Jesus Christ puts the demons to flight. Of old the tyrant pursued the people into the sea; in your case this headstrong, shameless demon, who is the origin of all evil, followed you even into the springs of salvation. The earlier tyrant was drowned in the sea; here the tyrant disappears in the water of salvation.

4 Nonetheless you hear a voice telling you to stretch out your hand and say to him as if he were there before you: 'I renounce you, Satan.'[5] I want to tell you why you stand facing west, for you need to know. The west is the region of visible darkness, and Satan is himself darkness and exerts his power in the dark. This is the meaning of the symbol of facing the west to renounce the prince of darkness and gloom. What then did you each stand and say? 'I renounce you, Satan, you evil and savage tyrant', meaning: 'I no longer fear your strength. For Christ has abolished it by allowing me to partake of his blood and his flesh, so as to destroy death by death through these his sufferings and to release me from perpetual slavery (cf. Heb 2.14–15). I renounce you, you subtle and crafty serpent. I renounce you, you schemer, who on the pretext of friendship introduced all wickedness and brought about the rebellion of our ancestors. I renounce you, Satan, author and partner in every evil.'

5 Then you are told to pronounce a second phrase: 'And all your works'. Satan's works are every sin, which you must renounce, in the same way that someone who has escaped from a tyrant has escaped from his weapons as well. Every kind of sin is numbered among the devil's works. But I want you to realize that your words, especially at such an awe-inspiring moment as this, are inscribed in God's invisible records.[6] So if ever you are caught doing something that contradicts your words, you will be judged a criminal. So renounce Satan's works, by which I mean all irrational actions and thoughts.

6 Then you say: 'And all his pomp'. These are the devil's pomp: a passion for the theatre, horse-races, hunting and all other such vain pursuits as those from which the saint begged God to free him when he said: 'Turn away my eyes from beholding vanity' (Ps 118 (119).37). Do not indulge in a passion for the theatre, where the actors put on indecent spectacles full of every kind of shameless obscenity, and effeminate men perform wild dances. Do not share

the passion of hunters who expose themselves to wild beasts in order to indulge their wretched stomachs; to pamper their bellies with food they become themselves food for the stomachs of savage beasts. To tell the truth, for the sake of their belly, which is their own God, they fight for their lives in single combat on the edge of a precipice.[7] Avoid the races, a mad spectacle which unseats the soul. All these things are the devil's pomp.

7 There are other things numbered among the devil's pomps, objects hung up in the temples of idols and at their feasts, such as meat and loaves, which are polluted by the invocation of abominable demons. For just as in the Eucharist the bread and wine before the invocation of the adorable Trinity was ordinary bread and wine, but after the invocation the bread becomes Christ's body and the wine Christ's blood, so too these foods which form part of Satan's pomp are of their own nature ordinary food, but are contaminated by the invocation of demons.[8]

8 Next you say: 'And your worship'. The devil's worship consists of prayers in the temples of idols, honours paid to lifeless idols, the lighting of lamps or burning of incense by springs and rivers. Some people have been tricked by dreams or demons into acting in this way, thinking they will even find a cure for bodily ailments, but you must have no part in such doings. Taking the auspices, divination, omens, amulets, writing on leaves, the use of charms or other spells – such things are the devil's worship. So avoid such actions, for if you give way to them after renouncing Satan and siding with Christ,[9] you will find the tyrant will treat you more savagely. Perhaps he treated you before as one of his family and spared you from some of the harshness of his service; but now that you have bitterly enraged him, not only will you lose Christ but you will learn what Satan is really like. You heard us telling you the story in the Old Testament about Lot and his daughters, didn't you? Wasn't he saved with his daughters when he reached the mountain, but his wife was turned into a pillar of salt, pilloried for all eternity to preserve the memory of the bad disposition she showed in looking back.[10] Think of your own good, then, and once you have put your hand to the plough (cf. Lk 9.62), don't turn back to the bitter concerns of this life. Escape to the mountain,[11] to Jesus Christ, to the stone cut without human hands which filled the world (cf. Dan 2.34–45).

9 So when you renounce Satan and trample underfoot every contract you have made with him,[12] you annul the old treaty made with hell, and there opens before you God's paradise which he planted in

the east, and from which our ancestor was expelled because of his disobedience. You symbolize this by turning from the west to the east, which is the region of light. Then you are instructed to say: 'I believe in the Father and in the Son and in the Holy Spirit and in one baptism of repentance.' I spoke to you at length about these things in the earlier instructions according to the grace God gave me.[13]

10 So be strengthened by these words, and be sober. For our enemy the devil, as we have just heard in the reading, is prowling round like a lion seeking someone to devour. In the past death was strong and devoured; but now in the time of the holy font of rebirth 'God has taken away all tears from every face'.[14] Now that you have put off the old man (cf. Col 3.9), you mourn no longer; having put on Jesus Christ, 'the robe of salvation' (Is 61.10 (LXX)), you are in festal mood.

11 These events took place in the outer room. God willing, when in our next explanations of the mysteries we enter the holy of holies, we shall learn the meaning of the rites which were celebrated there. To God the Father are glory, power and majesty with the Son and the Holy Spirit for ever and ever. Amen.

MYSTAGOGIC CATECHESIS 2

Concerning baptism

Reading: Rom 6.3–14: 'Do you not know that all of us who have been baptized into Christ Jesus have been baptized into his death? . . .'

1 Our daily explanations of the mysteries and our new instructions announcing new realities have a special value for you who have been made new and passed from the old state to the new. So I now have to put before you the sequel to yesterday's instruction so that you can understand the meaning of the rites which you celebrated in the inner room.

2 As soon as you entered, you took off your tunic, to show that you were putting off the old man with his deeds (cf. Col 3.9). Once you had taken it off you were naked, in this way imitating Christ naked on the cross, who in his nakedness 'disarmed the principalities and powers' and boldly 'triumphed over them' on the tree of the cross.[1] Since the hostile powers made their lair in our bodies, you can no longer wear that old tunic – of course I am not referring to this visible one but to 'the old man which was subject to the deceptions of its corrupting lusts'. May the soul that has once taken this old man off never put it on again, but rather say, like Christ's bride in the Song of Songs: 'I have taken off my tunic. How could I put it on?' (Cant 5.3). What a wonderful thing! You were naked in the eyes of all and felt no shame. In fact you were imitating the first man Adam, who was 'naked' in Paradise 'but not ashamed' (Gen 2.25).

3 Then, once you had removed your clothes, you were anointed with exorcised oil from the topmost hairs of your head to the lowest parts of your body, and became sharers in Jesus Christ, the true olive. You were cut from the wild olive and grafted on to the true olive, and began to share in the richness of the genuine olive.[2] So

the exorcised oil is a symbol of this share in the richness of Christ, and it wards off every trace of the enemy power.[3] For just as the breathing of the saints and the invocation of God burns like the fiercest flame and chases away the demons, so too the invocation of God together with prayer gives this exorcised oil such power that it can burn away the traces of sin and even repel the hidden powers of the evil one.

4 After this you were led to the holy pool of sacred baptism, just as Christ was taken from the cross to the tomb which stands before you.[4] Then you were each asked if you believed in the name of the Father and of the Son and of the Holy Spirit. You made the saving profession of faith and three times you were immersed in the water and came up from it again.[5] There in the font you symbolically re-enacted Christ's three-day burial. For just as our Saviour spent three days and three nights in the heart of the earth, so too when you came up the first time you were imitating Christ's first day in the earth and when you submerged his first night. A man in the dark can no longer see, but during the day a man lives in the light; so too when you submerged you could see nothing, as if it were night, but when you came up again it was as if you were in daylight. At the same moment you both died and were born; that saving water became your tomb but also your mother. So what Solomon said in another context could be adapted to you. For in his book he wrote: 'There is a time for giving birth and a time for dying' (Eccles 3.2 (LXX)). But with you it is the other way round: there is a time for dying and a time for being born, and one and the same time produces both results: your birth coincided with your death.

5 What a strange and wonderful thing! We did not literally die, we were not literally buried, we did not literally rise again after being crucified. We experienced these things only in symbols and representations; but salvation we experienced literally. Christ was really crucified and really buried and literally rose again, and all of this he did for our sake, so that by sharing his sufferings in imitation, we might gain salvation in truth. What unmeasured love this showed for mankind! Christ received the nails in his pure hands and experienced pain, and grants me salvation through sharing his experience without the pain and the toil.

6 No one should imagine that baptism only confers the forgiveness of sins and the grace of adoption, just as John's baptism only conferred the forgiveness of sins. We should be clear about this,[6] that just as baptism cleans away our sins and conveys the gift of the Holy Spirit, so too it represents Christ's sufferings.[7] This is the

meaning of Paul's words which you heard proclaimed just now: 'Do you not understand that we who were baptized into Christ Jesus were all baptized into his death? So we were buried with him through baptism' (Rom 6.3–4). Perhaps in writing this he had in mind people who believed that baptism conveys forgiveness of sins and adoption, but didn't yet realize that it contains a share by imitation in what Christ suffered in reality.

7 It was to teach us that what Christ suffered 'for us and our salvation'[8] truly and not in make-believe, and that we have become sharers in his sufferings – it was for this reason that Paul declared with such clarity: 'For if we have been planted with him in the likeness of his death, we shall be planted with him also in the likeness of his resurrection' (Rom 6.5). The expression 'planted with him' is well chosen, for it is here[9] that the true vine was planted, and we have been planted with him through sharing in the baptism of his death.[10] Concentrate all your attention on the apostle's words. He didn't say 'if we are planted with him in his death', but 'in the likeness of his death'. It was a real death that Christ really experienced, for his soul was separated from his body; and his burial was real, for his holy body was wrapped in a clean winding-sheet, and everything was done for him in reality. For us, however, there is the likeness of his death and his sufferings, but of salvation not the likeness but the reality.

8 Now that you have been given a full explanation of these truths, I urge you to keep them in your memory, so that I can say of you, unworthy though I am: 'I love you, because you always remember me and have kept the traditions which I passed on to you' (1 Cor 11.2 adjusted). God, who has brought you to life from the dead, has the power to grant you to 'walk in newness of life' (Rom 6.4). For to him is the glory and the power now and for ever. Amen.

MYSTAGOGIC CATECHESIS 3

Concerning the anointing with chrism

Reading: 1 Jn 2.20–8: 'And you have received the anointing from God and know everything . . .'

1 Now that you have been baptized and have put on Christ, you have been shaped to the likeness of the Son of God. For when God predestined us for adoption, he shaped us to the likeness of Christ's glorious body. So now that you have shared in Christ, you are correctly called 'christs' [anointed ones], so that God's words 'Do not touch my christs' applies to you (Ps 104 (105).15). You have become christs now that you have received the sacramental sign[1] of the Holy Spirit. Since you are images of Christ, everything which was done to you has a symbolic meaning.[2]

When Christ had washed in the River Jordan and shared the touch of his divinity[3] with the waters, he came up from them, and the Holy Spirit descended on him in substantial form, like resting upon like.[4] So too when you came up from the holy waters of the font your anointing took place, the sacramental sign of the anointing which Christ received. This anointing is the Holy Spirit, concerning whom blessed Isaiah spoke in the person of Christ in his prophecy concerning him: 'The Holy Spirit has come upon me; that is why he has anointed me and sent me to announce the good news to the poor' (Is 61.1).

2 Christ did not receive a human anointing with bodily olive-oil or *muron*;[5] it was the Father who anointed him with the Holy Spirit in proclaiming him Saviour of the whole world.[6] Thus Peter spoke of 'Jesus of Narareth, whom God anointed with the Holy Spirit' (Acts 10.38), and the prophet David proclaimed: 'Your throne, O God, lasts from age to age; the sceptre of your kingdom is a rod of righteousness. You have loved justice and hated wickedness; there-

fore God, your God has anointed you with the oil of gladness beyond your fellows' (Ps 44.7–8 (45.6–7)).

Just as Christ was truly crucified and buried and rose again, while you are privileged in baptism to be crucified, to be buried and to rise again with him in likeness, so it is with the anointing with chrism. He was anointed with the spiritual 'oil of gladness', that is, with the Holy Spirit, which is called the oil of gladness because it causes spiritual gladness; you were anointed with *muron* and became partners with Christ and began to share with him.

3 Beware of imagining that this is ordinary ointment. For just as after the invocation of the Holy Spirit the bread of the Eucharist is no longer ordinary bread but the body of Christ, so too with the invocation this holy *muron* is no longer ordinary or, so to say, common ointment, but Christ's grace which imparts to us his own divinity through the presence of the Holy Spirit.[7] To symbolize this truth you are anointed on your forehead and on your other senses. Your body is anointed with visible *muron*, while your soul is sanctified by the life-giving Spirit.

4 First you are anointed on the forehead so as to be released from the shame which the first sinner carried around everywhere, and to reflect the glory of the Lord with face unveiled (cf. Exod 34.29; 2 Cor 3.18). Next you are anointed on the ears, so as to be given the ears spoken of by Isaiah (50.4 (LXX)): 'And the Lord has given me an ear to hear', and by the Lord in the Gospels: 'He that has ears to hear, let him hear' (Mt 11.15). Next you are anointed on the nostrils, so that you may say, if you retain the sacred *muron*: 'We are Christ's sweet fragrance before God among those who are saved' (2 Cor 2.15). After this you are anointed on your breast, so that you may 'put on the breastplate of righteousness', and stand firm against 'the devil's wiles' (Eph 6.14, 11). For just as the Saviour went out and defeated his adversary after his baptism and the descent of the Holy Spirit, so too once you have been baptized and received the mystical anointing and put on the armour of the Holy Spirit, you have to stand against the power ranged against you and defeat it. For you can say: 'I can do all things in Christ who empowers me' (Phil 4.13).

5 Now that you have received the privilege of this holy anointing, you are called Christians, a name which truly reflects your birth. For before you were admitted to baptism and the grace of the Holy Spirit you had not properly qualified for the name though you were on the way to becoming Christians.

6 You must understand that the symbolic explanation[8] of this anointing with chrism is to be found in the Old Testament. For when Moses passed God's command on to his brother and installed him as high priest, he first made him bathe and then anointed him. Thus he was called the 'christ' – a word derived from the anointing. So too when the high priest made Solomon king, he anointed him after making him bathe in the Gihon (1 Kings 1.38–9). These rites were performed for them as a prefiguration,[9] but for you not as a prefiguration but in reality, because your salvation began with the one who was anointed in reality by the Holy Spirit. For he is truly the firstfruits and you are the whole lump (cf. Rom 11.16); if the firstfruits are holy, it is clear that the holiness will spread to the whole lump.

7 Preserve this anointing unstained, for it will teach you everything if it remains in you, as you have just heard blessed John saying in the course of his many reflections on the anointing with chrism. For this sacred gift is the spiritual protection for your body and salvation for your soul.

Long ago in ancient times blessed Isaiah proclaimed this prophecy: 'And the Lord will do this for all the nations on the mountain' (by the 'mountain' he means the Church both here and in other places, as when he says: 'And in the last days the Lord's mountain will be revealed' (Is 2.2 (LXX)). 'They will drink wine, they will drink gladness, they will be anointed with *muron*.' And to assure you that you are being told about this *muron* in a mystic sense he continues: 'Pass all these things on to the nations, for the Lord's decree applies to all the nations.'[10]

Now that you have been anointed with this holy *muron*, keep it pure and spotless within yourselves by making progress in good works and becoming pleasing to the 'pioneer of your salvation' (Heb 2.10), Christ Jesus, to whom is the glory for ever and ever. Amen.

MYSTAGOGIC CATECHESIS 4

Concerning Christ's body and blood

Reading: 1 Cor 11.23ff: 'For I received from the Lord the account which I passed on to you . . .'

1 This teaching of blessed Paul is sufficient to give us assurance concerning the sacred mysteries to which you were admitted when you became 'of one body' (Eph 3.6) and one blood with Christ. For we heard Paul declare just now: 'For on the night on which our Lord Jesus Christ was betrayed, taking bread and giving thanks he broke it and gave it to his disciples saying: "Take, eat, this is my body." And taking the cup and giving thanks he said: "Take, drink, this is my blood." '[1] Since then Christ himself taught us concerning the bread, saying: 'This is my body', who will dare to doubt any more? And since he has declared explicitly: 'This is my blood', who will ever hesitate and say it is not his blood?

2 Once at Cana in Galilee Jesus changed the water into wine by his own will. Isn't it reasonable then to believe that he changed wine into blood? When he was invited to a human wedding he performed this marvellous miracle; isn't it much more believable that he gave the 'sons of the bridegroom' (Mk 2.19) the enjoyment of his own body and blood?

3 So we receive with full assurance that what we are receiving is a share in Christ's body and blood. For in the form of bread you are given his body, and in the form of wine you are given his blood, so that by partaking of Christ's body and blood you may become of one body and one blood with Christ. In this way we become Christ-bearers, as his body and blood are spread around our limbs. Thus we become in blessed Peter's words 'sharers of his divine nature' (cf. 2 Pet 1.4).

4 In an address to the Jews Christ once said: 'Unless you eat my flesh and drink my blood, you do not have life within you' (Jn

6.53). Failing to understand the spiritual meaning of his words, they took scandal and departed, believing that the Saviour was urging them to cannibalism.

5 In the Old Testament there were 'Loaves of the Presence' (Exod 25.30; Lev 24.5–9; 1 Sam 21.2–6), but as they belonged to the Old Testament they came to an end. In the New Testament there is the bread of heaven and the cup of salvation, which sanctify both body and soul. Just as the bread is suitable for the body, so the Word is adapted to the soul.

6 So do not regard them as ordinary bread and wine, for they are the body and blood according to the Lord's declaration. For though your senses suggest this to you, let your faith reassure you. Do not judge by the taste, but draw from your faith unhesitating confidence that you have been granted Christ's body and blood.

7 Blessed David hints at what this means when he says: 'You have prepared a table before me in the face of those who afflict me.'[2] He means something like this: Before your coming the demons prepared for human beings a table that was polluted and defiled, filled with diabolical power; but after your coming, Lord, you prepared a table before me. When a man says to God: 'You have prepared a table before me', what else can it mean if not this mystical, spiritual table which God has prepared 'in the face of' the demons, that is, against or in opposition to them. The words are appropriate, for the one table involved communion with demons, the other involves communion with God. 'You have anointed my head with oil.' He anointed your head on the forehead with oil, by means of the seal which you receive from God, to make you 'the engraving of a signet: "Holy to the Lord"'.[3] 'And your cup which inebriates me, how strong it is!' (Ps 22 (23).5 (LXX)). As you can see, this refers to the cup which Jesus took into his hands and blessed saying: 'This is my blood which is shed for many for the forgiveness of their sins.'[4]

8 It is in reference to this grace that Solomon says enigmatically in Ecclesiastes: 'Come, eat your bread with gladness' (this spiritual bread). 'Come' (the author issues the saving invitation that offers happiness), 'and drink your wine with a good heart' (the spiritual wine), 'and let oil be poured over your head' (do you notice that the author is hinting at the mystic anointing with chrism?), and 'let your garments always be white', 'because the Lord has approved of your deeds'.[5]

Now that you have taken off your old garments and put on ones that are spiritually white, you must wear white always. Of course, I do not mean that you must always be dressed in white garments, but that you must always be dressed in garments that are *truly* white and shining and spiritual, so that you can say with blessed Isaiah: 'Let my soul rejoice in the Lord, for he has clothed me in the garment of salvation and arrayed me in the tunic of gladness.' (Is 61.10).

9 You have learnt with full assurance that what looks like bread, despite its taste, is not bread but Christ's body; that what looks like wine is not wine, despite what its taste suggests, but Christ's blood; and that this is what David long ago was referring to in the psalm: 'and bread strengthens the human heart, to make his face joyful with oil' (Ps 103 (104).15 (LXX)). So strengthen your heart by partaking of this bread in the knowledge that it is spiritual, and make the face of your soul joyful. So with a 'pure conscience' (1 Tim 3.9; 2 Tim 1.3), 'with face unveiled', 'and reflecting the glory of God', may you go forward 'from glory to glory' (2 Cor 3.18) in Christ Jesus our Lord, to whom is the glory for ever and ever. Amen.

MYSTAGOGIC CATECHESIS 5

Reading: 1 Peter 2.1ff: 'Therefore setting aside all evil and guile and slander . . .'

1 By God's goodness you have heard in the previous meetings all you needed to know about baptism, the anointing with chrism, and the partaking of Christ's body and blood. Now I must move on to what comes next, and today I shall set the coping-stone that is needed on the spiritual building.

2 So you saw the deacon giving water for washing to the bishop[1] and to the presbyters standing round God's altar. Of course, the deacon wasn't doing this because of any dirt on their bodies; that was not the reason: we didn't enter the church with dirt on our bodies in the first place. The washing was a symbol of our need to be cleansed of all our sins and transgressions. Since our hands stand for our actions, in washing them we are clearly symbolizing purity and blamelessness of action. Surely you heard blessed David's explanation of this rite: 'I shall wash my hands among the innocent, and walk around your altar, Lord' (Ps 25 (26).6 (LXX)). So to wash one's hands means not to be guilty of any sins.

3 Then the deacon calls out: 'Greet one another; let us kiss one another.' Don't take this kiss to be like the kiss friends exchange when they meet in the market-place. This is something different; this kiss expresses a union of souls and is a plea for complete reconciliation. The kiss then is a sign that our souls are united and all grudges banished. This is what our Lord meant when he said: 'If you are offering your gift on the altar and remember there that your brother has a complaint against you, leave your gift on the altar and go first and be reconciled with your brother and then come and offer your gift' (Mt 5.23–4). Thus the kiss is reconciliation, and so is holy, as blessed Paul implied when he proclaimed: 'Greet one an-

other with a holy kiss'; and Peter: 'Greet one another with the kiss of charity.'[2]

4 After this the bishop calls out: 'Lift up your hearts.'[3] For indeed at this most awesome[4] hour we ought to hold our hearts up to God and not keep them down below involved with the earth and earthly things. In effect then the bishop is telling you all at this moment to lay aside the cares of this life and domestic worries and hold your hearts up to the loving God in heaven.

Then you reply: 'We hold them up to the Lord', acknowledging by these words that you accept the bishop's instruction. Let no one present be disposed to say with their lips: 'We hold them up to the Lord', while in their thoughts keeping their mind involved with earthly cares. You should then keep God in mind at all times; but if human weakness makes this impossible, at least at this moment you should make this your ideal.

5 Then the bishop says: 'Let us give thanks to the Lord.' We should indeed thank him for calling us to so great a grace when we were unworthy, for reconciling us when we were his enemies, for granting us the privilege of receiving the 'Spirit of adoption' (Rom 8.15). Then you say: 'It is worthy and just.' For when we give thanks we perform a worthy and just action; but our Benefactor did not do what was just but what was more than just when he chose us to receive such great favours.

6 After this we call to mind heaven, the earth, the sea, the sun and the moon, the stars, every creature both rational and irrational, visible and invisible, the Angels, the Archangels, the Dominions, the Principalities, the Powers, the Thrones and the many-faced Cherubim,[5] saying in effect with David: 'Bless the Lord with me' (Ps 33.4 (34.3)). We also call to mind the Seraphim, whom Isaiah was inspired by the Holy Spirit to see standing round God's throne, using two wings to cover his face, two his feet, and two to fly, saying all the time: 'Holy, holy, holy, Lord Sabaoth.'[6] For the reason why[7] we recite this doxology which the Seraphim taught us is to share in the singing of the celestial armies.

7 Then, when we have sanctified ourselves through these spiritual hymns, we call upon the God who loves mankind to send down the Holy Spirit on the offerings so as to make the bread Christ's body and the wine Christ's blood, for whatever the Holy Spirit touches is made holy and transformed.

8 Then, after the completion of the spiritual sacrifice,[8] the worship without blood, we call upon God over this sacrifice of propitiation for the peace of all the churches, the stability of the world, for

kings, for our armies and allies, for the sick and the suffering, and in short for all who need help, and in intercession we all offer this sacrifice.

9 Then we commemorate those who have gone to their rest, first of all the patriarchs, prophets, apostles and martyrs, so that God may receive our petitions in answer to their prayers and intercessions. Then we pray for our holy ancestors and bishops who have gone to their rest, and in general for all who have gone to their rest before us, for we believe that great benefit will result for the souls for whom prayer is offered when the holy and most awesome sacrifice lies on the altar.

10 I would like to use a comparison to convince you of the truth of this. I know many people say: 'What good does it do for a soul to be commemorated in the offering once it has departed from this world, with or without sins?' Well then, suppose a king had banished some citizens who had offended him, and then their friends wove a garland and presented it to the king on behalf of the exiles. Wouldn't he grant them a remission of their punishment? In the same way, when we offer our petitions to God on behalf of the departed, even if they were sinners, instead of weaving a garland we offer Christ who was immolated for our sins, and thus, on their behalf and our own, we propitiate the God who loves mankind.

11 Then after this you make the prayer which the Saviour taught his own disciples. With a clear conscience[9] you name God as Father saying: 'Our Father who art in the heavens.' How great is God's love for mankind! Those who have recoiled from him and lie in the worst of plights are given so generous a pardon for their crimes and a gift of grace that he allows them to call him 'Father'. Our Father, who art in the heavens. One could take the 'heavens' to refer to those who bear the image of the heavenly man, those among whom God dwells and walks (cf. 1 Cor 15.49; Lev 26.11–12; Ezek 37.27).

12 'Hallowed be thy name.' God's name is holy of itself, whether we say so or not. However, since his name is sometimes profaned among sinners, according to the text: 'Through you my name is everywhere profaned among the gentiles' (Is 52.5; Rom 2.24), we pray that God's name may be hallowed among us. Not that his name used not to be holy and has now become holy; it becomes holy in us when we become holy and act in a way that is worthy of our sanctification.

13 'Thy kingdom come.' Only a pure soul can say 'Thy kingdom come' unreservedly. For only if we have paid attention to Paul's words: 'So do not allow sin to reign in your mortal body',[10] and

purify ourselves in deed and thought and word, will we be able to say to God: 'Thy kingdom come.'

14 'Thy will be done on earth as it is in heaven.' God's sacred and blessed angels do his will, as David said in the psalm: 'Bless the Lord, all you his angels, powerful and strong, who carry out his word' (Ps 102 (103).20). So when you make this prayer you are in effect saying: 'May your will be done in me on earth, Lord, as it is among the angels.'

15 'Give us this day our substantial bread.'[11] The ordinary bread we know is not substantial; but this holy bread is substantial in the sense that it is assimilated by the substance of the soul. This bread does not go down into the belly to be discharged into the privy; it is distributed throughout your whole constitution to the benefit of soul as well as body. 'This day' stands for 'every day', in accordance with Paul's saying: 'as long as there is a today to be named' (Heb 3.13).

16 'And forgive us our trespasses as we forgive those who trespass against us.' We have many sins, for we stumble in word and in thought, and many of our deeds deserve condemnation. 'And if we say that we have no sin, we lie', as John says (1 Jn 1.8). So we make an agreement with God, requesting him to pardon our sins as we forgive our neighbours' debts. So remembering how much we receive and how little we offer in return, let us forgive one another without delay or procrastination. The offences offered to us are slight and trivial and easily righted, but the offences we offer God are serious, and we must simply rely on his good will. So be careful not to debar yourself from receiving God's pardon for your serious sins because of the slight and trivial wrongs which you have suffered yourself.

17 'And lead us not into temptation', Lord. Do the Lord's words teach us to pray not to be tempted in any way? What do other passages say? 'A man who is not tempted is not tested';[12] and again, 'Count it all joy, brethren, when you meet with many kinds of temptation' (James 1.2). But it seems to me that to enter into temptation is not the same as to be drowned by temptation. For temptation is like a torrent which is hard to cross. Those who are not drowned in temptations get across because they are the best swimmers and are not dragged under; but those who go into the water without the same ability are drowned, just as, to give an example, Judas fell into the temptation of avarice and was unable to swim across, but was drowned both bodily and spiritually, and suffocated.[13] Peter on the other hand fell into the temptation of

denial, but though he fell into it, he was not drowned but swam across manfully and escaped from the temptation.

Listen to another passage speaking of the chorus of saints who have come through unscathed and give thanks for their release from temptation: 'You have tested us, O Lord, and tried us in the fire like silver; you have led us into the trap. You have loaded our backs with afflictions and raised men over our heads. We passed through fire and water, and you brought us out to a place of rest' (Ps 65 (66).10–12). Did you notice how confidently they spoke about crossing without being snared? 'And you brought us out to a place of rest.' To come to a place of rest means to be rescued from temptation.

18 'But deliver us from the Evil One.'[14] If the prayer 'lead us not into temptation' ensured that we would not be tempted in any way, he would not have said: 'But deliver us from the Evil One.' The Evil One is the demon ranged against us, from whom we pray to be delivered.

Then after the completion of the prayer you say 'Amen', sealing the prayer which God taught us with the word 'Amen', which means 'Let it be so'.

19 After this the bishop says: 'Holy things for the holy.' The offerings are holy, because they have received the descent of the Holy Spirit, and you are holy too because you have been granted the Holy Spirit;[15] thus the holy things are appropriate for holy people. Then you say: 'One is holy, one is Lord, Jesus Christ.' For truly there is one who is holy, holy by nature; for though we are holy, we are not so by nature, but by participation and discipline and prayer.

20 After this you hear the cantor to a sacred melody encouraging you to receive the holy mysteries. 'Taste and see', he sings, 'the goodness of the Lord' (Ps 33.9 (34.8)). Do not rely on the judgment of your physical throat but on that of unhesitating faith. For what you taste is not bread and wine but Christ's body and blood, which they symbolize.[16]

21 So when you approach do not come with your wrists extended or your fingers parted. Make your left hand a throne for your right, which is about to receive the King, and receive Christ's body in the hollow of your hand, replying 'Amen'. Before you consume it, carefully bless your eyes with the touch of the holy body,[17] watching not to lose any part of it; for if you do lose any of it, it is as if it were part of your own body that is being lost. Tell me, if someone gave you some golden filings, wouldn't you keep them safe and take care not to incur a loss through mislaying any of them? So

shouldn't you take much greater care not to drop any crumbs of what is more precious than gold or gems?

22 Then after receiving Christ's body, approach the cup of his blood. Do not stretch out your hands; bow down, say 'Amen' as a form of worship or adoration, and sanctify yourself by partaking of Christ's blood. While your lips are still moist, touch them lightly with your hands and bless your eyes, your forehead and your other senses. Then as you wait for the prayer, thank God for admitting you to these great mysteries.

23 Preserve these traditions inviolate and keep yourselves free from offence. Do not debar yourselves from communion,[18] and do not deprive yourselves of these holy and spiritual mysteries by incurring the stain of sin.

'May the God of peace sanctify you wholly, and may your body and your soul and your spirit be kept unscathed at the coming of our Lord Jesus Christ' (1 Thess 5.23), to whom is the glory for ever and ever. Amen.

NOTES

1 CYRIL'S LIFE

1 Jerome, *Chron.* (PL 27.683–4).

2 W. Telfer, *Cyril of Jerusalem and Nemesius of Emesa*, LCC 4, London, SCM Press, 1955, p. 19.

3 *pro . . . holōn hebdomēkonta etōn* (*Cat.* 6.20). Telfer, *Cyril*, pp. 37–8 has other arguments. The copyist gives 352 as the date for the *Catecheses*; this is not impossible. See sect. 3 below, note 5.

4 *tēn akolouthian tēs timēs*. For the Nicene canon see N.P. Tanner (ed.), *Decrees of the Ecumenical Councils*, London and Washington, DC, Sheed and Ward and Georgetown University Press, p. 9; J. Stevenson and W.H.C. Frend, *A New Eusebius*, 2nd edn, London, SPCK, p. 340.

5 See P.W.L. Walker, *Holy City, Holy Places? Christian Attitudes to Jerusalem and the Holy Land in the Fourth Century*, Oxford, Clarendon Press, 1990.

6 Socrates, *HE* 2.40; Touttée, PG 33.69–72.

7 Sozomen, *HE* 4.25; Theodoret, *HE* 2.22.

8 Theodoret, *HE* 2.23.

9 Socrates, *HE* 3.1; Sozomen, *HE* 5.4–5.

10 Theodoret (*HE* 3.10) gives a colourful account of this adventure.

11 Epiphanius, *Adv. Haer.* 73.37 (PG 42.472B, C).

12 Gregory of Nyssa (ed. G. Pasquali), Letter *On Pilgrimages* 2.10, 12 (*Gregorii Nysseni Opera* viii/2, Leiden, Brill, 1959).

13 Sozomen, *HE* 7.7; cf. Socrates, *HE* 5.8.

14 On Cyril's 'homoean' theology, see Sozomen, *HE* 4.25, and also p. 61. For Macedonius, see Sozomen, *HE* 4.26–7.

15 P. Nautin, 'La date du "de viris illustribus" de Jérôme, de la mort de Cyrille de Jérusalem et de celle de Grégoire de Nazzianze', *RHE* 56 (1961), 33–5.

2 JERUSALEM

1 For an account of recent archaeological research I am indebted to S. Gibson and J.E. Taylor, *Beneath the Church of the Holy Sepulchre, Jerusalem*, London, Palestinian Exploration Fund, 1994 (= GT). But see J.

Murphy-O'Connor's criticisms in *Revue biblique* 103 (1996), 301–3. See also A. Cameron and S.G. Hall, *Eusebius, Life of Constantine*, Oxford, Clarendon Press, 1999 (= CH), and Martin Biddle's beautifully illustrated *The Tomb of Christ*, Stroud, Sutton Publishing, 1999.

2 This is the story told in the *Golden Legend*; cf. R. Greenacre and J. Haselock, *The Sacrament of Easter*, Leominster, Gracewing, 1989, p. 68.

3 Jerome, *Com. Matt.* 27.33 (PL 26.209); GT 56–60.

4 Jn 19.41; Cyril, *Cat.* 13.32.

5 Lk 23.53; Cyril, *Cat.* 13.35.

6 GT 68–70; Jerome, *Com. Esa.* 1.2.9 (CSEL 73.33); Cassius Dio, *Hist. Rom.* 69.12.

7 GT 70, with references to Origen, *Com. Matt.* 24.15 (GCS 12.193–4); Bordeaux Pilgrim, *Itin.* 591.4 (CCSL 175.16); Jerome, *Com. Matt.* 24.15 (PL 26.177).

8 Eusebius, *Vit. Const.* 3.26.

9 GT 71.

10 Eusebius, *Onomastikon* 74.19–21; Jerome, Ep. 58.3 (PL 22.581); GT 68–9.

11 GT 68–9.

12 'sub praesentia matris suae' (Egeria, *Pereg.* 25.9).

13 Ambrose, *de ob. Theod.* 41–51; Socrates, *HE* 1.17; Sozomen, *HE* 2.1; Cyril, *Cat.* 13.4; *ad Const.* 3.

14 In an earlier article, 'Who Planned the Churches at the Christian Holy Places in the Holy Land?' (*StPatr* 18(1) (1985), 105–9), I overlooked this point, and suggested that Golgotha was discovered after the Tomb.

15 Cf. H.A. Drake, 'Eusebius on the True Cross', *JEH* 36 (1985), 1–22; J.W. Drijvers, *Helena Augusta: The Mother of Constantine and the Legend of Her Finding of the True Cross*, Leiden, Brill, 1991, pp. 83–6; GT 84–5.

16 Cyril, *Cat.* 4.10; 10.19; *ad Const.* 3.

17 Ambrose, *de ob. Theod.* 47–8; Socrates, *HE* 1.17; Sozomen, *HE* 2.1.

18 Constantine, *Oratio ad sanctorum Coetum* 1.18 (PG 20.1233, 1258–9).

19 593–4 (CCSL 175.39). 'Infant' is the conventional term for the baptized, who are 'reborn' in the font.

20 Eusebius, *Vit. Const.* 4.45; Socrates, *HE* 1.33.

21 See Introduction, sect. 4, p. 40. The evidence is set out in Biddle, *The Tomb of Christ*.

22 Telfer, *Cyril*, pp. 50–1. In another context, when referring to a structure extending *up to* the summit, Eusebius uses the preposition *eis*, not *epi*: 'raising the basilica [at Antioch] to an incredible height' (*eis amēchanon epairon hupsos*) (*Laud. Const.* 9; PG 20.1369B).

23 GT 84. The earliest statement that the apse was built where the Cross was found seems to be in the early sixth-century *Breviarius de Hierosolyma* (CCSL 175.109).

24 GT 77.

25 See W. Pullan, 'Jerusalem from Alpha to Omega in the Santa Pudenziana Mosaic', in B. Kühnel (ed.), *The Real and Ideal Jerusalem in Jewish, Christian and Islamic Art*, Jerusalem, Hebrew University, 1998, pp. 405–17.

26 *Holy City*, pp. 252–60. Cameron and Hall query these explanations (CH 274–7).

27 *Vit. Const.* 3.33; 3.28. Cyril, by contrast, regards the font as the Holy of Holies (*MC* 1.11).
28 J. Wilkinson, 'Jewish Influences on the Early Christian Rite of Jerusalem', *Le Muséon* 92 (1979), 347–59.
29 *de ob. Theod.* 46–8; PL 16.1464. It appears that Ambrose derived his account from a slightly earlier history written by Cyril's nephew Gelasius (cf. Drijvers, *Helena Augusta*, pp. 96–9).
30 On the legends concerning the finding of the cross, see Drijvers, *Helena Augusta.*
31 Ambrose, *de ob. Theod.* 46–8.
32 Cf. GT 78–9.

3 WORKS

1 See *Clavis patrum Graecorum*, ed. M. Geerard, Turnhout, Brepols, 1974–, 2.3585–3618.
2 Cyril, *Homily on Paralytic* 20; cf. L.P. McCauley and A.A. Stephenson, *St Cyril of Jerusalem*, Washington DC, 1970 (FaCh 64), pp. 221–2.
3 Philostorgius, *HE* 3.26; Sozomen, *HE* 4.5.1–5. Cf. E. Bihain, 'L'Épître de Cyrille de Jérusalem à Constance sur la vision de la croix', *Byzantium* 43 (1973), 266–7.
4 For an account of the MSS, their contents, and the titles they give to the works, see W.K. Reischl and J. Rupp (eds.) (RR), *S. Patris Nostri Cyrilli Hierosolymorum Archiepiscopi Opera quae supersunt Omnia*, Munich, Libraria Lenteriana, 1848–60, vol. 1, CXLVII–CXLIX; A. Piédagnel (ed.), *Cyrille de Jérusalem, Catéchèses Mystagogiques*, SC 126 *bis*, Paris 1988, pp. 21–3, 52–7. For a discussion of the authenticity of the *Mystagogics*, see E.J. Yarnold, 'The Authorship of the Mystagogic Catecheses Attributed to Cyril of Jerusalem', *Heythrop Journal* 19 (1978), 143–61.
5 As the modern system of numbering dates from the birth of Christ was not introduced until early in the sixth century, the date 352 was presumably the result of a later scribe's calculation.
6 The debate has been well summarized by Piédagnel, *Cyrille*, pp. 18–40.
7 McCauley and Stephenson, *St Cyril*, vol. 2, pp. 147–51.
8 See Piédagnel, *Cyrille*, pp. 22–3.
9 Piédagnel, *Cyrille*, pp. 24–5.
10 Cf. J.A. Jungmann (ET), *The Mass of the Roman Rite: Its Origins and Development (Missarum Sollemnia)*, New York, Benziger, 1955, reprint Blackrock, Four Courts Press, 1986, pp. 276–7, note 7.
11 For all these liturgical points, see Piédagnel, *Cyrille*, pp. 25–8.
12 With the exception of 18.33, which, as we have indicated above, Cyril may have added to the original text.
13 *Cat.* 3.3–4; 16.26; 17.35–7; *MC* 3.1–5. Cf. McCauley and Stephenson, *St Cyril*, vol. 2, p. 178; Yarnold, 'Authorship', pp. 157–9.
14 McCauley and Stephenson, *St Cyril*, vol. 2, pp. 146–7.
15 A. Doval, *Cyril of Jerusalem, Mystagogue: The Authorship of the Mystagogic Catecheses*, Patristic Monograph Series 17, Washington DC, Catholic University Press, 2001. Cf. Yarnold, 'Authorship'.

16 A. Renoux, 'Une version arménienne des catéchèses mystagogiques de Cyrille de Jérusalem?', *Le Muséon* 85 (1972), 147–53.
17 *MC* 3.2.
18 47.2, quoted on p. 40.
19 *MC* 2.5.
20 Jerome, *Contra Ioannem Hierosolymitanum* 7 (PL 23.360).
21 McCauley and Stephenson, *St Cyril*, vol. 2, p. 147.
22 Ed. M. van Esbroeck, *Le Muséon* 86 (1973), 283–304; cf. Yarnold, 'Authorship', p. 146.
23 *MC* 3.1: *tōi homoiōi epanapaumomenou tou homoiou.*
24 *Procat.* 1; *Cat.* 6.12; *MC* 1.1.
25 *kata krēmnon*: *Cat.* 4.20; *kata krēmnōn*: *MC* 1.6.
26 Cf. Rom 5.14, where Adam is the 'type' of Christ.
27 *Procat.* 1; *Cat.* 1.2; *MC* 1.1; 3.2–3; 4.2; 4.7–9.
28 *litos* (*MC* 1.7; 3.3); *psilos* (*MC* 3.3; 4.6); *koinos* (*MC* 3.3).
29 *Procat.* 15; *Cat.* 3.11; *MC* 3.1.
30 C. Beukers, 'For our Emperors, Soldiers and Allies', *VC* 15 (1961), 177–84.
31 Cf. E.J. Yarnold, 'Did St Ambrose Know the Mystagogic Catecheses of St Cyril of Jerusalem?', *StPatr* 12 (1975), 184–9.

4 LITURGY

1 See J.F. Baldovin, *Liturgy in Ancient Jerusalem*, Alcuin-GROW Liturgical Study 9, Bramcote, Nottingham, Grove Books, 1989.
2 Palladius, *Historia Lausiaca* 55.1.
3 M. Férotin, 'Le véritable auteur de la "Peregrinatio Sylviae". La vierge espagnole Etheria', *Revue des questions historiques* 74 (1903), 367–97.
4 P. Devos, 'La date du voyage d'Égérie', *Analecta Bollandiana* 85 (1967), 165–94. However, in a paper forthcoming in *StPatr*, 'The Date of the Itinerarium Egeriae', E.D. Hunt has queried several of Devos's arguments, and suggested a date a decade later, which would imply that the bishop of Jerusalem to whom Egeria refers was Cyril's successor John.
5 The text of both Egeria and Valerius is contained in *Égérie: Journal de Voyage (Itinéraire) et Lettre sur la B[se] Égérie*, SC 296, 1982. For English-speaking readers, there is a useful translation, with valuable illustrative material, by J. Wilkinson, *Egeria's Travels*, London, SPCK, 1971; 3rd edn, Warminster, Aris & Phillips, 1999.
6 J. Jeremias (ET), *Infant Baptism in the First Four Centuries*, London, SCM, 1960; K. Aland (ET), *Did the Early Church Baptize Infants?*, London, SCM, 1963.
7 Hippolytus, *Apostolic Tradition* (Botte), 17; Clement (*Stromata* ii.11.2); Origen (*Commentary on John*, 6.28.144).
8 M. Dujarier (ET), *A History of the Catechumenate: The First Six Centuries*, New York, Sadlier, 1979, p. 95.
9 W. Harmless, *Augustine and the Catechumenate*, Collegeville, Liturgical Press, 1995, p. 56.
10 See note 7 on the *Procatechesis*.

11 Cf. E.J. Yarnold, *The Awe-Inspiring Rites of Initiation: The Origins of the R.C.I.A.*, Edinburgh and Collegeville, T. and T. Clark and Liturgical Press, 1994, pp. 2–6. For Augustine's rites for admission into the catechumenate, cf. E.C. Whitaker, *Documents of the Baptismal Liturgy*, 2nd edn, London, SPCK, 1970, pp. 99–101.

12 The forty days of Lent were calculated variously in different parts of the world.

13 Egeria uses the technical term *competens*, which is mentioned in the modern Rite of Christian Initiation of Adults.

14 Egeria uses the everyday words for 'fathers' and 'mothers'.

15 *Phōtizomenoi* (*Procat.* 1; 12). In the Latin Church they were known as 'seekers' (*competentes*) or 'chosen ones' (*electi*).

16 *Procat.* 9. In the Latin Church the positive and negative aspects of this rite were called respectively 'insufflation' (blowing in', as when the risen Jesus breathed on the apostles to signify the gift of the Holy Spirit: Jn 20.22) and 'exsufflation' ('blowing away' the devil).

17 I.e. the baptized.

18 Egeria explains that, though the bishop understands Syriac, the translation is made by a presbyter who is always at hand to give a Syriac translation as the bishop speaks. Those who only understand Latin are given a private translation (47.3–4).

19 Maxwell Johnson has attempted to solve this problem; 'Reconciling Cyril and Egeria in the Catechetical Process in Fourth-Century Jerusalem', in P. Bradshaw (ed.), *Essays in Early Eastern Initiation*, Alcuin-GROW Liturgical Study 8, Bramcote, Nottingham, Grove Books, 1988, pp. 18–30.

20 *Pereg.*, 46.5–6. The 'church' is the Martyrium.

21 Cyril, *Cat.* 18.33. This paragraph was probably intended to replace 18.32, which implies that the final instructions are given immediately *before* baptism. Cf. above, p. 23, and Yarnold, 'Authorship'.

22 Augustine, Sermon 213.

23 For an attempt to reconcile Cyril and Egeria on this point, see Yarnold, 'Authorship', pp. 153–7.

24 *MC* 5.2–3; Mt 5.23–4: 'first be reconciled with your brother, and then come and offer your gift'.

25 Among these commentators are: L. Ligier (ET), 'The Origins of the Eucharistic Prayer: From the Last Supper to the Eucharist', *Studia Liturgica* 9 (1973), 161–85, esp. 179; E. Cutrone, 'Cyril's Mystagogical Catecheses and the Evolution of the Jerusalem Anaphora', *OCP* 44 (1978), 52–64; G.J. Cuming, 'The Shape of the Anaphora', *StPatr* 20 (1989), 333–45; J.R.K. Fenwick, *Fourth Century Anaphoral Techniques*, Bramcote, Nottingham, Grove Books, 1986, and *The Anaphoras of St Basil and St James: An Investigation into Their Common Origins*, OCA 240, Rome, 1992.

26 I have expounded this view in two articles: 'Anaphoras without Institution Narratives?', *StPatr* 30 (1997), 395–410; and 'The Function of Institution Narratives in Early Liturgies' (forthcoming).

27 See above, p. 21.

28 Either because not everyone could fit into the Anastasis, or in order to face the cross on Golgotha.

29 A. Kavanagh suggested that this dismissal at which the bishop lays his hand on the people is the origin of confirmation: *Confirmation: Origins and Reform*, New York, Pueblo, 1988.
30 'ipsa laetitia celebratur': *Pereg.* 26.11–12.
31 Actually Egeria says '*behind* the Cross' (35.2). If this is correct there must have been a separate chapel behind the Cross which is distinct from the Martyrium. However the Armenian Lectionary (39; see below) places the celebration *before* the Cross, i.e. in the courtyard at the foot of the jewelled cross, which would be the appropriate place for the annual passiontide Eucharist (see GT 78). Apparently the church at Sion had not yet been connected with the site of the Last Supper; cf. Wilkinson, *Egeria* pp. 38–9.
32 *Pereg.* 37.3. GT think the words 'behind the Cross' refer not to a separate chapel, but to the altar of the Martyrium where the first of the two Thursday Eucharists had been celebrated; see note 31.
33 *maximus labor*: *Pereg.* 43.1.
34 This is not to be confused with the Maccabean feast of Dedication (*enkainia*) mentioned in Jn 10.22, which is the feast of Hannukah or lights celebrated in November or December.
35 A. Renoux, 'Le Codex arménien Jérusalem 121', PO 35–6 (1969–71). J. Wilkinson's treatment of the subject in his edition of *Egeria's Travels* fails to take account of the Yerevan MS.
36 For a fuller treatment of this subject see Yarnold, *Awe-Inspiring Rites*, pp. 55–6.
37 The Eleona, Constantine's basilica on the Mount of Olives, not only commemorated the place of the ascension, but also incorporated the sacred cave where the Saviour 'initiated his disciples into the secret mysteries' (Eusebius, *Vit. Const.* 3.43). According to later tradition, this secret teaching included the Lord's Prayer.
38 Aristides of Athens, *Eleusinios* 256. The Greek word is *phrikōdēs*.
39 Lactantius, *Divinarum Institutionum Epitome* 18 (23). Lactantius, himself a convert from paganism, was the tutor of Constantine's son Crispus.
40 *Protrepticus* 2.21; cf. Hippolytus, *Refutatio* V.8.39ff.
41 Aristotle, frag. 15 (Ross).
42 H. Rahner, *Greek Myths and Christian Mystery*, London, Burns Oates, 1963, pp. 3–45. Rahner was of course far from suggesting, as some have done, that the influence of the pagan mysteries made itself felt as early as St Paul.
43 Cf. Yarnold, 'Who Planned the Churches?'.
44 Cf. T.D. Barnes, *Constantine and Eusebius*, Cambridge, Mass. and London, Harvard University Press, 1981, p. 36.
45 For Constantine's colourful devotion to the Passion, see above, p. 14.
46 Eusebius, however, takes the clue to the building to be Constantine's desire to build a new Jerusalem to replace the Jewish Temple: 'at the very saving Martyrium the new Jerusalem was constructed, facing the celebrated old one' (*HE* 3.33). J. Wilkinson argued that certain architectural features bear out Eusebius' interpretation ('Jewish Influences'). However Constantine's own letter to Macarius does not bear out this interpretation of the project.

47 Eusebius, *Laud. Const.* 9 (PG 20.1369C). However, Constantine's letter to Macarius, quoted above, indicates that his original scheme was more modest.
48 A. Grabar, *Martyrium*, Paris, 1946.

5 CYRIL'S USE OF SCRIPTURE, AND HIS THEOLOGY

1 See R. Murray, *Symbols of Church and Kingdom*, Cambridge, Cambridge University Press, 1975.
2 Origen, *de Principiis* iv.2.5, referring to Jn 2.6.
3 Cf. Diodore of Tarsus, Prologue on the Psalms, CCSG 6, p. 7.
4 Homily *de poenitentia* 6.4 (PG 49.320).
5 'Hierusolymis vero Cyrillus post Maximum sacerdotio confusa iam ordinatione suscepto, aliquando in fide, saepius in communione variabat': Rufinus, *HE* 1.23: PL 21.495 = Eusebius, *HE* 10.24: GCS 9/2, p. 989.
6 J. Lebon, 'La position de saint Cyrille de Jérusalem dans les luttes provoquées par l'arianisme', *RHE* 20 (1924), 181–210, 357–86; quotation on p. 383.
7 *Ēn pote hote ouk ēn* (*Cat.* 11.17).
8 A.A. Stephenson, 'St Cyril of Jerusalem's Trinitarian Theology', *StPatr* 11 (1972), 234–41; McCauley and Stephenson, *St Cyril*, vol. 1, p. 45.
9 Letter of Council to Pope Damasus (N.P. Tanner (ed.), *Decrees of the Ecumenical Councils*, London and Washington DC, Sheed and Ward and Georgetown University Press, 1990, i. 28).
10 McCauley and Stephenson, *St Cyril*, vol. 2, p. 235.
11 Glory: *Cat.* 6.1; worship: *Cat.* 16.4; wills: *Cat.* 15.25.
12 *Cat.* 7.5 (quoting Jn 8.49); *Cat.* 15.30.
13 Therefore his godhead *was* visible! *Cat.* 4.9. Cf. Tertullian, *Adversus Praxean* 27.
14 *MC* 3.3.

LETTER TO CONSTANTIUS

1 The artificial style of this letter is comparable to that of Constantine's letter to Macarius (see Introduction, sect. 2).
2 Socrates, *HE* 2.26–7; McCauley and Stephenson, *St Cyril*, vol. 2, p. 228.
3 Constantius reigned from 337 to 361.
4 See Introduction, sect. 2. Cyril says nothing of Constantine's vision of the cross which heralded his victory over Maxentius in 312.
5 It has been suggested that what Cyril describes is the well-known phenomenon of a parhelion.
6 When speaking of the cross as a 'boast', Cyril has such texts as Gal 6.14 and 1 Cor 1.31 in mind. Cyril evidently wants Constantius to use the cross as an emblem in battle, as his father had used the *labarum* or *chi-rhō* emblem as a military standard.
7 Telfer (*Cyril*, p. 198) indicates that at this time Constantius was a childless widower in need of an heir.

8 One MS adds: 'as you ever give glory to the holy and consubstantial Trinity, our true God, to whom all glory belongs for ever and ever. Amen'. However, as Cyril nowhere else uses the Nicene term 'consubstantial' (*homoousios*), preferring the term 'like' (*homoios*), and generally prefers scriptural language to philosophical, the sentence is likely to be an interpolation. See Introduction, sect. 4.

HOMILY ON THE PARALYTIC BY THE POOL

1 *kata ti.*
2 Literally: 'Do not examine the one who appears, but the one who works through the one who appears.' The context shows that Cyril does not mean that the man and the God are two distinct individuals.
3 Accepting Rupp's proposed reading of *se bastasanta* for the MSS's *sebasmata.*
4 'Human life' translates the Greek *oikonomia*, which is a common technical term for the Incarnation.
5 *Lithostrōtos* and *Gabbatha* are respectively the Greek and Aramaic terms translated here as 'paved with stones' (cf. Jn 19.13).
6 If this is the correct reading – the Greek text of this last sentence is in a very confused state – the 'father' is presumably Cyril's predecessor Maximus, and Cyril is preaching before becoming bishop.

PROCATECHESIS

1 It was preached at the beginning of Lent to the candidates who had given in their names ('enrolment', n. 1) for baptism ('enlightenment'; cf. Heb 6.4; Justin, 1 Apol 61.12) at Easter.
2 On Cyril's use of typology, see Introduction, sect. 5.
3 The 'Faithful' are the baptized; cf. *Procat.* 12.
4 The first of many appeals to the sanctity of the place where Constantine had built the basilica where Cyril was preaching.
5 Cf. *Procat.* 2.
6 Rom 6.11, 13. Cyril, as is his custom, comments on the passage which had been read during the service. On Cyril's Lectionary, see Introduction, section 4.
7 Cyril plays on the word 'catechumen'. The word is derived from the Greek *ēchē*, which means a sound or echo. The equivalent Latin term was *auditor* (hearer).
8 The *disciplina arcani* attempted to restrict knowledge of the most sacred rites and doctrines to those who had given in their names for baptism, or even to those who were baptized (see pp. 49–50). It is possible that Cyril is borrowing the language of the pagan mystery-religions (see pp. 52–5).
9 On the figurative interpretation of Scripture, see pp. 56–8.
10 I.e. you will be called 'Faithful' like God.

11 Cyril goes no further into the question of the validity of the baptism of schismatics which divided Pope Stephen and St Cyprian of Carthage in the third century.
12 Exorcism involved both 'exsufflation' (to blow away the devil) and 'insufflation' to introduce the breath of the Holy Spirit (cf. Jn 20.22).
13 On Cyril's systematic efforts to inspire awe in the candidates, see Introduction, pp. 50–2.
14 The Faithful are the baptized; the candidates who have been allowed to enrol for baptism are neither catechumens nor Faithful, and are so to speak in no-man's-land.
15 Cyril is alluding to a Syriac tradition that the males and females of every species were separated, presumably to prevent the population increasing during the year when they were confined to the ark. Adam's body was laid along the centre of the ark to keep the sexes apart.
16 Cyril is paraphrasing 1 Cor 14.34 and 1 Tim 2.12.
17 'Heard of God' is one of several interpretations of the name Samuel which Hannah gave to the son which God granted her in answer to her silent prayer (1 Sam 1.9–20).
18 A reference to the scented *muron*.
19 Christ = anointed. The reference is to the post-baptismal anointing. Cf. *MC* 3.1.
20 Cyril is more explicit about the equality of the Holy Spirit with the Father and the Son in *MC* 3.1, written perhaps thirty years later.
21 The newly baptized will go in procession from the baptistery into the Martyrium dressed in white baptismal robes and carrying torches. This is one of the earliest indications we possess for this practice.
22 Cyril hints at various elements in the rites, though the Discipline of Secrecy prevents him from speaking more explicitly.

CATECHESIS 3

1 Cf. *Procat.* 3–4.
2 On the seal and the invocation (*epiclesis*), cf. Introduction, sect. 3.
3 I.e. both water and Spirit.
4 Cyril seems to mean that the Spirit is given in the water; though by the time he delivered the *Mystagogic Catecheses* it had become the practice to confer the Spirit by means of a post-baptismal anointing (*MC* 3).
5 RR enclose the whole of this sentence in square brackets.
6 On the Discipline of Secrecy, see Introduction, sect. 4 under 'Mysteries'.
7 RR place the phrase 'for he was sinless' in square brackets.
8 The 'dignity' may be the name of 'Christ' which Cyril discusses in *MC* 3.
9 RR enclose the clause from 'for' to 'form' in square brackets.

CATECHESIS 4

1 The Creed was 'presented' to the candidates during the fifth *Catechesis* (see Introduction, sect. 4). The remaining thirteen Lenten Catecheses took the form of commentaries on the articles of the Creed.

2 Marcion (d. c. 160) distinguished between the loving God of Jesus Christ and the God of the Old Testament, who was the Creator and the stern legislator. It was a common Gnostic teaching that the creation of spirit was the work of the supreme divine being, while material things were created by a fallen inferior being.
3 Constantine removed just such a statue which the Romans had erected over Calvary. See Introduction, sect. 2.
4 Although Cyril rejects several of Arius' teachings in this paragraph, he still prefers to describe the Son as 'like' (*homoios*) the Father rather than 'consubstantial' (*homoousios*) with him. See Introduction, sect. 5.
5 By contrast Arius taught 'there was once when the Son was not'.
6 This was one form of the Adoptionist heresy.
7 Arius denied that the Son knew the Father.
8 In this context a distinction was often made between an idea in the mind, which was an immanent (*endiathetos*) word, and an idea or word which was uttered (*prophorikos*).
9 Origen taught that God, being eternally the Creator, created rational beings (*logikoi*) from all eternity.
10 The Docetists taught that Jesus' humanity was an illusory appearance (*dokēsis*); the Valentinians added that he had no material birth, but his mother was a mere conduit through which he passed.
11 Therefore his godhead *was* visible! This distinction between the events proper to Christ's humanity and those proper to his divinity is common in Latin, Antiochene and Syriac writers, though there are different ways of drawing it. Cf. E.J. Yarnold, '"Videmus duplicem statum". The Visibility of the Two Natures of Christ in Tertullian's *Adversus Praxean*', *StPatr* 19 (1989), 286–90.
12 I.e. Lazarus' body; cf. Jn 11.17.
13 Cf. Cyril, *ad Const.* 3; *Cat.* 10.19; Introduction, sect. 2.
14 Cyril seems not to envisage a doctrine of original sin.
15 The Gnostics taught that salvation consisted in freeing the soul from the constraints of matter.
16 I.e. in *Cat.* 3. If Cyril's 'day before yesterday' (*prōēn*) is to be taken literally, we have confirmation that the catechetical meetings did not take place every day (see Introduction, sect. 4).
17 See note 2 above on Marcion.
18 This version was known as the Septuagint (Seventy) after the seventy-two translators. Cyril's account of its composition is probably derived from the *Letter of Aristeas*.
19 It was not until the fourth century that the Church began to formulate a canon of the Old and New Testaments. In that century various lists appeared, differing somewhat one from another, such as Cyril's and (probably) the 'Muratorian Canon'. The Council of Rome held by Pope Damasus in 382 promulgated the first official list. Although Cyril does not classify every work not in the Jewish canon as 'apocryphal', as Protestant bibles were to do, he omits most of the Deutero-canonical OT works, but (unlike some lists) includes Hebrews in the NT.
20 In the Septuagint 1 and 2 Kings = 1 and 2 Sam; 3 and 4 Kings = 1 and 2 Kings in the Hebrew.
21 The Letter of Jeremiah = Baruch 6.

22 This Manichaean 'Gospel' is not to be confused with the Gnostic 'Gospel of Thomas' included among the Nag Hammadi documents, or with the 'Infancy Gospel of Thomas'.

CATECHESIS 5

1 The 'Faithful' are the baptized (cf. *Procat.* 2).
2 In addition to the two senses of 'faith' (*pistis*) distinguished in para. 2, the same word also denotes the object of faith, namely the Creed. This was kept secret from the candidates, and taught to them during Lent at the Presentation or Handing over of the Creed (see *Procat.* 12; Introduction, sect. 4). This Presentation took place at the end of *Cat.* 5.
3 By the end of his episcopate Cyril required the candidates to repeat the Creed formally to the bishop (*Pereg.* 46.5–6; Introduction, sect. 4).

CATECHESIS 10

1 Lists of symbolic titles of Christ are common in Greek and Syriac literature, sometimes, as here, with each title followed by a clause excluding the title's literal sense. Cf. Murray, *Symbols*, ch. 5 and pp. 354–63.
2 On this interpretation of the name 'Jesus', see below, para. 13.
3 The Arians (among others) held that Jesus was an ordinary man who was granted advancement or promotion (*prokopē*) to divine honours; cf. R.C. Gregg and D.E. Groh, *Early Arianism: A View of Salvation*, Philadelphia and London, Fortress Press and SCM, 1981.
4 Some MSS continue: 'who is also true God'.
5 The Fathers frequently identify the Lord who appears and acts in the OT with the pre-existent Christ.
6 Actually the verse 11.26 comes earlier.
7 This legend is to be found in Athanasius, *de Incarnatione* 36; it appears to be derived from Is 19.1.
8 Cyril was to develop his use of typology in the *Mystagogic Catecheses.*
9 Mk 13.2. Cyril characteristically invites his hearers to observe for themselves the sacred sites of which he is speaking.
10 Cyril bases his argument on the resemblance between 'Jesus' and *iasis*, which is a Greek word for 'healing'.
11 Christ = Messiah = Anointed.
12 On the wood of the cross, see Introduction, sect. 4.
13 Cyril seems to imply that the identity of the palm-tree was common knowledge.

CATECHESIS 11

1 *tupikōi.*
2 See *Cat.* 10.5 and note.
3 Cyril avoids using the term *homoousios*, preferring to speak of 'similarity' rather than identity. Some MSS add 'eternal from the eternal

Father', which was perhaps added in order to reject the Arian belief that 'there was when the Son was not'. Cf. *Cat.* 11.17.

4 Another reference to the theory that Jesus was 'promoted' or 'advanced' to divine honours; cf. *Cat.* 11.1.

5 Cyril is perhaps intending to refute two Arian arguments for the inferiority of the Son to the Father: (1) to be generated implies being later in time; (2) the generation of the Son took place by God's free choice.

6 The relationship between God and his Son was often regarded as analogous to that between a human being and his mind, his ideas and his spoken words (all denoted by the single Greek term *Logos*). Though already implied by Jn 1.1 ('In the beginning was the Word'), this vision owes its systematization to the Greek Apologists of the second century, especially Justin Martyr.

7 *enhupostatos.*

8 *prophorikon*; cf. *Cat.* 4.8.

9 The Greek word *archē* means both 'beginning' and 'principle'. Cyril in this paragraph argues against the Arian slogan that 'There once was when the Son was not'. Cf. *Cat.* 11.17.

10 Cyril understands the prophet's statement about the giving of knowledge as an allusion to the Law given by God to Moses.

11 Ps 44.7 (45.6), quoted in Heb 1.8, which was included in the reading of the day.

12 Ps 44.8 (45.7). On the Arian theory that the Son 'advanced' to divinity, see *Cat.* 10.5; 11.7.

13 The term 'Son–Father' is attributed to Sabellius, who maintained that the names Father, Son and Spirit did not imply any distinction in the godhead, but referred only to God's different operations in the world.

14 The notorious Arian slogan denying the eternity of the Son.

15 I.e. either to Arianism or Sabellianism.

16 On Cyril's preference for the formula 'like the Father' to the Nicene 'consubstantial with the Father', see Introduction, sect. 5.

17 Again Cyril is rejecting the two extremes of Arianism and Sabellianism.

18 Cyril can hardly mean that we should think of the Son only in his eternal godhead and not in his human reality, for the next three *Catecheses* are all about Jesus' birth, death and resurrection; he presumably means that to understand Christ's origins we need to go back beyond his human birth to his eternal existence.

19 A reference to Marcion and the various forms of Gnosticism; cf. *Cat.* 4.4.

20 Job 9.8 (LXX): 'figuratively' translates the Greek word *mustikōs*.

CATECHESIS 12

1 Cf. Exod 12.9. While using the Passover lamb as a symbol of Christ's divinity and humanity, Cyril is also speaking in veiled terms of the Eucharist.

2 This last error is that of Adoptionism; cf. *Cat.* 4.7.

3 The devil's defeat will come through the same means as his triumph, namely a virgin.

4 There exist carved figures of soldiers and slaves marked on the forehead with a cross. Liturgically the term 'seal' was applied to (1) the cross

traced with oil on the candidate's forehead, and (2) the whole rite of baptism. Cf. G.W.H. Lampe, *The Seal of the Spirit*, 2nd edn, London, SPCK, 1967.

5 Perhaps a reference to the tradition that when ascending Jesus left the marks of his feet on the Mount of Olives; see *Cat.* 14.23.

6 The representation of Mary as the second Eve was put forward by Justin Martyr and Irenaeus in the second century.

7 '*theou . . . koinōnos*'.

8 The theory that Jesus put an end to the devil's hold over sinful humanity by decoying him into attacking one who was God as well as man is expounded by several Fathers, such as Gregory of Nyssa, *Oratio Catechetica* 24.

9 Sections 17–32 are omitted here; they contain the Old Testament evidence concerning the time and place of the Saviour's birth and his birth from a virgin.

CATECHESIS 13

1 The Fathers frequently apply the word 'wood' to the 'tree' of Paradise and the 'cross' of Christ.

2 Cf. Num 25.7–8; 1 Tim 2.6. The application of the concept of 'ransom' to Jesus' saving work should not be used to justify the theory of vicarious punishment, i.e. the view that the Father vented his anger at our sins on his sinless Son.

3 RR bracket the second part of this sentence, but the sense is obscure without it.

4 The denial of the reality of Jesus' sufferings is an aspect of Docetism. See para. 37 below.

5 Perhaps a reference to the Magi, or to the Parthians whose conversion is implied in Acts 2.9.

6 The second part of para. 8 (omitted here) lists various details of the Passion without giving their scriptural 'testimonies'.

7 *theorētikēn.* On Cyril's exegetical method, see Introduction, sect. 5.

8 The sections omitted here give the testimonies for the thirty pieces of silver, the potter's field, the trials, the mockery and the crown of thorns.

9 Jer 11.19 (LXX). Cyril allows himself several digressions in the section. The main argument in paras 19 and 20 is that the cross is prophesied in many places in the Old Testament.

10 In *MC* 4 and 5.

11 *tupos*. On Cyril's use of typology, see Introduction, sect. 5.

12 The reason for saying that the baptism of martyrdom is attested in the gospels is given in *Cat.* 3.10. The term 'baptism in one's own blood' is found as early as *Apostolic Tradition* 19 (Botte).

13 By this time, in fact, most of the persecution of Christians was inflicted by other Christians. Cyril himself was exiled three times; see Introduction, sect. 1.

14 On the topography of Golgotha and the origin of the name, see Introduction, sect. 2.

15 Scholars do not accept Cyril's explanation of the origin of the name.
16 Ps 73 (74).12 (LXX). Both the Hebrew and the LXX read 'he', not 'you'.
17 I.e. the wood of the Tree of Knowledge and the wood of the cross.
18 *tupikon*.
19 On the Holy Sepulchre see Introduction, sect. 2.
20 Cf. para. 4 above.
21 The Mount of Olives gets its mention in connection with the ascension in *Cat.* 14.23.
22 The Bordeaux Pilgrim gave a similar description of Caiaphas' house less than twenty years before Cyril (*Itin.* 592 (CCSL 175, 16).
23 *huperanestōs*. The word is sometimes taken to mean 'towering above', a translation which Gibson and Taylor reject because 'the top of the rock . . . was only about two metres higher than the minimum *floor* level of the Constantinian Martyrium' (GT, 80). They accordingly propose the translation 'pre-eminent' adopted above.

CATECHESIS 14

1 We only have space to give Cyril's 'proofs' which have a connection with the Constantinian buildings.
2 Evidently the separate church of the Anastasis had not yet been built.
3 Although in Cyril's time in front of the tomb there was a porch, from which Cyril delivered his *Mystagogic Catecheses*, this was apparently set in front of the rock, not hollowed from it.
4 Cyril refers to *Cat.* 14.17.
5 RR detect a reference to the impression of Jesus' feet left in the rock. The conjunction of Bethlehem with the Mount of Olives may have something to do with Egeria's statement (*Pereg.* 42) that the vigil of the fortieth day after Easter was celebrated at Bethlehem. The 'heavenly gate' RR take to be the open roof of the church on the Mount of Olives; however, Egeria's accounts of the ceremonial there suggest that in her time the rites were still celebrated in an open place, and that the church of the Imbomon had not yet been built. See Introduction, sect. 4; Wilkinson, *Egeria's Travels*, pp. 14–16.

CATECHESIS 18

1 This 'handing over of the Creed' took place at the end of *Cat.* 5.
2 'Enlightenment' was a regular term for baptism; cf. Heb 6.4.
3 There is a problem here. While para. 32 suggests that the candidates will receive last-minute instructions *in advance* about the reception of the sacraments ('the order with which the called should enter . . .'), para. 33 states that instruction will be given *after* baptism, which in fact is what Cyril does in the *Mystagogic Catecheses*, where he explains why this arrangement is necessary (*MC* 1.1). Perhaps Cyril's practice changed over the long period of thirty years or more between the delivery of the *Catecheses* and that of the *Mystagogic Catecheses.* In that case, para. 33 may have been intended to replace para. 32. The fact

that some phrases in para. 32 are duplicated in para. 33 reinforces this hypothesis. See Yarnold, 'Authorship' esp. pp. 159–61.

4 In fact there are only five *Mystagogic Catecheses*. Cf. Yarnold, 'Authorship', pp. 153–7.

5 This summary corresponds closely with the contents of the *Mystagogic Catecheses*, except that, while the *reading* for *MC* 5 (1 Pet 2.1ff) would be appropriate for an instruction about 'how in future you ought to behave', the main *subject* of the last address is the Eucharist, with the teaching about behaviour squeezed into a brief allusion in the last paragraph. See Yarnold, 'Authorship', pp. 155–6.

MYSTAGOGIC CATECHESIS 1

1 Cyril gives two reasons why certain truths were kept secret from the new Christians until they were baptized and became known as the Faithful. See the discussion of the Discipline of Secrecy in the Introduction, sect. 4.

2 On typology, see Introduction, sect. 5.

3 Cyril's attitude to the Jews who were his contemporaries was far less complimentary.

4 Cf. Ex 12.7; 14.21–9. A less well attested reading in the MSS makes 'the enemy' rather than 'Pharaoh' the subject.

5 Cyril's description suggests that in the darkness the candidates cannot see the person who is directing them.

6 On Cyril's systematic efforts to inspire in the candidates a sense of awe, see Introduction, sect. 4.

7 The translation does its best with a corrupt text.

8 The water, the chrism, and the bread and wine each have an epiclesis recited over them, by which the Father is asked to send down his Spirit to transform the material elements into a vehicle of Christ's grace. See Introduction, sect. 4.

9 The Renunciation of Satan is followed by an act of 'Adhesion' to Christ, which here takes the form of a short profession of faith (para. 9); some other rites (e.g. Chrysostom, *Catéchèses Baptismales*, ed. A. Wenger, SC 50, 2.21; trans P.W. Harkins, Ancient Christian Writers 31, p. 53) include the explicit formula: 'I join your ranks (*suntassomai*), O Christ.' Thus the candidate abandoned service in Satan's ranks and entered the ranks of Christ.

10 Cf. Gen 19.26. Cyril's explanation contains two typical puns: pillar (*stēlē*)/pilloried (*estēliteumenē*); and salt (*hals*)/bitter (*halmuros*).

11 Lot and his family were told to seek refuge in the hills (Gen 19.17).

12 St Augustine describes a rite of trampling on cloth made of goat's hair (Sermon 216.10–11; PL 38.1082).

13 Cyril explains the trinitarian Creed in *Cat.* 6–18, and forgiveness through baptism in *Cat.* 1 and 2.

14 Phrases from several passages are paraphrased here: Is 25.8 (LXX); Tit 3.5; Apoc 7.17.

MYSTAGOGIC CATECHESIS 2

1 Col 2.15. For Cyril the stripping represents: (1) imitation of the stripping of Christ; (2) putting off the old nature (cf. Eph 4.22); (3) the innocence of Paradise. In fact the baptistery was dark and the sexes were separated.

2 Cf. Rom 11.24. In fact the cultivated plant is grafted on to the wild one.

3 Cyril attributes both negative and positive effects to the anointing with olive-oil: it drives away demons and imparts grace. Similarly the rite of breathing on the candidate has the negative effect of blowing away the devil (exsufflation) and the positive effect of breathing in grace (insufflation); cf. *Procat.* 9.

4 According to Egeria, the bishop gave these, the *Mystagogic Catecheses*, at the entrance to the tomb; see Introduction, sect. 4.

5 In baptizing in the name of the Trinity, the bishop did not say: 'I baptize you in the name of the Father . . .', but asked the candidates if they accepted a trinitarian Creed. After the mention of each Person, the candidate was pushed once under the water. Cyril takes the triple immersion also as a symbol of Christ's three days in the tomb.

6 The Greek text of this first clause is unsatisfactory.

7 Literally: 'is the antitype of Christ's sufferings'. According to Cyril's theology of sacramental symbolism, to say that sacraments are symbols of a grace does not imply that the grace is not present truly: in baptism the share in Christ's death and resurrection, and in the Eucharist the share in his body and blood, take place no less truly than his own passion, but the reality is now at the level of liturgical representation rather than literal history. Symbolism is so important for Cyril that he seems to regard the symbolic share in Jesus' sufferings to be more important than forgiveness or adoption or the gift of the Spirit.

8 This clause occurs in the Nicene Creed, but not in the Creed which Cyril explains in the *Catecheses*.

9 I.e. in the very place where Cyril was speaking.

10 Jesus himself seems to have linked his baptism with his death: 'Can you . . . be baptized with the baptism with which I am baptized?' (Mk 10.38).

MYSTAGOGIC CATECHESIS 3

1 Here and below 'sacramental sign' translates *antitupon.* On Cyril's use of typology, see Introduction, sect. 5.

2 'Image' = *eikōn*; 'has a symbolic meaning' = *eikonikōs*.

3 Literally 'the skin of his divinity'. The reference is perhaps to Moses' skin which radiated the brightness of the divine presence (Exod 34.29). Para. 4 below refers to the same passage.

4 Cyril characteristically expresses the equality of the Son and the Spirit in terms of likeness rather than 'one substance' (*homoousios*).

5 *Muron* is the chrism or scented oil used for conferring the gift of the Holy Spirit.

6 I.e. at his baptism by John.

7 Accepting the minority reading *parousiāi* instead of Piédagnel's *parousias*. On the epiclesis, cf. *Procat*. 9.
8 *sumbolon.*
9 *tupikōs*.
10 Is 25.6–7 (LXX paraphrased). Cyril takes this quotation as a prophecy that God will extend the gift of the sacramental wine and chrism to the gentiles.

MYSTAGOGIC CATECHESIS 4

1 St Paul's account of the Last Supper does not include the words 'Take, eat', 'Take, drink'. In fact the word 'take' before 'drink' does not appear in the gospel accounts either, but it is found in some Egyptian liturgies, such as that of the Deir Balyzeh papyrus. Moreover, Cyril quotes the words 'This is my body/blood' in an order which is not to be found anywhere in the New Testament, though it is followed in the Palestinian Liturgy of St James. It seems likely therefore that Cyril is quoting from the liturgy here, which incidentally provides evidence that his liturgy included an Institution Narrative. Cf. Yarnold, 'Anaphoras' esp. pp. 405–6; 409–10. See Introduction, sect. 4.
2 This paragraph contains three quotations from the Septuagint version of Ps 22 (23).5.
3 A reference to the gold plate which Aaron wore (Exod 28.36). In *MC* 4 the 'seal' is connected with the post-baptismal anointing with *muron*, in the *Catecheses* with baptism itself; see Introduction, sect. 3.
4 Mt 26.28, omitting the words 'of the covenant'.
5 Cyril is alluding to the baptismal robe. The quotations in the paragraph are taken from Eccles 9.7–8 (LXX).

MYSTAGOGIC CATECHESIS 5

1 Cyril calls him the 'priest' (*hierei*). The description of the Eucharist begins with the Lavabo.
2 Rom 16.16; 1 Pet 5.14.
3 This dialogue introducing the Eucharistic Prayer is found as early as the *Apostolic Tradition* in the early third century, and occurs almost universally from that day to this.
4 On Cyril's expectation that the liturgy will inspire awe, see Introduction, sect. 4.
5 Cf. Ezek 10.21. Cyril paraphrases the Preface and Sanctus.
6 Cf. Is 6.2–3. There was a tradition in Egypt that the seraphim used their wings to cover the divine face, not their own (cf. Origen, *de Principiis* iv.3.14). This is one of several indications of Egyptian influence on Cyril's liturgy; see G.J. Cuming, 'Egyptian Elements in the Jerusalem Liturgy', *JTS* 25 (1974), 117–24.
7 Reading *dia touto*.
8 Since Cyril appears to pass directly from the epiclesis (para. 7) to the Intercessions (para. 8), the conclusion is often drawn that Cyril's liturgy had no Institution Narrative. I argue against this theory in

Introduction, sect. 4, where there is also a brief discussion of his understanding of eucharistic sacrifice and of the real presence.

9 The Syrian, Byzantine and Latin liturgies similarly affirm the presumption involved in addressing God as Father: 'audemus dicere' ('Let us pray with confidence to the Father', 'we have the courage to say').

10 Rom 6.12.

11 Cyril's argument requires one to take the Greek word *epiousios*, which is translated 'daily' in the familiar form of the Lord's Prayer, to mean instead 'substantial'. Ambrose also knows this explanation (*de Sacramentis* 5.24).

12 This is not a direct quotation from Scripture; perhaps the nearest equivalent is in Rom 5.3–4.

13 A reference to Judas' suicide (Mt 27.5).

14 The Fathers frequently interpreted the last petition of the Lord's Prayer as a request for deliverance from the evil *spirit* (masculine) rather than from evil itself (neuter).

15 Most liturgies contained a double epiclesis, invoking the Holy Spirit first on the bread and wine, and then on the communicants.

16 *antitupou*.

17 Theodore of Mopsuestia similarly instructs the communicants to apply the body of Christ to the eyes and also to kiss it (*Bapt. Hom.* 5 (6, 16).28; Yarnold, *Awe-Inspiring Rites*, p. 242). Cf. Murray, *Symbols*, p. 60.

18 'Communion' (*koinōnia*) denotes sharing in the common life of the Church as well as in the sacrament.

BIBLIOGRAPHY

Aland, K. (ET), *Did the Early Church Baptize Infants?*, London, SCM, 1963.

Baldovin, J.F., *Liturgy in Ancient Jerusalem*, Alcuin-GROW Liturgical Study 9, Bramcote, Nottingham, Grove Books, 1989.

Barnes, T.D., *Constantine and Eusebius*, Cambridge, Mass. and London, Harvard University Press, 1981.

Beukers, C., 'For Our Emperors, Soldiers and Allies', *VC* 15 (1961), 177–84.

Biddle, M., *The Tomb of Christ*, Stroud, Sutton Publishing, 1999.

Bihain, E., 'L'Épître de Cyrille de Jérusalem à Constance sur la vision de la croix', *Byzantium* 43 (1973), 266–7.

Cameron A., and S.G. Hall, *Eusebius' Life of Constantine*, Oxford, Clarendon Press, 1999 (= CH).

Cuming, G.J., 'Egyptian Elements in the Jerusalem Liturgy', *JTS* 25 (1974), 117–24.

—— 'The Shape of the Anaphora', *StPatr* 20 (1989), 333–45.

Cutrone, E., 'Cyril's Mystagogical Catecheses and the Evolution of the Jerusalem Anaphora', *OCP* 44 (1978), 52–64.

Devos, P., 'La date du voyage d'Égérie', *Analecta Bollandiana* 85 (1967), 165–94.

Doval, A., *Cyril of Jerusalem, Mystagogue: The Authorship of the Mystagogic Catecheses*, Patristic Monograph Series 17, Washington, DC, Catholic University Press, 2001.

Drake, H.A., 'Eusebius on the True Cross', *JEH* 36 (1985), 1–22.

Drijvers, J.W., *Helena Augusta: The Mother of Constantine and the Legend of Her Finding of the True Cross*, Leiden etc., Brill, 1991.

Dujarier, M. (ET), *A History of the Catechumenate: The First Six Centuries*, New York, Sadlier, 1979.

Fenwick, J.R.K., *Fourth Century Anaphoral Techniques*, Bramcote, Nottingham, Grove Books, 1986.

—— *The Anaphoras of St Basil and St James: An Investigation into Their Common Origin*, OCA 240, Rome, 1992.

Férotin, M., 'Le véritable auteur de la "Peregrinatio Sylviae". La vierge espagnole Éthéria', *Revue des questions historiques* 74 (1903), 367–97.

Geerard, M. (ed.), *Clavis patrum Graecorum*, Turnhout, Brepols, 1974–.

Gibson, S., and J.E. Taylor, *Beneath the Church of the Holy Sepulchre Jerusalem*, London, Palestinian Exploration Fund, 1994 (= GT).

Grabar, A., *Martyrium*, Paris, Collège de France, 1946.

Greenacre, R., and J. Haselock, *The Sacrament of Easter*, Leominster, Gracewing, 1989.

Gregg, R.C., and D.E. Groh, *Early Arianism: A View of Salvation*, Philadelphia and London, Fortress Press and SCM, 1981.

Harkins, P.W. (trans. and ed.), *St John Chrysostom: Baptismal Instructions*, Westminster, Md and London, Newman Press and Longmans Green, 1963.

Harmless, W., *Augustine and the Catechumenate*, Collegeville, Minnesota, Liturgical Press, 1995.

Hunt, E.D., 'The Date of the Itinerarium Egeriae', *StPatr* 38 (2001), forthcoming.

Jeremias, J. (ET), *Infant Baptism in the First Four Centuries*, London, SCM, 1960.

Johnson, M., 'Reconciling Cyril and Egeria in the Catechetical Process in Fourth-Century Jerusalem', in P. Bradshaw (ed.), *Essays in Early Christian Initiation*, Alcuin-GROW Liturgical Study 8, Bramcote, Nottingham, Grove Books, 1988.

Jungmann, J.A. (ET), *The Mass of the Roman Rite: Its Origins and Development (Missarum Sollemnia)*, New York, Benziger, 1955; reprint Blackrock, Ireland, Four Courts Press, 1986.

Kavanagh, A. *Confirmation: Origins and Reform*, New York, Pueblo, 1988.

Lampe, G.W.H., *The Seal of the Spirit*, 2nd edn, London, SPCK, 1967.

Lebon, J., 'La position de saint Cyrille de Jérusalem dans les luttes provoquées par l'arianisme', *RHE* 20 (1924), 181–210, 357–86.

Ligier, L. (ET), 'The Origins of the Eucharistic Prayer: From the Last Supper to the Eucharist', *Studia Liturgica* 9 (1973), 161–85.

McCauley, L.P., and A.A. Stephenson (trans. and ed.), *St. Cyril of Jerusalem*, The Fathers of the Church 61 and 64, Washington, DC, Catholic University of America Press, 1969–70.

Maraval, P., *Égérie, Journal de voyage*, SC 296, Paris, Cerf, 1982.

Murray, R., *Symbols of Church and Kingdom*, Cambridge, Cambridge University Press, 1975.

Piédagnel, A. (ed.), *Cyrille de Jérusalem, Catéchèses Mystagogiques*, SC 126 *bis*, Paris, 1988.

Pullan, W., 'Jerusalem from Alpha to Omega in the Santa Pudenziana Mosaic', in B. Kühnel (ed.), *The Real and Ideal Jerusalem in Jewish, Christian and Islamic Art*, Jerusalem, Hebrew University, 1998, pp. 405–17.

Rahner, H. (ET), *Greek Myths and Christian Mystery*, London, Burns Oates, 1963.

Reischl, W.K., and J. Rupp (eds.), *S. Patris Nostri Cyrilli Hierosolymorum Archiepiscopi Opera quae supersunt Omnia*, Munich, Libraria Lentneriana, 1848–60 (= RR).

Renoux, A., *Le Codex arménien Jérusalem 121*, PO 35–6, 1969–71.

—— 'Une version arménienne des catéchèses mystagogiques de Cyrille de Jérusalem?', *Le Muséon* 85 (1972), 147–53.

Stephenson, A.A., 'St Cyril of Jerusalem's Trinitarian Theology', *StPatr* 11 (1972), 234–41.

Stevenson, J. and Frend, W.H.C., *A New Eusebius*, 2nd edn, London, SPCK, 1987.

Tanner, N.P. (ed.), *Decrees of the Ecumenical Councils*, London and Washington, DC, Sheed & Ward and Georgetown University Press, 1990.

Telfer, W., *Cyril of Jerusalem and Nemesius of Emesa*, LCC 4, London, SCM Press, 1955.

van Esbroeck, M., 'Une homélie sur l'église attribuée a Jean de Jérusalem', *Le Muséon* 86 (1973), 283–304.

Walker, P.W.L., *Holy City, Holy Places? Christian Attitudes to Jerusalem and the Holy Land in the Fourth Century*, Oxford, Clarendon Press, 1990.

Wenger, A. (ed.), *Jean Chrysostome: Huit Catéchèses Baptismales*, SC 50, Paris, Cerf, 1957.

Whitaker, E.C., *Documents of the Baptismal Liturgy*, 2nd edn, London, SPCK, 1970.

Wilkinson, J., 'Jewish Influences on the Early Christian Rite of Jerusalem', *Le Muséon* 92 (1979), 347–59.

—— *Egeria's Travels*, London, SPCK, 1971; 3rd edn, Warminster, Aris & Phillips, 1999.

Yarnold, E.J., 'Did St Ambrose Know the Mystagogic Catecheses of St Cyril of Jerusalem?', *StPatr* 12 (1975), 184–9.

—— 'The Authorship of the Mystagogic Catecheses Attributed to Cyril of Jerusalem', *Heythrop Journal* 19 (1978), 143–61.

—— 'Who Planned the Churches at the Christian Holy Places in the Holy Land?', *StPatr* 18(1) (1985), 105–9.

—— '"Videmus duplicem statum". The Visibility of the Two Natures of Christ in Tertullian's *Adversus Praxean*', *StPatr* 19 (1989), 286–90.

—— *The Awe-Inspiring Rites of Initiation: The Origins of the R.I.C.A.*, Edinburgh and Collegeville, Minnesota, T. & T. Clark and Liturgical Press, 1994.

—— 'Anaphoras without Institution Narratives?', *StPatr* 30 (1997), 395–410.

—— 'The Function of Institution Narratives in Early Liturgies', Rome, OCA, forthcoming.

INDEX